Ambiguous Realities

Ambiguous Realities

WOMEN IN THE MIDDLE AGES AND RENAISSANCE

Edited by CAROLE LEVIN and JEANIE WATSON

WAYNE STATE UNIVERSITY PRESS DETROIT 1987

Library of Congress Cataloging-in-Publication Data

Ambiguous realities.

  Bibliography: p.
  Includes index.
  1. Women in literature—History. 2. European
literature—Renaissance, 1450–1600—History and
criticism. 3. Literature, Medieval—History and
criticism. 4. Women—History—Middle Ages, 500–1500.
5. Women—History—Renaissance, 1450–1600. I. Levin,
Carole, 1948–   . II. Watson, Jeanie, 1943–   .
PN56.5.W64A49   1987   809'.89287   87-21671
ISBN 0-8143-1872-X (alk. paper)
ISBN 0-8143-1873-8 (pbk. : alk. paper)

TOC

For Our Parents
Charlotte and Frank Kern Levin
Doris and Ores Watson

Contents

Contents

Contributors

Sara J. Eaton is an assistant professor of English at Northwest Missouri State University. She has taught courses in the Renaissance and in writing at the University of Minnesota and at Augsburg College in Minneapolis. This essay is part of a larger work in progress that studies the uses of the demonstrative in Renaissance drama.

Deborah S. Ellis received her doctorate from Berkeley in comparative literature and medieval studies. She has published articles and reviews on medieval literature and medieval women in such journals as *English Studies, Essays in Arts and Sciences,* and the *Journal of Women's Studies in Literature,* and is at work on a book on Chaucer and the medieval image of women. She is currently assistant professor of English at Southwestern University.

Janis Butler Holm received her doctorate from the University of Michigan and is now assistant professor of English at Ohio University, where she also teaches in the Women's Studies Program. She has edited a critical edition of *The Mirrhor of Modestie* and has published several essays on sixteenth-century attitudes toward women. An earlier version of "The Myth of a Feminist Humanism" received an award from the Women Educators group at the 1984 American Educational Research Association Convention.

Constance Jordan is an assistant professor of English and comparative literature at Columbia University. She is the author of *Pulci's Morgante: Poetry and History in Fifteenth-Century Flor-*

ence and various articles and reviews on Montaigne, Spenser, and women in Renaissance literature in such journals as *Renaissance Quarterly* and *Studies in Philology*. Jordan is currently at work on a study of Renaissance defenses of women and the origins of modern feminism.

Eileen Kearney is assistant professor of religious studies at the University of Pennsylvania. She has published essays on Peter Abelard and Peter the Lombard in *The Encyclopedia of Religion* and is working on a major study of Peter Abelard.

N. Elaine Lawson is employed by the Ministry of Agriculture of the government of Canada in Ottawa. She holds a degree in history and political science from Glendon College, York University, Toronto.

Carole Levin is associate professor of history at State University of New York at New Paltz. She has published articles both on propaganda and on images of women in Tudor England in various periodicals including *The Sixteenth-Century Journal* and *The International Journal of Women's Studies* as well as the essay collections *Silent But for the Word* and *Women in the Middle Ages and Renaissance: Literary and Historical Perspectives*. She recently received the Monticello Fellowship to work at the Newberry Library on her study of the images of queenship in Renaissance England.

Dennis Moore is an assistant professor in the Rhetoric Program of the University of Iowa and author of *The Politics of Spenser's Complaints and Sidney's Philisides Poems*. His work in progress includes a study of Henry Howard's *Dutiful Defense of the Lawful Regiment of Women* (1590).

Cary J. Nederman is lecturer in political science at the University of Canterbury, Christchurch, New Zealand. He previously taught at York University, Toronto, and the University of Alberta. He has published widely in medieval, history, and politics journals on topics in the history of political thought.

Shirley F. Staton is associate professor of English and former Women's Studies Coordinator at Purdue University Calumet. She has published on Sylvia Plath's stories in *Women & Literature* and on Renaissance literature in *Literature/Film Quarterly* and *Iowa*

State Journal of Research. Staton recently published a critical anthology, *Literary Theories in Praxis.* She has been awarded grants from Lilly Library of Indiana University, Purdue University, and the Indiana Committee for the Humanities, and has been selected as a National Endowment for Humanities Institute participant.

Betty S. Travitsky has taught at Brooklyn College, Touro College, and the Jerusalem College for Women. She has held a National Endowment for the Humanities Summer Fellowship and a Mellon Postdoctoral Fellowship and is a participant in the ongoing colloquium, "Women and the Renaissance," which meets at the Folger Shakespeare Library. She is the editor of *The Paradise of Women,* a critical anthology of writings by Renaissance Englishwomen; her articles have appeared in such journals as *The Bulletin of Research in the Humanities* and *English Literary Renaissance.* Her essay in this collection is the outgrowth of her current study of portrayals of female criminals in the Renaissance drama.

Jeanie Watson is associate dean of the Brown College of Arts and Sciences and associate professor of English at Southwestern University. Her work on Romantic and Victorian poetry and children's literature has appeared in *Prose Studies, The Journal of Pre-Raphaelite Studies, Children's Literature,* and elsewhere. She is the editor of Warren W. Wooden's *Children's Literature of the English Renaissance.* She is currently working on Coleridge and the fairy tale tradition.

Valerie Wayne is an associate professor of English at the University of Hawaii at Manoa. She has published essays and reviews on Christine de Pizan, feminist criticism of Shakespeare, the shrew in medieval and Renaissance drama, and Vives' *Instruction of a Christian Woman* in such journals as *Biography, Shakespeare Studies, Essays in Criticism,* and in the essay collection *Silent But for the Word.* She is completing a critical edition of Edmund Tilney's dialogue on marriage, *The Flower of Friendshippe* (1568).

Karen F. Wiley Is assistant dean of the college and assistant professor of French at Gettysburg College. She has written articles on Montaigne, Louise Labe, and Marguerite de Navarre. Her current interests include Marguerite de Navarre and Bonaventure Des Periers. She has coauthored (with Susan O. Whitebook) a review grammar study guide, *Tour de Grammaire,* and has contributed a chapter on using journal techniques in language classes in *The Journal Book.*

Acknowledgments

The idea for this collection began with a series óf special sessions on women in the Middle Ages and Renaissance organized by Janis Butler Holm and Carole Levin for the 1984 International Conference on Patristic, Medieval, and Renaissance Studies at Villanova University. We would, therefore, like to thank Professor Holm for all of her work in the initial stages of the project and Thomas Losoncy and Joseph Schnaubelt, conference co-chairmen, for their generous support.

In addition, we especially appreciate Joan B. Williamson's help in reading and selecting the essays for the book.

Finally, we also wish to thank Paul Merrix, who encouraged the project; Karen Wiley, Rozalyn Levin, and Dennis Moore, who each read portions of the manuscript; and Ruth Elwell, who provided the index for this volume.

Carole Levin
Jeanie Watson

Introduction

Carole Levin

⤴ The predominant cultural expectations for women in medieval and Renaissance Europe, as propagated and institutionalized by both the medieval Church and the literate aristocracy, were quite straightforward. The ideal woman was to be chaste and obedient; she was to be busy in the home and silent outside it. The Church provided two models for women: Eve, the temptress, and Mary, the Mother of God; thus society viewed women as either pure and virginal or filled with the carnal lust of the deceitful Eve. In either case, the culture stereotyped women as inferior and childlike both in their intellect and their being and, consequently, as essentially different from men. Because women's nature was "other," it was a nature to be feared. The misogyny so pervasive in the patriarchal structure of medieval and Renaissance society was a response to this fear and an attempt to keep women safely within their prescribed roles where they could present no danger to men.[1]

Although these powerful, albeit contradictory, cultural images of women were dominant from the twelfth through the sixteenth centuries, they do not adequately reflect the reality of women's lives in medieval and Renaissance Europe. This reality was much richer and much more ambiguous than the cultural stereotypes could admit. While questions about women's position in the period are complex and often clouded by the influence of the stereotypes themselves, we do know that women of all classes worked hard, not only inside the home but often outside it as well. In addition, women played important parts in political, social, and economic change. The further one reads in the texts of the Middle Ages and Renaissance, the less uniformity and more ambiguity one finds about what woman's role actually was.

Only recently has scholarship begun to pay serious attention to these ambiguities and to explore fully their significance. It is now evident that the emergence of feminist criticism in the last decade has had an enormous impact on the way we read medieval and Renaissance history and literature. Our questions and areas of investigation are different, and they are more inclusive than they once were. Whereas traditional studies of the period have often ignored the significance of women's role and status in society, the recognition that gender is a significant category of study has allowed feminist criticism to begin to analyze such issues as the role and status of women within the culture and the impact of sex-role stereotyping on the development of women and men. Earlier in this century, works by such authors as Eileen Power, Alice Clark, and Mary Beard focused on the importance of women's roles and images in medieval and Renaissance Europe. In the last few years, these important insights have been greatly expanded by such scholars as Joan Kelly, Natalie Davis, Diane Bornstein, Lawrence Stone, and many others. Kelly's early suggestion that when we look at women's experience we must reassess the way we periodize history and Davis's work on women's experience serving both as safety valve and agent for change within society have been particularly provocative in asking us to rethink many of our assumptions. Feminist scholarship has caused us to pose new questions that elicit more information about the image of women and the position they played in society and, in the process, to expand our knowledge of the entire culture of the Middle Ages and Renaissance.

By asking questions of specific literary, historical, and theological texts, the essays in the present collection illuminate a number of important issues about women in the Middle Ages and

Renaissance: 1) the changes in attitude toward women in the culture of Western Europe from the twelfth through the sixteenth century, primarily in England and France; 2) women's roles and status within that society; 3) the dichotomy between the public and private spheres for women; 4) the prescription for women's behavior and the image of the ideal woman; 5) the difference between the perceived and actual audience of the medieval and Renaissance writers. And, finally, these essays demonstrate the ways in which traditional texts can be reread and reinterpreted because of the impact of feminist criticism.

The essays in *Ambiguous Realities* fall into three categories: role and representation in medieval and Renaissance texts, rereadings of medieval and Renaissance literary texts, and role and representation in English Renaissance texts. The essays in the first group examine conflicting ideologies concerning women's capabilities in the late Middle Ages and early Renaissance. The ambiguities of an author's perspective in presenting models for women is delineated in the initial essay of the first group, "Boccaccio's In-Famous Women: Gender and Civic Virtue in the *De mulieribus claris*," by Constance Jordan. Boccaccio's contemporaries saw *De mulieribus claris* as a work that cast doubt on the Pauline notion that the ideal for women was silence and chastity. Jordan argues that while scholars have often read this work as an exception to Boccaccio's usual hostility toward women, *De mulieribus claris* is far more ambiguous; what Boccaccio produced—by presenting avarice and lust as essential feminine characteristics—was a subtle but devastating attack on the concept he claimed to be defending. The few women Boccaccio considers to be positive models all come to unfortunate ends. The ironies inherent in Boccaccio's presentation reflect the tensions in early Renaissance Italy when women were becoming more involved in the social and economic system.

One of the women Boccaccio uses as an example is Zenobia, a third-century Roman woman whom medieval and Renaissance writers often present as an ideal model of behavior. In her essay "Zenobia in Medieval and Renaissance Literature," Valerie Wayne analyzes the image of Zenobia. Interestingly, her findings support Jordan's reading of Boccaccio. Additionally, Wayne shows that works that celebrate women permit us to glimpse the conflict between women's experience and the cultural norms that influence their lives, and she illuminates this conflict in expectations by tracing literary representations of Zenobia.

Eileen Kearney's essay, "Heloise: Inquiry and the *Sacra Pagina*," gives a rather different perspective on the twelfth century, since she focuses on a female author. Kearney's essay demonstrates that Heloise's intellectual ability and insight went beyond that of being simply the pupil of Peter Abelard. Concentrating on the author's commentary on the *sacra pagina,* Kearney presents Heloise as an articulate and brilliant thinker who, through her penetrating study of sacred literature, participates in the twelfth-century transformation of theology. Kearney's analysis of Heloise's critique of the ways the prescriptions from the Rules of Benedict are inappropriate for women shows us how Heloise raises challenging questions about the nature of women's religious commitment.

In the final essay in the first group, "The Frivolities of Courtiers Follow the Footprints of Women: Public Women and the Crisis of Virility in John of Salisbury," Cary J. Nederman and N. Elaine Lawson concentrate on the misogyny they see inherent in the twelfth century by affording a textual analysis of John of Salisbury's *Policraticus* which illustrates his fear that feminine influence would weaken the feudal political structure. The apprehension of women's nature and potential power apparent in John of Salisbury's writing reflect the more general psychological need of those in power to keep women out of the public sphere.

The use of the insights of feminist scholarship to reinterpret literary texts is especially evident in the next set of essays in the volume. As earlier essays in the collection show, many medieval writers present the appropriate sphere for women as the private one. In her essay "Domestic Treachery in the *Clerk's Tale*," Deborah S. Ellis gives us an author who challenges the idea that the home is secure and instead presents the home as a place where abuses of power can easily take place. Ellis examines the changes Chaucer makes from his sources in the story of Patient Griselda to show how this tale works as "an emblem of domestic treachery," an important motif in a number of Chaucer's works.

Jeanie Watson's essay, "Enid the Disobedient: The *Mabinogion's Gereint and Enid*," deals with another woman who has been seen as a Patient Griselda: Enid. Watson argues, however, that the *Mabinogion* story of "Gereint and Enid" educates the reader, as well as Gereint, toward a revisionist view of women and men and their place in the world. The women in this story, while remaining beautiful, pure, and "feminine," insist on speaking and being heard, on taking action both in the home and outside it; the female ideal becomes, in this process, much more androgynous. Gereint, on the other hand, learns that a man cannot be uxoriously inactive nor mindlessly aggressive, and, thus, the male ideal also becomes more androgynous and realistic.

Karen F. Wiley's essay, "Communication Short-Circuited: Ambiguity and Motivation in the *Heptaméron*," also asks us to reread a traditional text from a fresh perspective. Wiley argues that the levels of motivation in the *Heptaméron* each have their own manner of communication: public, social, and personal. She gives evidence, for example, that Marguerite de Navarre's technique of "short-circuited communication" allows her to use ambiguity of discourse not only to protect the social order but also to assure the reader's participation in the work.

The impact of a feminist perspective is especially apparent in Shirley F. Staton's essay, "Reading Spenser's *Faerie Queen*—In a Different Voice." Staton uses the insights of psychologist Carol Gilligan on modern sex-role development to explore the idea that Book III, in addition to addressing a specifically female audience, also attempts to depict women's experience. Staton argues that Gilligan's analysis of the ways in which females learn to be "feminine" sheds light on what critics have perceived as a "loose" structure in Book III.

The third group of essays in the collection considers the ideologies about women's nature and potential in the latter part of sixteenth-century England when a woman herself was ruler. While Elizabeth's reign may well have been a catalyst for theoretical discussion, the fact of a powerful woman on the throne did not necessarily lead to higher status for women in general, as the following essays demonstrate.

Sara J. Eaton's work on "Presentations of Women in the English Popular Press" cautions us about the difficulties in using such popular works as courtesy literature, pamphlets, and ballads published during the English Renaissance to learn about women's lives. Eaton argues that many of the authors were less concerned about realistically portraying women than with presenting rhetorical constructions within the neo-Platonic tradition. The praise and dispraise that English rhetoricians used in their cultural stereotypes do not, Eaton suggests, tell us about women's lives in society but about male belief, attitudes, and fears about women.

Betty S. Travitsky's essay, "The *feme covert* in Elizabeth Cary's *Mariam*," discusses Elizabeth Cary's problems with her family and society caused by her being a woman of strength and independence. Cary publicly professed her conversion to Catholicism and was severely punished for this action. Despite the problems she experienced, Cary continued her creative and intellectual endeavors, and Travitsky demonstrates how the author's own difficult experiences are reflected in the way she depicted married women in her drama, particularly *Mariam*. Travitsky further argues that the play serves as a painful reminder of the fact of woman's subordination in marriage in Renaissance England.

While Travitsky's work examines the views of a specific woman, Janis Butler Holm's essay, "The Myth of a Feminist Humanism: Thomas Salter's *The Mirrhor of Modestie*," looks more generally at women's status in the English Renaissance. Holm examines the question of women's education, centering her discussion on Thomas Salter's tract *The Mirrhor of Modestie*. She argues that while there were some exceptional, learned, aristocratic women in this period, we must not assume from these few examples that women were generally encouraged to move into new cultural spheres. Rather, suggests Holm, works on women's education argue for traditional expectations for women's behavior.

Set against the pervasive cultural stereotypes, however, were also some Renaissance works that presented women as having courage and insight. Carole Levin's essay, "'I Trust I May Not Trust Thee': Women's Visions of the World in Shakespeare's *King John*," analyzes the treatment of women characters in Shakespeare's play. She argues that the women are more honest, at least with themselves, and more realistic about the world they live in than the male characters. Nonetheless, while the women in *King John* are more clear-sighted, they are also powerless.

Finally, in his essay "Recorder Fleetwood and the Tudor Queenship Controversy," Dennis Moore also asks us to examine the ambiguity toward women as powerful and significant human beings so evident in the Middle Ages and Renaissance, this time centering the discussion on attitudes toward queenship present in sixteenth-century England. Moore relates William Fleetwood's *Itinerarium ad Windsor* to the Tudor controversy over whether a woman might rightfully rule. Fleetwood, a loyal Elizabethan, argues that they certainly can; at the same time, his argument demonstrates the unique and anomalous nature of the queen's position, since Elizabeth was a ruler in a society that saw her gender as a limitation and did not present other women with opportunities for positions of authority.

While a number of the essays in *Ambiguous Realities* provide us with new interpretations of well-known texts, others introduce us to works that, although little known, can also shed fresh light on the way people in medieval and Renaissance Europe considered the position and nature of women. From all of these contributions, we learn how many layered and ambiguous the conception of women was from the twelfth through the sixteenth centuries, as indeed it is in any period. In addition, the variety of perspectives on the image and reality of women's lives in the Middle Ages and Renaissance represented in this collection demonstrates the wide range of feminist scholarship in literature, history, and theology. Scholarship has traditionally explored the male side of human experience. The essays in this volume are part of the work that is redressing that imbalance and presenting us with a vision that includes all of humankind.

Note

1. For a brief overview on the question of images of and attitudes toward women in the Middle Ages, see the works of Frances and Joseph Gies, Eileen Power, and Shulamith

Shahar. The view of woman as Eve was specifically set forth at the end of the fifteenth century in *Malleus Maleficarum,* or *The Hammer of the Witches.* Each of the essays in this collection provides the reader with an extensive list of critical works, and I would refer the reader to the specific essays for further bibliography, as well as to the bibliographic essay at the end of the collection.

Works Cited

Beard, Mary. *Woman as a Force in History.* New York: Macmillan, 1946.

Bornstein, Diane. *The Lady in the Tower: Medieval Courtesy Literature for Women.* Hamden, Conn.: Archon Books, 1983.

Clark, Alice. *Working Life of Women in the Seventeenth Century.* New York: Dutton, 1919.

Davis, Natalie. *Society and Culture in Early Modern France.* Stanford, Calif.: Stanford University Press, 1975.

Gies, Frances, and Joseph Gies. *Women in the Middle Ages.* 1978. New York: Barnes and Noble, 1980.

Gilligan, Carol. *In a Different Voice.* Cambridge, Mass.: Harvard University Press, 1982.

Kelly, Joan. *Women, History, and Theory.* Chicago: University of Chicago Press, 1984.

Power, Eileen. *Medieval Women.* Edited by M. M. Posten. Cambridge: Cambridge University Press, 1975.

Shahar, Shulamith. *The Fourth Estate: A History of Women in the Middle Ages.* Translated by Chaya Galai. London: Methuen, 1983.

Stone, Lawrence. *The Family, Sex, and Marriage in England, 1500-1800.* New York: Harper and Row, 1977.

Summers, Montague, trans. *Malleus Maleficarum.* London: J. Rodker, 1928.

ONE

ole and Representation
in Medieval and Early
Renaissance Texts

Boccaccio's In-Famous Women: Gender and Civic Virtue in the *De mulieribus claris*

Constance Jordan

o the Magnifico's judgment in Castiglione's *Libro del Cortegiano* that Boccaccio was "no friend of women," the *De mulieribus claris* (Concerning Famous Women) may be considered an exception. Modeled on Plutarch's *Mulierum virtutes* (The Virtues of Women), it appears to represent praiseworthy examples of womankind, historical as well as legendary. As Plutarch's text served to question the Aristotelian image of woman as possessing the cardinal virtues only in a "mode of subordination," so Boccaccio's seems intended to cast doubt on the Pauline notion of woman as best realized in her silence and chastity. To writers of later defenses of women, such as Galeazzo Capella, Syphorien Champier, and Sir Thomas Elyot, the *De mulieribus* served as a source of exempla confirming the civic virtue of women throughout history.[1]

Yet careful readers must see that this work is not epideictic in any sustained and direct manner but rather pervasively critical. It is important to realize how devious Boccaccio's rhetorical strategies actually are, how subtly he subverts his own stated intentions. In the Proem to his collection he establishes the parameters of its discourse by identifying the criteria by which he has chosen the women he represents. The "fame" they possess is not in every case to be understood in the narrow sense of that term, "so that it always is seen to correspond to virtuous action," but more generally to designate a condition of "being very well known throughout the world" (Proem 24).[2] Boccaccio's model here is ancient history, where he claims that he has read not only of the Gracci and the Scipioni but also of Hannibal and the miser, Crassus. Following the practice of humanist historians, he declares that he intends to instruct his reader by means of exempla, to praise worthy deeds and to condemn iniquitous ones.[3] So described, the rhetorical program of the *De mulieribus claris* seems unexceptionable; indeed, it seems to indicate that its author will exhibit a kind of detachment and the free exercise of historical judgment that is missing from his earlier *De casibus virorum illustrium* (Concerning the Fortunes of Famous Persons), a work obviously linked to medieval notions of Fortuna and the inexorable movement of her wheel.

Yet the reverse is actually the case. In the text of the *De mulieribus* Boccaccio fails, quite deliberately I think, to follow the rhetorical program he has set forth in its Proem. In fact, few of his portraits depict women leading lives that exhibit *virtus;* rather, they describe women who appear to be more or less reprehensible, more or less ineffectual, or simply pathetic. While Boccaccio's opening remarks to each of his histories sometimes lead one to expect praise, he almost always exhibits the evidence that follows in a negative light and in perspectives so bizarre and unfamiliar that it seems designed to threaten his reader's sense of what is decent and appropriate. In case after case, Boccaccio's accounts of the strength, wit, and resourcefulness of women are rendered deeply ironic by reference to feminine garrulousness, avarice, and lust.

The doubleness of this text, confounding categories of praise and blame, constitutes its great interest, even, arguably, its charm. It would be a mistake to write it off merely as a cunning vilification of women, a sophisticated version of the misogynist side of the *querelle des femmes.* For what is at stake is Boccaccio's ability to compel belief—and most especially his own—in an ordered political world, a just and fixed hierarchy of creatures. He turns against his intention to submit women to the same kind of historical judgment he believes is appropriate for men because he perceives that the concept of a truly genderless *virtus* will undermine the social order, effectively doing away with the power of men to determine the nature and welfare of family life. Among his many portraits there is scarcely one that is not more or less colored by a condemnation of the woman's audacity in venturing into a world reserved for men.

For the few women whose "masculine" *virtus* Boccaccio does not overtly reprove, he reserves a piously noted but unfortunate end—military defeat, suicide, imprisonment, exile—usually undergone for the sake of a father, husband, or son. The vast majority of his famous women, if they are not clearly vicious, are either fraudulent, in that their virtue is actually a mask for some secret vice, or effectively punished for violating accepted social norms. Thus Boccaccio implies that a woman's fame, or *claritas*, is a form of notoriety, a concept possibly derived from Vergil's portrait of Dido's fame (so conspicuously different from that of Aeneas), but in any case common to many discussions of women in antiquity.

It is probably impossible fully to account for the obvious ambivalence in Boccaccio's treatment of his topic in this text. It is unlikely that anyone as skilled in rhetorical procedures as the writer of the *Decameron* could remain unaware that he represents his subject with irony, yet this may have been the case in the *De mulieribus*. Evidence necessary to validate a psychoanalytic interpretation would be difficult to obtain and perhaps inconclusive, however much Boccaccio's other works, notably the *Corbaccio,* as well as his troubled childhood make plausible such an approach. What the critic can do, on the other hand, is to demonstrate how these portraits are rendered ironic and to propose for consideration certain historical circumstances that may have made such a treatment attractive.

Boccaccio dedicates the *De mulieribus* to Andrea Acciaiuoli of Florence, the Countess of Altavilla. He speaks of it as a work "in praise of women" and goes on to say that the countess herself exemplifies a *virtus* equal to that of the most distinguished ladies. He further claims that "God in his generosity has filled your spirit with that which nature has denied the weaker sex" (Dedica, 18,

27

20).[4] For this reason, he goes on to say, her name is Andrea, which is Greek for *man*. That is, he compliments her by suppressing her actual gender and by rhetorically reconstituting her as male through an act of language, a naming, which is also a sign of divine generosity (*liberalitas*).

In keeping with his compliment to the countess Andrea, that women are great insofar as they are men, the bulk of the Proem is devoted to a representation of what may be termed a humanistic feminism—the view that the excellence of women may be perceived in their participation in the *vita activa,* or public life, as much as in domestic and contemplative activities. Indeed, because they are inherently less fit for this kind of endeavor than men, "since they are by nature soft and feeble physically and weak mentally," they are the more to be commended. To illustrate his concept of feminine *claritas,* Boccaccio states that he chooses examples from pagan antiquity since Christian women follow a higher law:

> The ladies of sacred history, following the way and the directions of their holy Teacher, often discipline themselves to tolerate adversity almost beyond human consideration. Pagan women, by contrast, attain [glory]—and with what a strength of spirit—either by a certain gift or instinct of nature; or better, because they are spurred on by a spark of the fleeting splendor of the world. (Proem 26)[5]

He concludes by declaring that his treatise will fill in a blank page of history, giving to women who attain a merely secular greatness a place comparable to that reserved for Christian women in the history of the Church.

This prefatory material seems straightforward. Evidently demonstrating a commitment to the value of civic as opposed to religious virtue, Boccaccio appears to redefine the nature of the *vita activa* so that women can participate in it and thus to endorse a single standard of virtue for men and women. It is only when he begins his histories that the ambivalence of his position in this prefatory material becomes apparent. Each of his portraits of famous women could be said to constitute a negative example, one that discourages rather than encourages emulation. Considered as a totality, the text seems to function as a *concessio,* a refutation of its apparent thesis.

It is important to recognize how contentious Boccaccio's argument might have appeared even to him and certainly to his contemporaries. What was at issue, finally, was not so much whether women were capable of civic virtue but rather whether it was desirable for them to cherish and to foster these kinds of abilities *as a class.* In dealing with this issue Boccaccio confronts and rewrites Aristotelian texts on the nature of women. Aristotle derives his notion that women are politically inferior to men from the fact that he considers them morally as well as physically weak, having the virtues only in a mode of subordination and not of command. By contrast, Boccaccio begins by assuming that men and women are morally equal (however unlikely women were in practice to exhibit moral strength), perhaps because the Church itself subscribed to the spiritual equality of men and women. But when he finds that by conceding and even extolling the moral virtue of women he may be thought to imply their political and social equality with men, he has recourse to irony and paradox.

Boccaccio's histories can be divided into several categories: histories celebrating the arts, histories celebrating arms and political triumphs, histories celebrating devotion to family, and histories of vice.

Eloquence, whether manifest as poetry or oratory, is the art in which Boccaccio's women most often excel, and in his representation of them the nature of his conflict is evident. In part, his histories reveal his fear that a woman's cultivation of eloquence jeopardizes the least stable of the two specifically womanly virtues: silence. In part, he also recognizes that eloquence is the skill that might enable women most directly to participate in public life. The simplest of his strategies is to term the eloquent woman a "man" and thus to deny her sex. The Roman Hortensia is praised for arguing in the Senate against a tax levied on Roman women "with such an inexhaustible and effective eloquence that to her admiring audience she appeared to have changed her sex and spoken as her father, [the orator] Hortensius reborn" (lxxxiv:332).[6] Similarly, the poetess Proba became so adept at writing Vergilian poetry that her metrical version of the Vulgate, pieced together from scraps of the *Eclogues, Georgics,* and the *Aeneid,* is said to be indistinguishable from the verse of her master:

> She chose now whole lines, now some parts, suiting them to her subject with remarkable skill . . . so that no one, unless most expert, could distinguish the linkages . . . so that an ignorant reader could easily have thought that Vergil had lived in the time of the Apostles. (xcvii:392, 394)[7]

Proba conforms to the conception of woman proposed in the pseudo-*Economics,* in which woman is portrayed as conserving what her husband has invented or acquired.[8] Proba's poetic function is limited to re-presenting what male poets have written and does not extend to changing the canon.

The case of Iole appears to be an inversion of that of Hortensia. "Malicious by nature" (*erenata fraudibus*), she thinks it "more honorable" (*plus decoris*) to have overcome Hercules by lasciviousness than by war. She reduces him to an ignominious uxoriousness, seating him in a feminine manner among women (*sedere femineo ritu . . . inter mulierculas*), and demanding that he tell tales of his deeds (*narrare fabellas laborum suorum;* xxiii:100). Here the eloquent man is perceived as effeminate, the victim of feminine guile designed to control him; having made Hercules eloquent, Iole can be said to speak *through* him. And just as Hortensia's speech makes her appear as eloquent as her father, so Iole's eloquence, displaced onto her lover, makes him appear as one of her handmaidens. In neither instance does Boccaccio's famous woman speak persuasively in a natural feminine voice. If she is eloquent and chaste, she is a "man"; if she is sexual, her partner does the speaking but at the price of his masculinity.

Artful women are sometimes characterized as endowed with superhuman gifts: the Queen of Sheba, for example, pursues the wisdom of Solomon not with study (*studium*), that is, human effort, but through God's grace (*donum Dei;* xliii:184). More often, they are associated with diabolical forces. Boccaccio wonders whether Tiresias's daughter, Manto, who learned pyromancy from her father, did not mix with her art the work of the devil (*opus diabolicum*). In any case, he calls her virginity "spoiled by evil arts" (*nephastis suis labefactare;* xxx:126, 128). Circe is the classic case of the learned woman as witch-goddess: she attracts Ulysses' men with eloquent speech (*sermo ornatus*), and later they appear "deprived of human reason" (*ratio humana subtracta;* xxxviii:156). Boccaccio permits himself to generalize on the basis of this example: "We can understand this very well if we consider the habits of men and women; for there are many Circes about, and there are many men who are turned into beasts through lust."[9] This universal kind of change seems to have affinities with Iole's transformation of Hercules. In both cases, a woman's art is represented most powerfully as a stimulus to lust. This alters men for the worse; they become effeminate or bestial.

Feminine eloquence that is least subject to Boccaccio's covert criticisms is associated with chaste women. Marcia, the artist, is first praised for her virginity, "conquering that fleshly desire to which even great men have sometimes succumbed" ("superato carnis aculeo, cui etiam prestantissimi non nunquam succubuere viri"; lxvi:266). It is then noted that she not only takes up painting and sculpture because she despises "woman's work" (*ministerium muliebris*) but also that she portrays women exclusively, because, following classical style in which human figures are represented nude, she would either have had to execute "imperfect men" (*vires imperfecti*) or subject herself to a "virgin's shame" (*pudor virginis;* ibid.). Commending Cornificia the poetess for writing verse that causes her to equal her brother Corneficius in fame, Boccaccio goes on to deplore women who do not exert themselves intellectually but instead "think that they are not useful for anything except a man's pleasure, bearing and feeding children; if they wished to apply themselves to study, they would have at their disposal all the means that are required to make men famous" (lxxxvi:338).[10]

These stories place the eloquent woman in an interesting double bind. On the one hand, her art, which is seen as effacing or utterly subduing her sexuality, is termed a good thing, since her sexuality is debilitating and without it she can become a "man" (Hortensia, Proba, Corneficia). But on the other hand, it is also seen as affecting male sexuality, and this is ambiguous: if it stimulates desire, it transforms men to lesser creatures (Circe, Iole); if it re-presses desire, it castrates men, making them "imperfect" (Marcia). Feminine self-expression cannot therefore be approved by men; however it is conducted, whatever the mode of its production, it jeopardizes male sexuality either by denying it and thus testifying to a limitation of their control over women or by indulging it and testifying to a loss of their self-control.

These intricate relationships are made further problematic by histories that turn on dramatic paradoxes. Two of Boccaccio's elo-quent women are in fact untutored; moreover, their natural elo-quence manifests itself in silence. Leena, a prostitute, is arrested for plotting the death of the tyrant Aminta. She bravely withstands tor-ture, and finally, rather than give away her fellow conspirators, she bites out her tongue: "not less glory is owed her tongue, first mute and then cut off, than that which was owed to the tongue of Demos-thenes, able to pronounce such ornate orations" (1:204).[11] The freed-woman Epicari is arrested for plotting against Nero; she too with-stands torture, refusing to divulge the secrets of the conspiracy. Fearful that she will not be able to remain silent forever, she hangs herself in her cell: in this way Epicari "gives the lie to the old proverb that women are silent only about what they do not know" ("veteri frustrato proverbio, quo docemur tacere quod nesciunt mulieres"; xciii:378). In both of these cases feminine speech is paradoxically voiced when the organs of speech are destroyed: they achieve *claritas* by virtue of unspoken speech. Furthermore, this art of keeping silent is achieved by women who have not been in-structed in how to be "eloquent." Therefore a wholly natural art, it suggests that an educated eloquence in a woman is destructive and to be discouraged.

Perhaps the most arresting of all Boccaccio's histories of women who have mastered the arts of discourse is that of the legendary Pope Joan, in which both the discipline of study and virile talents are wholly nullified by the effects of her biologically feminine body.

Following her lover to England, Joan was thought by all to be a cleric and so "busied herself in the study of Venus and of letters." On the death of her lover she was recognized to be superior to all others (*pre ceteris excellens*), furnished with wonderful knowledge (*predita scientia mirabili*). As a private person (*privata*) she retains her honesty (*honestas*), but when she is elected to the pontificate, "it happened that she was carried away with burning lust . . . so it happened that the pope conceived." In due course she gives birth, "without obstetrical assistance and in a public street; thus she showed that, except for her lover, she had fooled all men" (ci:416, 418).[12]

In many respects the history of Pope Joan conforms to the general pattern of histories of eloquent women. At the outset her talents allow her to achieve a masculine identity; she is "honest" (presumably faithful to her lover) as long as she remains a private person. When she enters the public arena, however, she experiences intense desire and becomes the victim of her physical being, which gives her away twice over: by revealing her sexual identity, it destroys her public role. Her parturition is monstrous, for in labor she lacks the assistance of other women, and she gives birth in public, outside the circle of family. As an event, her motherhood figures her grotesqueness: she is a person of learning, in a position of the highest public trust (of Christian souls), and also a woman who has borne a child. That Boccaccio regards the union of these functions as scandalous is partly indicated when he notes that the clergy of Rome avoids the avenue where the birth occurred, bypassing it on side streets. Furthermore, it makes explicit what other histories imply, that is, that the womanly virtue of silence is bound up with a second virtue proper to women: chastity. The woman who speaks is often the woman who lusts after men; if she speaks well, her lust is likely to be more intense.

Boccaccio's histories of politically powerful women reveal a similar tendency to associate the acquisition of *claritas* with the preservation or, conversely, the loss of chastity. Many of them represent the integrity of the woman's body as a metaphor of the independent state; her chastity then seems to function as a guarantee of the freedom of her people. Correspondingly, the lust of the male attacker signifies the threat of political tyranny.

The history of Lucretia is typical of these relationships. Married to Collatinus, she is judged by Boccaccio to be the most chaste of Roman matrons. But her virtue only excites Sextus, the son of Tarquinius Superbus, the tyrant. He rapes her, she denounces him publicly, and then kills herself for shame. Boccaccio concludes that her action "restored not only her honor that the undisciplined youth had violated by his vile act, but also made possible the restoration of Roman liberty" (xlviii:196).[13] A comparable outcome follows the rape of Virginea, the daughter of Verginius, an honorable plebeian, and the betrothed of the tribune Icilius. During the period when Rome was governed by the *decemviri,* she was raped by Appius Claudius. Responding to this dishonor, her father stabs her to death in a city street, declaring: "Beloved daughter, I give you back your liberty in the only way I can." Consequently, "because of actions of Verginius and Icilius, in conjunction with a . . . secession of the plebes, the *decemviri* were forced to resign their office and to restore to the people the liberty they had taken away" (lviii:240).[14]

These histories also resemble that of the wife of Orgiagonte, King of Galatia, in important respects. Here military defeat is made coincident with the conqueror's rape of the defeated queen; her liberty is represented as incomplete without her revenge upon the rapist. Overcome and made the prisoner of the Roman consul, Manlius, Orgiagonte's queen is raped by a Roman centurion. After ransom has been arranged and she is unchained, she commands two of her slaves to behead the centurion as he is counting the ransom money. Hiding his head under her cloak, she leaves the Roman prison and returns to her husband with her prize. Commenting on the history, Boccaccio terms her the queen "of the tribe of Lucretia" and declares that "while her liberty was *not yet entirely restored* [that is, while she was still in the enemy's power (my italics)] . . . the shame of the outrage to her body . . . not only encouraged her, a brave woman, to face prison and death, but also, the avenger of a crime, to bring it about that the swords of her slaves fell on the head of the wicked adulterer" (lxxiii:296).[15] His point is clear: Orgiagonte's queen would not have been made free merely by paying a ransom because her freedom is morally as well as politically constituted. More precisely, her political freedom is only realized when she regains her moral purity.

Boccaccio's history of Dido reestablishes these values on a more imposing scale: the physical integrity of this queen both signifies and ensures the political independence of her state. Following Petrarch rather than Vergil and Dante, Boccaccio relates that the widowed queen, famous throughout Africa for her laws and customs, has vowed to remain faithful to the memory of her husband. But when a neighboring king, Massitanus, threatens to destroy Carthage if she refuses to marry him, her people become fearful. They proceed to trick her into declaring that her country must come before all else: "Are you ignorant that we are born for our fathers and the fatherland?" ("An ignoratis quia patri nascamur et patrie?") she asks them. Having realized that for her this means she must agree to marry her besieger if she wishes to prevent the destruction of her city, she arranges to keep her pledge to her people and her vow to her dead husband in the only way left to her: suicide. On her funeral pyre she declares (with deliberate irony): "I go to my husband" ("ad virum vado"; xlii:174, 176). How this action ensures the independence of her Carthaginians is represented more realistically in an earlier and fuller version of her history that Boccaccio tells in the *De casibus virorum illustrium*. There, having agreed to marry Massitanus, Dido asks for a delay during which she fortifies her city against the barbarian's army. Satisfied that it is safe, she kills herself (2.10.134–142). What is implied in the *De mulieribus* is here made explicit: the impregnable walls of her city appear to be the political correlative of her inviolate physical self. Its independence is guaranteed by her refusal to allow herself to be possessed. In the *De mulieribus* her subjects honor her as the "mother of her people" (*mater publica*).

In both accounts it is clear that Dido's political role is maternal. In the context of her tragic history the identification renders ironic her earlier speech about patriotism as patriarchal. Since motherhood is a subordinate rather than a dominant role, she must have only a disembodied ghostly spouse if she is to be authoritative.

Indeed, Boccaccio's description of her government colors the question of patriotism with romance themes and motifs in ways no government by a man could be imagined as doing. Had Dido been a man, her allegiance to her country, *patria,* would have been like an allegiance to her father, *pater,* as she herself insists allegiance ought to be for her subjects. As a king, she would have conceived of her political duty as a father's responsibility for his family, that is, it would have involved the kinds of loyalty, service, and obedience that characterize relations between a superior and his subordinates. As a queen, by contrast, her allegiance is understood in terms of a woman's rather more ambiguous obligations, chiefly those established at the time of her marriage with her husband. Merely by being a woman—and especially a marriageable one—she is constantly made vulnerable to a usurpation of the powers of government by an actual husband. Boccaccio does not suggest that this is a matter for law to resolve by forbidding gynocracy but rather that it is a phenomenon of culture, an expression of the symbolic language of power that partly reflects and partly determines the nature of sexual and social relations.[16]

In his history of Veturia, the mother of Coriolanus, Boccaccio elaborates the basic elements of the story to illustrate the danger to the state that is posed by the sexuality of a politically powerful woman. Attempting to placate her rebellious son, Veturia assumes the leadership of the Roman women; in a sense she symbolizes the womanhood of the Roman state engaged, in this instance, in an effort to return an errant citizen to his proper civic duty. But her words imply that her son's error is somehow her fault:

> I see now that my fertility is against me and the interests of the country. While I thought to have reared a son and citizen, I [now] realize that instead I have brought forth a hateful and implacable enemy. Indeed, it would have been better had I never conceived. If I had been sterile, Rome would have been safe, free from enemy assault; and I, [now] miserable, would have been able to die in a free country. (1v:222)[17]

It is symbolically significant that it is a son of a politically minded mother, rather than father, who is portrayed as outside the city, a rebel to its laws. If the woman's chaste body is identified with the state that is secure in its defenses, a woman's fertile body must stand for the converse of this. As Boccaccio represents her, Veturia is chiefly memorable not as a woman whose powerful eloquence saves the state but rather as one whose sexuality nearly brings about its ruin.

The history of Cleopatra reveals a different but equally negative view of the politically powerful woman. Boccaccio depicts her entirely as a creature of appetites. She is never described as having governed but only as having sought illicit unions with powerful princes from whom she demands rewards—towns, states, territories—for sexual favors. She is characterized as possessed of a "lust for governing" (*libido regni*), but as her career unfolds, the object of her desire is repeatedly revealed to be not a city or state but its prince (lxxxviii:346). She acquires much territory—from Pompey, Caesar, Antony—but her conquests are wholly erotic. Boccaccio practically implies that Cleopatra cannot experience an effort of will in other than a sexual way. In contrast to a man, who represents the head of the body politic or the rationality directing civic affairs, this woman represents the body itself, its most basic and elemental desires. Her failure to govern is then a physically determined fact, a logical product of her femininity.

For Boccaccio only a single queen, Zenobia of Palmyra, achieves a commendable *claritas,* and her career ends in military and political defeat. She conforms to the principal requirements for an essentially feminine virtue: she is chaste as a maid, eschewing the company of men; she is chaste and loyal as wife, submitting to the desire of her husband only for the sake of children, following him to battle when necessary; she is prudent and courageous as a widow, guarding the welfare of her sons and their state. But her forces are overcome by Roman armies, and at last she is led captive in the triumph of the victorious Roman general, Aurelianus. This defeat culminates in what appears to be a symbolic adjustment of status: "The triumph over, conspicuous for its prizes and treasure, Zenobia lived *in private among the other Roman women* to the end of her days" (my italics; c:414).[18] The statement effectively calls into question this queen's extraordinary abilities, suggesting that if they have not actually been misdirected, they are at least capable of considerable redirection. In the end Zenobia is no different from a decent Roman matron.

Boccaccio's histories of women who attain *claritas* through purely heroic activity are generally typified by his accounts of Amazon warriors who are by nature chaste: Marpesa, Lampedace, Orizia, Antiope, Pentesilea, Camilla, Tamyris. One of the women in this category who diverges from the stereotype is remarkable for the fact that her virile heroism also entails the sacrifice of her children, much as if the two kinds of activity represented in bearing arms and bearing children were fundamentally incompatible. Ipsicratea, Mithradates' queen, follows him on his campaigns, cutting her hair, wearing armor, riding chargers into battle. For all this "she did not receive adequate reward." In his old age, Mithradates kills their son in a fit of anger, is then besieged by another son, and finally "lest his wife and other children outlive him, poisoned Ipsicratea who with her deeds had given him so much help during her life" (lxxviii: 314).[19] These events suggest that, whatever the considerations of public policy, Mithradates at last takes steps to rid himself of what he perceives (and perhaps has always perceived) as a threat to his own power: a virile wife and her children, one of whom (like Veturia's son) is shown to be a rebel.

Together these histories compose Boccaccio's complex image of relationships between men and women who for various reasons have achieved fame through actions customarily performed by men: bearing arms, leading military exercises (campaigns, battles, escapes from prison), excelling in diplomacy and government. While these activities might in themselves benefit the people on whose behalf they are done, they are also, in relation to a larger scheme of social values, disruptive of the normal social hierarchy and therefore to be discouraged. The sexuality of the politically powerful woman is especially dangerous: it is often the means by which she acquires power from men, and, if it results in her having children, the offspring often threaten the state with rebellion or civil war.

This conception of the politics of sexuality may reflect at some level Boccaccio's sense of the perils of allowing married women the right to possess and bequeath property. After all, the child who expects to inherit only from his father is less likely to disobey him than one who is assured of his mother's possessions as well. The history of Veturia concludes with a long and ostensibly moralistic diatribe against allowing women to wear jewels and precious clothing. In relation to the preceding story this makes little sense; if, however, it is considered in relation to Boccaccio's representation of relationships of power within the family, it may be thought to reveal something of his worries about the purely political—in contrast to the moral—consequences of women's wealth.

Boccaccio reserves his unqualified praise for women who have suffered both for their determination to remain chaste and, most important, for the sake of male relatives, especially husbands but also sons. Several of these histories relate the virtuous suicides of these devoted women; others tell of long periods of trial and fidelity.

Dido's is an example of a virtuous suicide; Lucretia also dies for her own and her husband's honor. Portia dies for love of her husband (lxxxii); Pompeia Paulina, Seneca's wife, attempts suicide for the same reason but is saved at the last moment (xciv). Hippo throws herself into the sea rather than be raped by pirates (liii). The wives of the Cimbrians, captured and imprisoned with their children by their enemies led by the Roman Gaius Marius, kill their children and then commit suicide rather than undergo the humiliation of enslavement. To Boccaccio this virtuous action recovers (rather inexplicably) the honor lost by their Cimbrian husbands: "By fleeing . . . slavery and dishonor, they [the women] reveal that their husbands were conquered not by force but by fortune" (lxxx:322, 324).[20] The hidden point surely is that a man's honor is in part if not at times wholly vested in the behavior of his wife.

Several of Boccaccio's noble wives rescue their husbands from dishonor (or are the cause of their honor) or death. Argia, wife of Polyneices, recovers her husband's corpse, which is lying behind enemy lines, in order to give it a proper burial (xxix). Virginia, the wife of the plebe Lucius Volupnius, defends her husband's reputation from the criticisms of patrician women (lxiii). Penelope's fidelity to Ulysses is rehearsed (xl); it compares to the devotion of young Antonia, who, after the early death of her husband, remains cloistered in her sister-in-law's house for the rest of her life (lxxxix).

A couple of histories record a wife's rescue of her husband. Ipermestra, the daughter of Danaus, saves her husband Lynceus from her father's attempted murder (xiv); the wives of the Menii exchange places with their husbands in prison, condemned to death by the Spartans for attempting to overthrow the state. The latter case provokes Boccaccio to enlarge on true love in marriage: "Every cloud of sensuality having dissipated, realizing that no honest effort ought to be spared for the safety of a friend, they felt devotion within the depths of their hearts, and determined to rescue their husbands" (xxxi:132, 134).[21] The contrast between self-centered love (*sensualitas*) and the spirit of self-sacrifice (*pietas*) underscores the relative inflexibility of Boccaccio's conception of love between human beings. It is not *until* sensuality—or the life of the senses and the body—is transcended that anything worthwhile is experienced.

Two instances of wifely endeavor are especially remarkable because they elicit from Boccaccio precise descriptions of what he considers the true form of *claritas* available to a woman. Triaria follows her husband into an enemy city and fights at his side: "Great is the force of conjugal love in a pure heart. To these [women there is] no fear as long as their husbands' honor is exalted" (xcvi:390).[22] And Sulpicia follows her husband into exile, bent on sharing with him every discomfort and privation:

> The woman does not know how to be a wife who refuses to bear with her husband the blows of fate, weariness, exile, poverty, and to march against dangers with a strong will. This is a woman's war, these are her battles, her victories, her most conspicuous triumphs: to overcome with honesty, with fortitude and with a chaste spirit the feebleness, the comforts, and the obsessions of family life. From this derives their fame and eternal glory. (lxxxv:336)[23]

It is significant here that in the course of his celebration of Sulpicia's courage Boccaccio slips into metaphor; in fact, the nature of the struggle this woman undergoes alters as the passage proceeds. It is in the first place a struggle to confront physical and objective hardships of exile; it is finally a struggle to transcend the moral limitations of a conventional wifely existence. As a result, Sulpicia appears to have been denied a real part of her story; her important battles no longer take place on actual ground and over real conflicts but rather in her mind and against aspects of her own nature.

This transvaluation of the terms upon which a woman gains *claritas* recalls Boccaccio's earlier transformation, in the histories of Leena and Epicari, by paradox of a woman's true eloquence: she speaks well when she is silent. Both kinds of slippage are characteristic of the arguments in moralistic treatises directed at women for the next two centuries: exhortations to moral perfection, to be realized in a vague, hypothetical world of feeling about which nothing certain can be known, are substituted for counsel concerning experiences of an objective reality about which reasonable persons might agree or disagree.

Among the many histories in this collection it is difficult to find one in particular that conveys clearly the anxiety and frustration that seems so often to pervade, in one way or another, Boccaccio's idea of a woman who is worth praising because, as he states in his Proem, she has been enflamed "by a spark of the fleeting splendour of the world." But in the bizarre fates of two very different women, the princess Dripertua and the legendary Niobe, something of the conflict between the writer's stated intention and the text he actually writes is evident.

Dripertua is a faithful daughter to her father, Mithradates, whom she follows even after his defeat by Pompey. Her energy and devotion are all the more remarkable, Boccaccio writes, because she is reported by ancient historians to have been born with a double set of teeth and "to [have given] in her time a monstrous spectacle of herself to all the people of Asia" ("monstruosum de se spectaculum Asyaticis omnibus tribuit evo suo")—a misfortune for which she does not blame her father (lxxv:302). The image of Dripertua's teeth is strikingly suggestive. It implies that beneath her filial devotion is a certain ferocity that could have been directed against her

41

father for his part in giving her this attribute and that might be directed at other men (the second set evokes the image of a *vagina dentata*) should they attempt to take her from her father. This daughter's devotion is therefore deeply ambiguous, superficially correct yet charged with hostility and fear.

Boccaccio's version of Niobe's story follows the plot of the legend; what is remarkable are his observations on Niobe's plight. Since nature has made women mild and submissive, he concludes:

> It is no wonder . . . if divine anger is more prompt and judgment more cruel against proud women [than against proud men] each time they exceed the limits of their feeble condition, as stupid Niobe did, fooled by the tricks of Fortune and ignorant of the fact that the generation of many children is not a work [indicative] of the *virtus* of the person who bore them but of nature who directed the benevolence of heaven to the mother. (xv:80)[24]

In other words, Niobe can claim no *virtus* as a mother, for the excellence of her children is owing to Fortune and not to the care she has lavished on them. Her story is thus a thoroughly negative version of the various histories celebrating women as men. As such, it points to the most formidable of Boccaccio's inconsistencies. Throughout the *De mulieribus* he has ostensibly praised but actually made suspect the woman who gains *claritas* by participating in public activities; he has commended her for virile qualities while at the same time demonstrating how dangerous these qualities cause her to become. Here he denies a woman *claritas* for performing those essentially private tasks that by implication he has suggested are her privilege and duty. In effect he reduces her to a biological machine, a conduit through which the next generation passes into life. Once again Boccaccio's argument lapses into paradox.

I have suggested that the *De claris mulieribus* functions rhetorically as a *concessio,* a figure of thought in which a proposition—in this case that the *virtus* of women is praiseworthy—is made in order to be discredited. In what kind of a world of discourse, and specifically of *political* discourse, would Boccaccio have been moved to make such a statement and to what end?

The absence of any explicit discussion in the text itself of the reasons for such an argument makes the task of interpretation difficult; nevertheless certain points are quite clear. For Boccaccio the notion of a woman who attains *claritas* is charged with feelings of mistrust. Throughout his histories such women are shown breaking through conventional limits to feminine behavior, effacing distinctions between the sexes, abandoning their customary places in the social order. Comparable instances of feminine rebelliousness are rare in other of Boccaccio's historical works of this period, but one—in the *De casibus* concerning Brunhildis, Queen of the Franks—seems especially significant.

In this work Boccaccio intends to illustrate that the goddess Fortuna works to punish tyrannical and overbearing governors. The principal exception to his thesis is the dramatic history of Brunhildis. Recalling sources in Ovid, Boccaccio has Brunhildis speak in her own defense and deny that Fortune is anything more than a trope, a figure of thought designed to mask the fact that real historical explanations are unavailable or unacceptable to the historian.[25] In effect, her accusation jeopardizes the significance of the entire text and its vision of history as Providential. The importance of this incident to readers of the *De mulieribus* is that the voice subverting the moral assumptions upon which the text bases its understanding of historical events is that of a woman.

The history of Brunhildis gives a focus to Boccaccio's own uncertain politics: it indicates his perception that the threat of social chaos is posed not by a tyrant but by a figure representing the socially subordinate, typically represented (as instituted in Scripture) by a woman. Brunhildis's effrontery does not necessarily indicate that Boccaccio saw that women were gaining social and economic power (although perhaps this is also the case) but rather that he feared that the system by which power was allocated was in danger of breaking down. Throughout the *De casibus* Boccaccio's political opinions find constant expression in the texts of the individual histories that make up the treatise. In essence he adopts two opposing points of view on the distribution of power: he lashes out against tyrannical government when he speaks of the former Florentine dictator, the so-called Walter of Athens. But he is also critical of the *popolo*—the large class of artisans, merchants, and bankers whose collective greed, he says, overrides any concern with the common good. While he insists that a ruler is to be responsive to the will of his subjects, he also paints these subjects as unruly and feckless. In other words, his effort to define, and in a sense to redefine, the elements of good government is marked by fear of figures both of authority and of subordination. His willingness to believe in the judgment of either is evidently undercut by misgivings created by his knowledge of the nature of political and business activities in Florence.

The *De mulieribus* shows the same kind of tension between attitudes that are in theory mutually exclusive. It proposes to redefine another relationship of authority and subordination—in this case of the authoritative male over the subordinate female—and to perceive in the subordinate the *virtus* that might justify in certain cases a self-authorized and independent behavior. Yet this attempt at the redefinition of a kind of political (sexual and familial) relation repeatedly ends in irony, much as if Boccaccio regarded, whether consciously or not, any change in the customary arrangements for the distribution of power as too risky and preferred finally to affirm a more traditional political order.

By virtue of its contradictions Boccaccio's text on women exemplifies certain of the important developments that were to occur in European historical writing, in which for the next two centuries every aspect of the institution of political power came under review. In these texts a wide spectrum of possible forms of government are the subject of repeated discussion, and the problems of assigning and enforcing political and religious authority elicit a variety of responses, both liberal and conservative. In its depiction and condemnation of famous women the *De mulieribus* represents an early effort to comprehend and respond to some of the ideas that were to feature in this debate. Its ambivalence indicates that Boccaccio, like many other humanist writers, saw the classical past both as exemplary of an admirable (and in this case genderless) *virtus* and as a source from which traditional moral and political (in this case gender-linked) positions might be affirmed.

Notes

1. For Aristotle's discussion of the political status of women, see most importantly the *Politics* 1, 5; 1260a 5–8. For a useful discussion of Plutarch's *Mulierum virtutes,* see Stadter; on women and the state in antiquity, see Okin, 15–96; for a survey of learned thought on the position of women in the Renaissance, see Maclean, 47–81. Many of the defenses of women that appeared in print throughout the early sixteenth century adapted Boccaccio's histories to their own generally unambiguous ends; Capella's *Della eccellenza et dignita delle donne* (1526), Champier's *Nef des dames vertueuses* (1515), and Elyot's *Defence of Good Women* (1540) are merely representative. For an early study of the *De mulieribus* that recognizes its latent contradictions, see Hortis.

2. . . . ut semper in virtutem videatur exire . . . illas intelligere claras quas quocunque ex facinore orbi vulgato sermone notissimas novero. . . . All translations are my own.

3. The *De mulieribus claris* was begun in 1361 and continuously revised to 1375. A late work, it is part of a group of writings in Latin, including the *De genealogia deorum gentilium* (1350–1360, revised to 1375) and the *De casibus virorum illustrium* (1355–1374), that show the influence of Petrarch and Boccaccio's own increasing concern with religious orthodoxy and political order—a concern that may to some degree reflect Boccaccio's direct involvement in the civic affairs of Florence during the busy period from 1350 to 1358. In particular, Boccaccio's immediate model for the *De mulieribus* is Petrarch's *De viris illustribus.* For a discussion in English of these works and their relation to Boccaccio's political activities, see Branca, 97-127.

4. . . . quod sexui [in] firmiori natura detraxerit, id tuo pectori Deus sua liberalitate miris virtutibus superinfuserit. However disingenuous we may find Boccaccio's argument here—that a woman is praiseworthy insofar as she "is" a man—it is similar to that of Plutarch in the *Mulierum virtutes,* and a regular feature of most later defenses of women. In societies like those of Renaissance Europe where social and political order were thought to depend on maintaining a strict hierarchy of persons, where the very concept of equality was rarely expressed and usually philosophically suspect, to praise a creature by identifying it as qualitatively higher on creation's ladder than it in fact is may not be so back-handed a compliment as it might seem. What is remarkable, and unique to Boccaccio, is the development of these notions of value and worth in the histories that follow.

5. He quippe ob eternam et veram gloriam sese fere in adversam persepe humanitati tolerantiam coegere, sacrosancti Preceptoris tam iussa quam vestigia imitantes; ubi ille, seu quodam nature munere vel instinctu, seu potius huius momentanei fulgoris cupiditate percite, non absque tamen acri mentis robore, devenere.

6. . . . eamque perorando tam efficaciter inexhausta facundia agere, ut maxima audientium admiratione mutato sexu redivivus Hortensius crederetur.

7. . . . nunc hac ex parte versus integros, nunc ex illa metrorum particulas carpens, miro artificio in suum redegit propositum . . . ut, nisi expertissimus, compages possit advertere . . . ut huius compositi ignarus homo prophetam pariter et evangelistam facile credat fuisse Virgilium.

8. . . . in id egit mollitiei deditum, ut etiam inter mulierculas, femineo ritu sedens, fabellas laborum suorum narraret.

9. Ex quibus satis comprehendere possumus, hominum mulierumque conspectis moribus, multas ubique Cyrces esse et longe plures homines lascivia et crimine suo versos in beluas.

10. . . . quasi in ocium et thalamis nate sint, sibi ipsis suadent se, nisi ad amplexus hominum et filios concipiendos alendosque utiles esse, cum omnia que gloriosos homines faciunt, si studiis insudare velint, habeant cum eis comunia.

11. Quo equidem non minus, et muta prius et inde precisa eius lingua, splendoris consecuta est, quam florida persepe oratione apud suos valens meruerit forsitan Demosthenes.

12. . . . [actum est] ut, que privata precipuam honestatem servaverat, in tam sublimi evecta pontificatu in ardorem deveniret libidinis . . . actum est ut papa conciperet . . . obstetrice non vocata, enixa publice patuit qua fraude tam diu, preter amasium, ceteros decepisset homines.

13. . . . cum . . . non solum reintegratum sit decus, quod feditate facinoris iuvenis labefactarat ineptus, sed consecuta sit romana libertas.

14. Qua possum via, dilecta filia, libertatem tuam vendico . . . opere Virginii ac Icilii facta secunda plebis secessione, actum est ut decemviri coacti abdicarent imperium et romano populo quam occupaverant libertatem linquerent.

15. . . . necdum satis erat mulieris libertas reddita, cum labefactati corporis indignatio . . . inpelleret ut nec iterum, si oportuerit, subire cathenas, tetrum intrare carcerem et cervicem prebere securibus expaverit animosa femina, inclita scelesti facinoris ultrix, quin servorum gladios constanti iussu in caput infausti stupratoris adigeret.

16. The political problem Boccaccio addresses implicitly here in the story of Dido— that is, the extent to which a ruling queen can be governed by her husband, if at all—is not really solved before the middle of the sixteenth century when arguments involving the succession of Elizabeth I and Mary Stuart clarify the difference between a woman in the capacity of wife and a woman in the capacity of governor. In the former capacity she is subject to her husband, regardless of his status, but only in affairs that have strictly to do with the conduct of their marriage. In the latter capacity her husband is subject to her; in effect, he is as much her subject as anyone else in affairs of the realm. He can claim no special privileges or power. The classic formulation of this distinction is by Aylmer.

17. Satis, me miseram, adverto fecunditatem meam patrie michique fuisse adversam; ubi filium et civem peperisse arbitrabar, hostem et infestissimum atque inflexibilem peperisse me video. Satius quippe non concepisse fuerat: potuerat sterilitate mea Roma absque oppugnatione consistere et ego misella anus in libera mori patria.

18. Sane consumato triumpho thesauro et virtute spectabili, aiunt illam privato in habitu inter romanas matronas cum filiis senuisse.

19. Hypsicratheam, que tot vite sue subsidia laborando prestiterat, ne illi superviveret, veneno assumpsit.

20. . . . dumque servitutem et turpitudinem laqueo obstinate fugerent, non viribus, sed fortune crimine suos homines superatos ostendunt.

21. . . . sublata sensualitatis nebula, advertentes quoniam nil honestum pro salute amici omictendum sit, ex intimis cordis latebris excitata pietate, ut viros periculo eximerent.

22. Ingentes in sano pectore coniugalis amoris sunt vires: nulla illis, dum modo viri gloria extollatur, formido.

23. . . . sed cum viris, exigente fatorum serie, subeundi labores, exilia perpeti, pauperiem tolerare, pericula forti ferre animo: que hec renuit, coniugem esse non novit. Hec uxorum spectanda militia, hec sunt bella, he victorie et victoriarum triunphi conspicui. Molliciem luxumque et angustias domesticas honestate et constantia ac pudica mente superasse, hinc illis est fama perennis et gloria.

24. Quam ob rem mirabile minus si in elatas dei proclivior ira sit et iudicium sevius, quotiens eas sue debilitatis contingat excedere terminos, ut insipiens Nyobes fecit, fortune lusa fallacia, et ignara quoniam ample prolis parentem fore, non virtutis parientis, sed nature opus esse, in se celi benignitatem flectentis.

25. This is an extraordinary story and merits further study. Boccaccio, in the guise of the historian, is engaged in interviewing the ghost of Brunhildis, who laments that she cannot succeed in getting Boccaccio to believe her own account of her life. She declares: "This is the misfortune that comes to those who are unhappy: no one believes them" (Infelicium hoc vetus infortunium est, ut eis egrius prestetur fides.) And again: "Alas, how miserable I am! You think I am a liar. Thus the saying goes: 'Fortune is like this: it takes away belief in the words of those from whom it has taken all other goods'" (Me miseram, quia infelix sum! mendacem existimat iste. Dictum est: Sic Fortuna facit: horum verbis aufert fidem quibus bona cetera abstulit; 9.1:750, 756). For the dictum on Fortune, see Ovid *Epistolae ex Ponto* 2.3, 10.

Works Cited

Aristotle. *Politics.* Loeb Classical Library 264. Cambridge, Mass.: Harvard University Press, 1972.

Aylmer, John. *An Harborowe for Faithfull Subjects.* Strasborowe, 1559. Facsimile reprint, The English Experience, no. 423. New York, 1972.

Boccaccio, Giovanni. *De casibus virorum illustrium.* Tutte le Opere 9. Milan: Mondadori, 1983.

―――. *De claris mulieribus.* Tutte le Opere 10. Verona: Mondadori, 1967.

Branca, Vittore. *Boccaccio: The Man and His Works.* Translated by Richard Monges. New York: New York University Press, 1976.

Hortis, Attilio. *Le Donne famose descritte da Giovanni Boccacci.* Rivista Triestina di Scienze, Lettere ed Arti. Vol. 6. Trieste, 1877.

Maclean, Ian. *The Renaissance Notion of Woman.* Cambridge: Cambridge University Press, 1980.

Okin, Susan Moller. *Women in Western Political Thought.* Princeton, N.J.: Princeton University Press, 1973.

Ovid. *Tristia. Ex Ponto.* Loeb Classical Library 151. Cambridge, Mass.: Harvard University Press, 1975.

Stadter, Philip. *Plutarch's Historical Methods: An Analysis of Mulierum Virtutes.* Cambridge, Mass.: Harvard University Press, 1965.

Zenobia in Medieval and Renaissance Literature

Valerie Wayne

uring the Middle Ages and the Renaissance, women were sometimes damned not with faint praise but with extensive and effusive adulation. While titles proclaim their fame and worth—*Concerning Famous Women, The Legend of Good Women, The Defence of Good Women, The Nobility of Women,* and one more explicitly desperate instance, *A Woman's Woorth, defended against all the men in the world*—the texts themselves often contradict their titles through affirming an association of strength and virtue with men and masculinity. These texts that celebrate women therefore permit us to glimpse the conflict between women's experiences and the cultural norms that influenced their lives, even though most of the texts tried to perpetuate those norms.[1] As I consider here the literary representations of a woman named Zenobia, I will be especially concerned with three issues involved in that encounter between a person and her culture: definitions of gender difference, injunctions on sexual pleasure, and descriptions of domestic role.

Zenobia is an especially useful medium for these concerns because her life was often recounted as an *exemplum* by medieval and Renaissance writers. Boccaccio, Chaucer, Lydgate, Christine de Pizan, Juan Luis Vives, Helisenne de Crenne, Sir Thomas Elyot, Agrippa,

Zenobia as warrior, from a miniature in *Le Livre des femmes nobles et renomées,* a French translation of Boccaccio's *De claris mulieribus.* Early fifteenth century. British Museum Royal 16 G.V. By permission of the British Library.

William Bercher, Antony Guevara, William Painter, George Pettie, Ariosto, Ben Jonson, George More, Barnabe Rich, Daniel Tuvil, and Thomas Heywood[2]—all commend her prowess, her fortitude, her chastity, or her learning. She was a kind of woman warrior of the third century who was descended from the rulers of Egypt, grew up in the forests where she learned to kill wild animals, married a prince of Palmyra and conquered the Eastern Empire with him, then ruled that city-state in Syria as a regent for her sons after her husband died, and was eventually defeated by the Roman emperor, Aurelian. The principal source for her life was the *Historia Augusta,* a collection of biographies of Roman emperors, caesars, and usurpers living from A.D. 117 to 284 that was written about 395. Although the *Historia* has been described by one modern scholar as a "fictional history" that "carries a mass of fabrications,"[3] it was a recognized classical authority during the eras we are considering, and the writers who used it were less concerned to write factual history than to recount lives for didactic purposes. They presented their readers with a public version of the self, one influenced by and conveying social and cultural values. For this reason, their treatment of a woman who did not suit all the conventional categories of feminine behavior becomes especially interesting when they register astonishment at her achievements and adjust their accounts to serve various normative purposes.

Typically feminine behavior usually prevented women from having their lives recounted at all. In his preface to *Concerning Famous Women,* Boccaccio laments the small recognition women have received from previous writers, but he admits parenthetically how unqualified most of them were to perform conventional heroic acts: "If men should be praised whenever they perform great deeds (with strength which Nature has given them), how much more should women be extolled (almost all of whom are endowed with tenderness, frail bodies, and sluggish minds by Nature), if they have acquired a manly spirit and if with keen intelligence and remarkable fortitude they have dared undertake and have accomplished even the most difficult deeds?" (xxxvii). Boccaccio's subjects in his book therefore rarely succeed as women: if their behavior is conventionally feminine, it is too weak to merit much attention; if it is not, they deserve attention not as women but as aberrant creatures who have succeeded in spite of their sex. Of Artemisia, for example, who became a woman warrior after her husband died, Boccaccio inquires: "What can we think except that it was an error of Nature to give female sex to a body which had been endowed by God with a magnificent and virile spirit?" (127). Those women whom Boccaccio treats are often exceptional because they combine female bodies with "manly," "magnificent," or "virile" spirits—spirits that cannot be seen but can be inferred from the accomplishment of "difficult deeds." This combination of body and spirit is technically an "error of Nature," as Boccaccio suggests of Artemisia. Zenobia's life shows evidence of a similar "error" since she gained physical strength from her early life in the woods: "Having thus overcome feminine softness, she was so strong that by her strength she surpassed the young men of her age in wrestling and all other contests" (226). Boccaccio's book on women therefore becomes a collection of exceptions, strong but aberrant tokens, not a clear confirmation of women's worth.

Boccaccio treats Zenobia not only in this collection on women but in another gathering of lives, *The Fates of Illustrious Men,* remarking as he does so that the Emperor Aurelian could lead Zenobia ceremoniously in triumph "since she had put aside the characteristics of a woman for those of a man" (209). Chaucer, who used both sources from Boccaccio for *The Monk's Tale,* also includes Zenobia's life as the only woman's among the seventeen tragic lives retold by the Monk. She appears in an unambiguous female role only after she has been defeated and publicly shamed. The changes are plainly set forth at the end of his account: she who frightened kings and emperors is now the object of people's gazes; she who wore a battle helmet and won towns by force now wears on her head a vitremyte, a woman's cap; and she who bore a scepter of flowers now bears a distaff. If Zenobia's masculine spirit qualified her for fame in Boccaccio's accounts, in Chaucer's she becomes womanly through defeat.

These versions of Zenobia's life authorize an aberrant creature whose existence cannot be denied but who is an apparent contradiction—a strong woman. The contradiction arises from correlations assumed to exist among the terms of two sets of binary oppositions. The first set—male versus female—viewed the sexes as opposite to each other rather than similar or complementary. The second opposition—strong versus weak—was derived from descriptions of the physical body. Often these descriptors were applied beyond the body to the internal or entire being, which was referred to as "nature," "spirit," or "heart." Men's bodies were said to be strong, and then their nature was inferred to be strong; women's bodies were seen as weak, so their natures were thought to be weak, too. Since hierarchy and value are implicit in all binary oppositions, this inference of "nature" from physical description made explicit what was presupposed all along: that men were superior to women not only physically but in moral worth, just as weak natures were assumed deficient to strong ones. When Zenobia performed deeds that implied strength or capability, her actions contradicted the correlation between women and weakness. To explain her within the framework of these oppositions, the writers shifted to the other term to describe her as an "unnatural" conjunction of female and male characteristics. The practice created a third category of admirably aberrant women who were valued in contrast to "natural" women because they were more like men.

Praising such women does not celebrate them as androgynous or bisexual individuals who combine female and male characteristics in a positive synthesis; nor does it deconstruct the opposition between femininity and masculinity by challenging those categories and their dependence on a fixed concept of identity (Moi, 12–15). Instead it accounts for the existence of some women who were not clearly inferior to men by attributing to those few some male characteristics. Finally the practice valorizes masculinity and reasserts the inferiority of women. And it lasted a long time. In the sixteenth century, Juan Luis Vives praised Catherine of Aragon for her tenacity in trying to preserve her marriage to Henry VIII by saying that she had "a man's heart, by the error and fault of nature" (Watson, 10). If the fault was nature's, it nonetheless produced an improvement upon woman's nature, so it was still better to be an aberration than to be a woman. William Painter works with the same antitheses in 1567 when he says of Zenobia, "of a woman, she cared but onely for the name, and in the facts of Armes she craved the title of valiant" (97v). When noting her custom of always being present at battle and showing herself "more hardie than any of all the troupe," he adds that this is "a thing almost incredible in that weake and feble kynde" (97v–98). Such behavior must have appeared incredible to those for whom these oppositions seemed so fixed and firm that they had become fundamental to their interpretation of experience.

The values associated with the oppositions so prevalent in medieval discussions of women appeared to shift when some humanists sought grounds for arguing that women were superior to men. Sir Thomas Elyot provides conventional definitions of the sexes in his *Defence of Good Women:* "Nature made man more strong and couragiouse, the woman more weake fearefull and scrupulouse, to the intente that she for her feblenesse shulde be more circumspecte, the man for his strengthe moch more adventurouse" (36). Then he converts these differences to an argument for women's superiority on the grounds that women are more prudent than men and that the virtue of prudence is a superior mark of a rational being: "The power of reason is more in the prudente and diligent kepynge, than in the valiaunt or politike geatyng," and "Prudence, whiche in effect is nothyng but reason, is more aptly applied to the woman, whereby she is more circumspecte in kepynge, as strengthe is to the man, that he maye be more valiaunt in geattynge" (44–45). Elyot assumes the correlations between the two sets of oppositions but instead of inferring "nature" from the physical body he introduces a new category—reason—that he applies equally to both sexes. He values the exercise of this rational faculty more than physical strength. So a woman's self-defense from her position of physical weakness becomes superior to a man's activity in combat. When he presents Zenobia as a confirmation of these arguments, he has her speak as a character only after she has been defeated by Aurelian. That formidable woman who once invaded Mesopotamia enters the dialogue by remarking, "Ye have caused me to do, that I have used verye seldome. . . . To be out of myne owne house at this tyme of the nyghte" (52–53). Her reluctance, her fear of "infamy" (53), is a positive quality for Elyot, one that confirms her prudence and her reason. A profound suspicion of the outside world and its effect upon a woman's reputation lies behind this account.

More radical was the disassociation of moral nature and physical strength that was always implicit within the binary oppositions. It was Christine de Pizan who questioned the connection. "A large and strong body never makes a strong and virtuous heart," she says, "but comes from a natural and virtuous vigor which is a boon from God, which He allows Nature to imprint in one reasonable creature more than in another" (37). She challenges the association between strength and nature, asserting instead the presence of another "Nature" that serves as an intermediary between God and the individual, imprinting strength of heart or courage irrespective of gender. For Christine, then, good or strong women might exist without contradiction, and those women who are monstrous or unnatural are associated not with physical strength, but with evil. "For to tell the straight truth, there is nothing which should be avoided more than an evil, dissolute, and perverted woman, who is like a monster in nature, a counterfeit estranged from her natural condition, which must be simple, tranquil, and upright" (18). She also identifies a compensation for women's physical weakness. "If Nature did not give great strength of limb to women's bodies, she has made up for it by placing there that most virtuous inclination to love one's God and to fear sinning against His commandments" (37). One problem with Christine's revision is that, as she posits women's virtue as a compensation for their physical weakness, she makes them the primary bearers of her culture's moral and religious values.

Christine also resorts to a concept of "Nature" when she revises these definitions of the sexes. Like others, she uses the term to identify some agency of natural order, one that for her has its source directly in God. In restructuring that order she shows the effects of her own interpretations of experience on her perceptions of herself and other women. She can do so because the term "Nature" is used by all of these writers to invoke an order that is social and cultural, not "natural"; hence the word can be redefined. Jonathan Dollimore has shown that some Renaissance writers like Montaigne and Francis Bacon were aware of the relativism behind this procedure, as when the former observes that "the lawes of conscience, which we say to proceed from nature, rise and proceed of custome," or the latter remarks that "moral virtues are in the mind of man by habit and not by nature" (16). Christine, too, may have understood how much she was altering previous patterns as she wrote: she describes the approach behind her *Book of the City of Ladies* as *antiphrasis,* a method that permits her to speak against what previous writers like Boccaccio have said about women (Callies, 269). But the more important point for our understanding of these eras is that the oppositions of gender difference, of men as strong and women as weak, were so fundamental to perceptions at the time that they functioned like other ideologies discussed by Dollimore: "Both Althusser and Montaigne see ideology (or custome) as so powerfully internalised in consciousness that it results in misrecognition; we understand it (insofar as we 'see' it at all) as eternally or naturally given instead of socially generated and contingent" (17–18). The contradictions associated with women in these works are a function of just such a misrecognition, so that when these male writers set out to praise women, the norms they use presuppose male superiority so fully that they denigrate women even as they praise them. Their stated intentions are, if not beside the point, nonetheless subverted by their own procedure.

If these concepts are socially contingent, they are also subject to change over time, and the arguments for women's superiority made by Elyot and Christine de Pizan do represent some historical changes in thinking about women. While the Middle Ages celebrated Zenobia for deeds writers thought of as masculine, Renaissance writers gave more emphasis to her typically feminine qualities. One effect of this change was that the issue of her gender became less important than the control of her sexuality and her assumption of a conventional role, for once a writer accepted Zenobia as a woman, she was a potential temptation and a potential wife.

Boccaccio was the first to comment at some length on her sexual behavior, but the material was always available to make her an exemplar of chastity. According to all the accounts of her life that treat this subject, Zenobia never slept with her husband except to conceive children by him, and she regularly abstained from her husband's bed long enough to see whether she had conceived before sleeping with him again. During pregnancy she would not let him touch her. Boccaccio comments: "How praiseworthy was this decision in a woman! It is clear that she thought sexual desire is given to men by Nature for no other reason than to preserve the species through continuous procreation, and beyond this it is a superfluous vice. However, women having similar moral scruples are very rarely found" (228). What is presented here as Zenobia's opinion about sexual desire was the opinion articulated by most writers through the middle of the sixteenth century—that sexual pleasure was permissable, if at all, only in conjunction with procreation. The earliest accounts of Zenobia's life show her putting this injunction into literal practice. Christine de Pizan includes a remark that suggests the practice might have been a function of religious preference—"This maiden despised all physical love and refused to marry for a long time, for she was a woman who wished to keep her virginity for life" (52)—and the remark combined with what else we know about Zenobia's life might suggest it was also a function of personal preference. But for most of these writers it was enough that her actions showed a strict adherence to religious injunctions on married sexuality.

The medieval writers were not especially concerned with this aspect of Zenobia's life, however: Christine de Pizan gave it very brief treatment, and Chaucer's Monk viewed it from the perspective of her husband, Odenathus: "Al were this Odenake wilde or tame, / He gat namoore of hire" (3481–3482). Yet Zenobia's chastity becomes central in Juan Luis Vives' conductbook of about 1529, *The Instruction of a Christian Woman,* where she appears at some length in a chapter called "Howe [the wife] shulde lyve betwene her husbande and her selfe privatly" (el^v). He praises her enthusiastically: "Who wolde thynke that this woman had any luste or pleasure in her body? This was a woman worthy to be had in honour and reverence whiche had no more pleasure in her naturall partes than in her fote or her fynger. She had be worthy to have borne children withouten mannes company whiche never desyred it but only for children: orels to have brought them forthe without payne which gate them without pleasure" (e4ᵛ–e5). Vives is clearly delighted with Zenobia's sexual restraint, not only because it accords with religious standards of marital chastity, but because it shows that she is devoid of sexual feeling. He admires her so much that he finds her worthy of an immaculate conception or an exemption from the curse of the Fall. Absence of sexual pleasure within a woman is for him a sign of extraordinary virtue—because, of course, it provides a far greater assurance of chastity than the mere exercise of restraint. For there is nothing to restrain.

There is also, in this view of her, nothing to entice. The advantage from a man's perspective is that she becomes responsible for controlling sexuality in men, and those who emphasized the virtues of female chastity were, primarily, male authors. Perhaps the appropriation of the woman warrior for the exemplar of chastity, which appears also in the case of Spenser's Britomart, is made on the assumption that such women were more able to use their strength to control their own sexual responses, or that they had fewer responses to control. When someone like Zenobia was viewed as a woman rather than a man *manqué,* the issue of her chastity became much more important, and the change suggests a greater concern with the desires that such a woman was capable of arousing.

One other way of controlling the desires of both sexes was to restrict women through a rigidly defined role: to domesticate them more than desex them. That means was pursued by Elyot in his *Defence of Good Women.* He takes up Zenobia's life only after she has been defeated by the Emperor Aurelian and is confined to an estate where she lived like a Roman matron with her children. However, Zenobia does recount her life before her defeat, and considerable emphasis is placed upon her study of moral philosophy when she was young. Her governance of the kingdom of Palmyra after her husband's death is also treated at some length. It might have been possible for Elyot to apply these discussions of education and governance to arguments for an extension of women's spheres of activity, but instead they are interpreted in a very limited way. Of education he has Zenobia say: "For by my studye in moral philosophy . . . I perceyved, that without prudence and constancy, women mought be broughte lyghtely into errour and foly,

57

and made therfore unmete for that companye, wherunto they were ordeyned: I meane, to be assistence and comfort to man through theyr fidelitie" (55–56). Zenobia learned the fidelity appropriate to a wife from her education, and this effect of it is stressed far more than her ability to educate her own children or to write the epitomes or histories she is said to have composed. Of her government Elyot has her explain: "And to the intente that the name of a woman, shulde not amonge the people be had in contempt, I used so my procedynges, that none of them mought be sayd, to be done womanly. Wherfore I sate alway abrode amonge my nobles and counsaylours, and sayde myne opinion, so that it seemed to theym all, that it stode with good reason" (61–62). Here "womanly" behavior is assumed to be silent and poorly reasoned; Zenobia's government appears unwomanly but reliable when she speaks her mind and reasons persuasively. Yet Elyot himself never reasons from Zenobia's performance that women are capable of governing outside their homes. Finally his praise for her government seems intended to guide women as domestic managers, and that is what Elyot himself suggests in his preface to the *Image of Governance:* "My litle boke callid the defence of good women, not only confoundeth villainous report, but also teachith good wives to know well their dueties."[4] Their primary duties are to stay at home and devote all of their energies to their husband and children.

Elyot does explicitly intend that his book will confound those who speak disparagingly of women. He says in his dedication that after reading Zenobia's life, he desired that it should be read in English, "wherby women (specially) moughte be provoked to imbrace vertue more gladly, and to be circumspecte in the bryngynge up of theyr children" (1). Then he remembers "the ungentyll custome of many men, whiche do set theyr delyte in rebukynge of women, althoughe they never receyved displeasure, but often tymes benefyte by theym" (2). So he tells the story of Zenobia's life as evidence against antifeminist views, preceding it by an argument between two characters, Candidus and Caninius, who are advocates for and against the sex. Nothing he says about women is as ambiguous, as snide, or as ironic as Boccaccio's frequent remarks. And the debate between the two men is plainly concluded in favor of women's superiority. Is it not, then, unfair to charge Elyot, of all these authors, with contradicting or subverting his own assertions?

I do not think so, for the virtue that he accords to women is so fugitive and cloistered that it needs to be rigidly defined before it can exist at all. It seeks no test in the world at large, and its ability to endure one is questionable. The prudence Elyot proclaims as women's greatest strength is a timid acceptance of a social order that keeps them at home and encourages men to seek them there. Just as he proposes no changes in previous definitions of sexual difference or injunctions on sexual pleasure, so Elyot advocates no activities for women such as those Zenobia herself engaged in. His treatment of her life only after she is defeated by the Emperor Aurelian is analogous to the defeat she suffers from her confinement to a domestic role in his account. Although he argues for women's superiority, Elyot is the only writer who focuses primarily on Zenobia's life after that defeat. Christine de Pizan had simply ignored it. Elyot makes it his subject, for it allows him to illustrate a superiority that depends upon excluding women from activities where reason cannot be equated with prudence because it has a larger application. Elyot's role for married women is much like that described as the "angel in the house," but the role finds its beginnings here over three hundred years before Coventry Patmore's poem of that name.[5] If Vives' version of Zenobia's life makes her look nearly frigid, Elyot's shows her as a willing captive. Together these accounts describe the chaste domestic, a role that is tamer than the warrior woman and more fully restricted yet is remarkably similar to it at a sexual level, for both views of Zenobia remove her from the field of desire. The woman-warrior and the woman-domestic are both safe—they are sexually unapproachable and not eligible to arouse men's feelings. The primary claim for their virtue finally has less to do with women's goodness than with men's, for they serve as a guarantee of men's sexual control.

After reviewing nearly all of the literature on women in the Renaissance, Linda Woodbridge remarks that its view of women "was an unstable compound. Even the Renaissance mind, shot through with paradox from infancy, could not indefinitely hold in colloidal suspension the theory that women were weak and the fact

Zenobia as wife, from a drawing by Inigo Jones of Ben
Jonson's *Masque of Queenes,* presented at Whitehall on 2
February 1609. Zenobia's part was played by the Countess
of Derby. In *The Masque of Queenes, by Ben Jonson, with
the Designs of Inigo Jones.* London: The King's Printers,
1930. By permission of the British Library.

that the women one knew were strong, the theory that virtuous women never left the house and the fact that seemingly virtuous women one knew worked in shops and attended the Globe" (325–326). The disjunctions she observes are just those I have tried to point out, yet there is little indication that the suspension did not hold to the seventeenth century and, in many respects, far beyond it, or that writers in any number became more conscious of the gap between theory and fact or cultural norm and individual experience. One reason may be that the very act of writing about women not only perpetuated the norms applied to them but gave an appearance of harmony between those norms and their subjects. When a woman like Zenobia led an army or ruled a city-state, her very life challenged accepted notions of female behavior, much as Elizabeth I's did when she assumed the English throne. By making Zenobia's life into an *exemplum,* writers could to some degree control it, bring it into better alignment with the norms most important to them, and commend themselves in the process for acting on behalf of her and her sex. Elizabeth I devised a similar identity on her own behalf in presenting herself as a Virgin Queen, and the image she chose showed even greater sexual restraint than that in the manly woman or the chaste domestic, as if only a virgin might be entrusted with Elizabeth's degree of political power. The *exempla* created about Zenobia served a similar function—not just to perpetuate cultural norms, but to assure oneself and others that they had been met, that women were weak, chaste, and homebound even though one of them grew up in the woods, fought wild animals, led an army, drank with her troops, and governed wisely. So if the goals of these writers were not entirely achieved or are not satisfactory to some of us now, that is because the presuppositions that prompted the *exempla*—that men are the standard of value by which others are judged and that masculinity as well as femininity is defined in a specific and limiting way—are implicit within them. The writers are trapped by their own norms, by what is so fundamental to their interpretation of experience that they call it "Nature."

Representations of Zenobia's life did not end with the seventeenth century. Since the publication of accounts of the archeological digs in Palmyra in 1753 and treatment of her life in Gibbon's *Decline and Fall of the Roman Empire* in 1776, no fewer than eight novels, two poems, a melodrama, and an opera have been published based on her life.[6] Walter Savage Landor has her die with Rhadamistus in one of his "Imaginary Conversations." Edgar Allan Poe incorporates her as Signora Psyche Zenobia, alias Suky Snobbs from Philadelphia, and teaches her to write for magazines in his essay "How to Write a Blackwood Article." Nathanial Hawthorne casts her as his heroine in *The Blithedale Romance,* describing her as a "high-spirited Woman, bruising herself against the narrow limitations of her sex"[7]: she is at least shown as far more conscious of those social norms than in any previous account, a change that reflects the influence Margaret Fuller had upon that fictional portrait. And the influence from life to literature could work the other way around: in 1813 the eccentric Englishwoman, Lady Hester Stanhope, who was traveling in the romantic eastern Mediterranean, made an entry into Palmyra that she later described as the greatest triumph of her life. She was envisioning herself in the role of its first queen (Browning, 70).

Zenobia was also the precursor of that figure now associated with the dilemma of nineteenth-century women writers—the madwoman in the attic. The Lady Zenobia Ellrington appears in Charlotte Brontë's first love story, written about 1830 when she was fourteen. Lady Ellrington is a tall, strong, dignified woman who lapses into fits of rage when her love for a marquis is not returned. Fannie Ratchford's study of the Brontës' juvenilia shows how Charlotte used Lady Ellrington for the character of Bertha Mason in *Jane Eyre* (204–207). Sandra Gilbert and Susan Gubar use the same character to represent the predicament of the woman writer, and their adaptation is equally appropriate to the historical Zenobia, who studied philosophy with Longinus, knew Latin and Greek, and composed histories—or, as Elyot put it, "eloquent stories" (52). When Elyot remarks that a woman in Zenobia's situation at the end of her life would have had time to write since her children were all grown and she was confined to an estate, he shows little understanding of the problems of an intelligent, sequestered woman that Gilbert and Gubar explore so fully.

So she was transformed from medieval warrior and Renaissance wife to woman writer of the nineteenth century, and in the twentieth century Zenobia changed at least one more time—into a car. In 1926 two American women, Rose Wilder Lane and Helen Dore Boylston, set out to drive from Paris to Albania in a Model T Ford named Zenobia, and their journey is recorded in a book called *Travels with Zenobia.* There is something entirely appropriate about this last incarnation of Zenobia. Instead of being a mere vehicle for others' travels, including my own, as a modern machine she may finally escape the constraints of "Nature," sexuality, domesticity, madness, and authorship. Women are not always confined by them either. Like Model T Fords, they may be seen steaming down some street in southern France, around a bend in the Balkan states, or over the Delaware River on the Tacony Palmyra Bridge on a dusty quest to find out a new route, some terrible beauty, and a different future.

Notes

I would like to thank my colleagues Joseph Chadwick and Craig Howes for their generous help on this essay.

1. Most commentators on these texts, from Wright and Camden to Dusinberre and Jordan, consider praises of women as evidence of more positive attitudes towards women in medieval and Renaissance society. Jordan even uses the word "feminism" to describe humanist treatises such as Elyot's *Defence of Good Women.* I have tried to show in this essay why I consider the term inappropriate and why such texts do not represent an unambiguous advance for women. Woodbridge articulates similar views.

2. Boccaccio, *Concerning Famous Women,* 226–230, and *The Fates of Illustrious Men,* 207–210; Chaucer, *The Monk's Tale,* 2247–2374; Lydgate 8.666–742; de Pizan, 52–55; Vives, D4^v and e4^v–e5; Crenne, 100; Elyot, *Defence of Good Women,* 51–66; Agrippa, E5^v; Bercher, 100; Guevara, see Bush, 33–34; Painter, 95–100^v; Pettie, 221; Ariosto, 37.5.5–6; Jonson, 336–337; More, E6^v–E7^v; Rich, 3; Tuvil, 43–44; and Heywood, 231 and 379. Harbage, 74, also lists a lost play called *Zenobia* performed in England between 1580 and 1592. In quoting from these authors, I have expanded contractions and modernized i, j, u, and v where necessary.

3. Syme, 6 and 1. His conclusion regarding a composition date (ca. 395) appears at 90.

4. Elyot, *Four Treatises,* 208.

5. Gilbert and Gubar, 22–29; Woolf, 57–63; Houghton, 341, 375–379.

6. Hirsh, 188–190, provides a list in his footnotes, which may be supplemented by Vaughan's novel and Albinoni's opera. The best archeological account is in Browning.

7. Hawthorne, 2–3. Hirsh discusses Hawthorne's use of William Ware's novel at 183. Poe also used it.

Works Cited

Agrippa, Cornelius. *Of the Nobilitie and Excellencie of Womankynde*. Translated by David Clapham. London, 1542. Ann Arbor, Mich.: University Microfilms, Reel 71.

Albinoni, Tomaso Giovanni. *Zenobia, Regina de Palmireni*. New York: Garland, 1979.

Ariosto, Ludovico. *Orlando Furioso Translated into English Heroical Verse by Sir John Harington (1591)*. Edited by Robert McNulty. Oxford: Clarendon Press, 1972.

Bercher, William. *The Nobility of Women (1559)*. Edited by R. Warwick Bond. London: Roxburghe Club, 1904.

Boccaccio, Giovanni. *Concerning Famous Women*. Translated by Guido A. Guarino. London: George Allen and Unwin, 1964.

―――. *The Fates of Illustrious Men*. Translated by Louis Brewer Hall. New York: Frederick Ungar, 1965.

Browning, Iain. *Palmyra*. Park Ridge, N.J.: Noyes Publications, 1979.

Bush, Douglas. *Mythology and the Renaissance Tradition in English Poetry*. Rev. ed. New York: Norton, 1963.

Callies, Valerie. Review of *The Book of the City of Ladies*, translated by Earl Jeffrey Richards. *Biography* 7, no. 3 (1984): 266–276.

Camden, Carroll. *The Elizabethan Woman*. Rev. ed. Mamaroneck, N.Y.: Paul J. Appel, 1975.

Chaucer, Geoffrey. *The Works of Geoffrey Chaucer*. Edited by F. N. Robinson. 2d ed. Boston: Houghton Mifflin, 1957.

Crenne, Hellisenne de. *A Renaissance Woman: Helisenne's Personal and Invective Letters*. Translated and edited by Marianna M. Mustacchi and Paul J. Archanbault. New York: Syracuse University Press, 1986.

Dollimore, Jonathan. *Radical Tragedy: Religion, Ideology, and Power in the Drama of Shakespeare and His Contemporaries*. Chicago: University of Chicago Press, 1984.

Dusinberre, Juliet. *Shakespeare and the Nature of Women*. London: Macmillan, 1975.

Elyot, Sir Thomas. *The Defence of Good Women*. Edited by Edwin Johnston Howard. Oxford, Ohio: Anchor Press, 1940.

―――. *Four Political Treatises by Sir Thomas Elyot*. Edited by Lillian Gottesman. Gainesville: Scholars' Facsimiles and Reprints, 1967.

Gibbon, Edward. *The Decline and Fall of the Roman Empire*. Edited by J. B. Bury. 3 vols. New York: Heritage, 1946.

Gibson, Anthony. *A Womans Woorth, defended against all the men in the world*. London: John Wolfe, 1599.

Gilbert, Sandra M., and Susan Gubar. *The Madwoman in the Attic: The Woman Writer and the Nineteenth-Century Literary Imagination*. New Haven, Conn.: Yale University Press, 1979.

Harbage, Alfred, and S. Schoenbaum. *Annals of English Drama, 975–1700*. 2d ed. Philadelphia: University of Pennsylvania Press, 1964.

Hawthorne, Nathaniel. *The Blithedale Romance*. Edited by Seymour Gross and Rosalie Murphy. New York: Norton, 1978.

Heywood, Thomas. *Gunaikeion*. London, 1624. Ann Arbor, Mich.: University Microfilms, Reel 890.

Hirsh, John C. "Zenobia as Queen: The Background Sources to Hawthorne's *The Blithedale Romance*." *Nathaniel Hawthorne Journal* (1971), pp. 182–190.

Houghton, Walter E. *The Victorian Frame of Mind, 1830–1870*. New Haven, Conn.: Yale University Press, 1957.

Jonson, Ben. "The Masque of Queens." In *Plays and Masques,* edited by Robert M. Adams. New York: Norton, 1979.

Jordan, Constance. "Feminism and the Humanists: The Case of Sir Thomas Elyot's *Defence of Good Women.*" *Renaissance Quarterly* 36 (1983): 181–201.

Landor, Walter Savage. "Rhadamistus and Zenobia." In *Complete Works,* 16 vols., edited by T. Earle Welby, 1:270–273. London: Chapman and Hall, 1927.

Lane, Rose Wilder, and Helen Dore Boylston. *Travels with Zenobia: Paris to Albania by Model T. Ford.* Edited by William Holtz. Columbia: University of Missouri Press, 1983.

Lydgate. *The Fall of Princes.* Edited by Henry Bergen. London: Early English Text Society, 1924.

Moi, Toril. *Sexual/Textual Politics: Feminist Literary Theory.* London: Methuen, 1985.

More, George. *Principles for Yong Princes.* London, 1611.

Painter, William. *The Palace of Pleasure.* 2d tome. London, 1567. Ann Arbor, Mich.: University Microfilms, Reel 259.

Pettie, George. *A Petite Pallace of Pettie his Pleasure.* London, 1576. Ann Arbor, Mich.: University Microfilms, Reel 1390.

Pizan, Christine de. *The Book of the City of Ladies.* Edited by Earl Jeffrey Richards. New York: Persea, 1982.

Poe, Edgar Allan. "How to Write a Blackwood Article." In *Complete Works,* 17 vols., edited by James A. Harrison, 1:269–282. New York: T. Y. Crowell, 1902.

Ratchford, Fannie Elizabeth. *The Brontës' Web of Childhood.* New York: Columbia University Press, 1941.

Rich, Barnabe. *The Excellencie of Good Women.* London, 1613. Ann Arbor, Mich.: University Microfilms, Reel 858.

Syme, Sir Ronald. *The Historia Augusta.* Bonn: Rudolf Habelt, 1971.

Tuvil, Daniel. *Asylum Veneris; or, A Sanctuary for Ladies.* London, 1616. Ann Arbor, Mich.: University Microfilms, Reel 1,012.

Vaughan, Agnes Carr. *Zenobia of Palmyra.* New York: Doubleday, 1967.

Vives, Juan Luis. *The Instruction of a Christian Woman* (1529?). Facsimile in *Distaves and Dames: Renaissance Treatises for and about Women,* edited by Diane Bornstein. New York: Scholars' Facsimiles, 1978.

Watson, Foster. *Vives and the Renascence Education of Women.* London: Edward Arnold, 1912.

Woodbridge, Linda. *Women and the English Renaissance: Literature and the Nature of Womankind, 1540–1620.* Urbana: University of Illinois Press, 1984.

Woolf, Virginia. "Professions for Women." In *Women and Writing,* edited by Michele Barrett. New York: Harcourt Brace Jovanovich, 1980.

Wright, Louis B. "The Popular Controversy over Woman." In *Middle-Class Culture in Elizabethan England.* Chapel Hill: University of North Carolina Press, 1935.

Heloise: Inquiry and the *Sacra Pagina*

Eileen Kearney

ttempting to recover something of the reality of Heloise's life and thought is a challenge, not only in the reading and reconstruction of texts but also in recognizing the multiple and divergent factors that influenced her thought both consciously and unconsciously. For example, although clearly in touch with the innovative theological developments of her time, Heloise nonetheless works within the accepted doctrinal norms concerning the role and status of women. In this she reflects the same ambiguity that is constant in a tradition that extols the woman of virtue but does so by measuring women against values and norms understood and articulated by men. This essay proposes to bring forward Heloise's insight into only one aspect of her experience that she discussed in view of the inner struggle she faced when living out the norms of the Benedictine Rule. Unhappy with the prescriptions of the Rule as written for men, she strives to alter these to conform to the needs of women. As she clarifies the issues, Heloise discovers a theological principle that assures the basic equality of the sexes. Nonetheless she is caught by her own adherence to philosophical and biological principles of inequality. Heloise does not and indeed cannot escape this twelfth-century dilemma.

Precise historical data on Heloise is limited, and details of her birth, probably around 1100, are unknown.[1] We do know that she was the niece of Fulbert, a canon at the cathedral of Notre Dame on the Ile de la Cité. We also know that she studied at the Convent of Argenteuil, a few miles north of Paris, and prior to meeting Peter Abelard, she was certainly trained in the arts of grammar and rhetoric. Historically, the significance of Heloise has always depended upon her relationship with Peter Abelard, which began sometime around 1114 or 1115 when Fulbert brought Master Peter into his residence as her teacher. The two became the paradigm of star-crossed lovers; their subsequent tragedy and the end-story of their lives as Abbess and Abbot has been immortalized throughout the centuries (Dronke, *Abelard*). This is, in fact, what history best remembers about Heloise.

Modern scholarship, prompted perhaps by Gilson's examination of their relationship in his study, *Heloise,* and in his essay, "Abélard," (83–89) or by the renewal of interest in the authenticity question,[2] has taken a new look at Heloise (Radice, Bourgain). Textual analysis illustrates her skill as a writer (Dronke, "Heloise" and "Heloise's *Problemata*"). Recent studies dealing with the history of the Paraclete raise the question of the potential significance of Heloise in her role as Abbess of the Paraclete (*Cartulaire;* Waddell, "Peter Abelard" and *Twelfth Century Hymnal*). One essay examines Heloise's view of the monastic ideal as formulated in her letters (Georgianna).

But there is an aspect of Heloise's career that has not been considered: her interest in and practice of commenting on the *sacra pagina.* Heloise's writings deserve to be considered from a theological perspective, since in the twelfth century, she stands as an articulate and at times brilliant thinker who took part in the transformation of theology from its essentially moral and monastic character to the kind of scientific discipline we now associate with the theology of the schools.[3] In fact, it is precisely those elements which characterize this transformation that are at work in her theological writings: the new and challenging questions (Landgraf, Flint); the struggle to recover a sense of harmony when faced with the problem of contradictory teachings;[4] and the increasing reliance on discursive inquiry as it opened the way for men and women to discover meaning from the *sacra pagina* through a critical investigation of texts.[5]

Only a few works of Heloise are extant today.[6] However, in addition to some personal letters, two texts clearly illustrate how she was engaged in this sort of penetrating study of sacred literature. In the *Problems of Heloise,* the author writes a brief introductory letter to Peter in which she tells him of the difficulties experienced in trying to understand the meaning of certain passages of Scripture. Each of the forty-two questions raised are resolved by a solution of Abelard.[7] Heloise's Letter-Preface, although very brief, tells us a great deal about the Abbess of the Paraclete. For example, Heloise emphasizes that rather than serving as a means of conversion, this sacred study raises many perturbing questions. And in some of her questions, Heloise lines up conflicting scriptural passages just as Abelard had done with his own collection of patristic sources in the *Sic et non.*[8] Like the students who followed the lectures of Peter, her interest is explicitly focused on the meaning of passages that for one reason or another raise difficulties of interpretation.

It is, however, in another work that Heloise best illustrates her skill in the burgeoning theological methods of the early twelfth century. Heloise writes a long letter to Peter in which she makes two requests: first, that he compose a treatise on the origin of nuns and, second, that he accommodate the discipline of the Rule of Benedict for a community of women.[9] The letter gives precise evidence of how her method compares with the way that the masters were approaching theology by relying on dialectics. Under their influence, the contemplative ambiance for *lectio divina* was gradually being replaced by an analysis of Scripture and the Fathers, informed by the principles of logic, textual criticism, and the creative appropriation of doctrine. Heloise's letter, which describes in depth the inadequacy of the Benedictine Rule when imposed on women, reflects the analytical character of the new theology. In particular, three aspects of her approach are most noteworthy: first, while Heloise scrutinizes the Rule in detail, she actually uses the evidence of the text to establish the point of her argument that the Rule, as written, cannot serve women; second, she uses critical inquiry to shape this argument so that Peter can see the dilemma she faces; and third, she resolves this problem in such a way that her discussion of theological issues leads to a new formulation of doctrine.

A Critique of the Rule of Benedict

Although Heloise opens and closes her letter with some personal comments to Peter, she soon sets before him the issue at hand: she wants a Rule of Life that is suitable for women. She notes that none of the Fathers imposed a Rule upon women and that furthermore, Benedict specifically wrote his Rule for men. "I wonder," she asks, "what Benedict would do if he had written for women?"[10]

Point by point, Heloise refers to thirteen chapters of the Rule in which the directives are inappropriate for women, and she explains why:[11] for example, the clothing described is designed for men (242.18–22; R 160), and the required manual labor is also suitable only for men (243.20–21; R 161–162). In addition, she mentions practices that endanger either the spirit of celibacy or of silence:[12] the prescription that allows the Abbess to entertain both male and female guests (242.23–243.7; R 161–162) and the legislation that requires a male to read the Gospel during evening prayer (242.22–23; R 160). She also believes that the practice which requires a formal commitment from a candidate within a one-year period does not allow sufficient time to evaluate a person's constancy (243.22–25; R 161).

As Heloise continues, it is increasingly apparent that the Rule with its prescriptions (which the nuns must profess) cannot in fact be fulfilled precisely because it is intended for men. In her eyes, this presents an ethical dilemma (Dronke, "Heloise's *Problemata*").

However, she also knows that this problem could be eliminated if, officially, legislation were either changed or relaxed. The practice of dispensation from obligations or of modifying a law as a concession because of particular needs or circumstances that make it impossible to fulfill the law had always been part of the Christian life.[13] Heloise points out several examples within the Rule itself where Benedict prescribes such moderation and accommodation of legislation according to need. For example, he allows wine and meat to be taken as a concession (244.14–15; R 163), and he teaches that the Rule is only a beginning step; one should use discretion in its implementation (247.3–9; R 168). Along with Benedict's insistence on discernment, Heloise adds other authorities whose teachings support her own belief that the "letter" of the Rule is not absolute.[14] Of course, she relies on Scripture,[15] but she also turns to experience: to the contemporary practices of the Canons of St. Augustine (245.34–35; R 165), to the nature of the female body (245.37–38; R 165), and to what she understands of masculine and feminine psychology (253.7–11; R 178).

We can see that Heloise has read her text meticulously; and just as other scholars of the time were beginning to indicate when their commentary was a personal opinion or teaching, so too Heloise makes her reader aware that this reflection is her very own.[16] Other aspects of her theological method also parallel the practice of theology in the schools. First of all, Heloise has worked within a hierarchy of authority: the Fathers take precedence over Benedict. Even more significantly, the text is discussed not by commenting on each chapter in sequence but by lifting out a series of difficulties: Heloise cites the text only and precisely where its prescriptions are unsuitable for women and where its counsels offer the reader a means of accommodating the law. Thus, while she lets Peter know that she is careful and judicious, her dilemma as Abbess is acutely described. And she insists on a resolution of her problem: How, in fact, can she impose legislation that cannot and should not be followed?

Inquiry and the *Sacra Pagina*

Heloise's encounter with the Rule of Benedict forces her to raise serious, probing, and challenging questions about the religious commitment of women. At the heart of her inquiry, though, is her acceptance of a principle of male superiority: women are the weaker sex (R 160, 161, 162, 164–165).[17] This inequality pervades all areas of human life including the physical roles and duties of women, the lower rank of women in social and institutional hierarchies, and the spiritual dependence of women both on male models of sanctity and male standards for ascetical practices.[18] It is not as if some women do not achieve more than some men but only that in so doing they excel according to male standards. This bind cannot be put "right" in its twelfth-century context. But Heloise does surprise us by the rigor with which she investigates the logical consequences of the principle when applied to religious life: if women must profess a Rule that is written for men, they must, in fact, fail.

We have already seen how Heloise analyzed the Rule by establishing the text as the cause of an inevitable discrepancy between theory and practice. But this is only the beginning of her reflection. The Abbess of the Paraclete does more than show Peter her predicament. Heloise's letter continues to probe the issue by a critical discussion of the question at hand: Granted the Rule and its prescriptions, how can it be accommodated for women?

Heloise's reliance on the question as a literary and theological frame for her critique of the Rule is no accident. Beryl Smalley's research consistently highlighted the significance of such queries as one hallmark of the transformation of theology in the twelfth century (*The Study of the Bible,* 66–82). At the school of St. Victor, as well as in Paris and throughout the West, scholars were increasingly engaged in discursive inquiry as a method of theological discourse. What we are beginning to sense today, though, is that this approach was not restricted to the schools. Heloise is a perfect example of how the new theological methods were penetrating all intellectual circles. With Abelard as her teacher, she was of course in a privileged position. Nonetheless, if we examine her writing on the *sacra pagina* in detail, her personal skill and expertise begin to emerge.

Furthermore, Heloise will advance her thought through discursive inquiry. She continuously questions the meaning of ideas, and with each query and response, she brings the discussion through a series of progressive steps that eventually show how women can be free. She begins by citing Benedict's advice to abbots, urging them to preside with prudence and consideration, always attentive to the needs of the weak (244.13–15; R 163). Then she looks to common sense and states that to have the same Rule for both men and women is contrary to reason (243.40–244.1; R 163–164). Such remarks, woven in and out of her discussion, can seem insignificant and even dated, yet they support each step of her inquiry. And if we lift out the major developments of her thought from the fuller context of these reflections, the logical sequence of her thought becomes obvious:

> 1) Men and women are not equal; it is therefore unreasonable to expect both to follow the same rule (243.40–245.8; R 164).
>
> 2) There is no patristic precedent for such an imposition (245.10–13; R 164).
>
> 3) The Gospels, especially the Beatitudes, are the essence of Christian life: we should not strive to be more than Christian (245.7–8; R 164).
>
> 4) This is what is sufficient for women: . . . if we live continently and without possessions, wholly occupied by the service of God, and in so doing equal the leaders of the Church themselves in our way of life or the religious laity or even those who are called Canons Regular and profess especially to follow the apostolic life . . . (246.16–17; R 166).
>
> 5) . . . it is clear that virtues alone win merit in the eyes of God, and that those who are equal in virtue however different in works, deserve equally of God (250.30–33; R 174).

One could easily miss the power of her argument: women equal men. Heloise has logically lifted the question out of both an ideological and practical context and placed the issue in the theological arena: before God, women and men are equal. But, granted the prescriptions of the Rule as given, how can this be effectively realized? Heloise knows that dispensation[19] can be granted and, as noted, includes several illustrations of such practice in referring to the Canons who eat meat and wear linen (245.30–33; R 165) and to Benedict's advice that, rather than a daily recital of the Psalms, the monks may spread out the recitation over a full week (247.10–13; R 168).[20] She also mentions the teaching of Chrysostom who encouraged young widows to remarry (245.15–18; R 165) and of Jerome who cautioned against rashness in taking vows (245.21–25; R 165).

But mere precedent for dispensation or concession in history is not enough to assure Heloise in this case. The Abbess seeks a rationale in the sacred doctrine of Scripture. Of all the authorities she mentions, it is the teaching of Paul that is at the heart of her own understanding and plea. She cites Paul's Letters to Timothy and to the Romans, stressing in all cases the Pauline precept of justification through faith (248.40–249.15; R 171–172). It is this primacy of the interior disposition over and against all practice that becomes the doctrinal focus for Heloise. This is the turning point for her argument, and she has brought it forward carefully and clearly. Its authority is without question on every count: reason, logic, precedent, and its verity as the Divine Word.

Heloise can now be very precise in her request for the Paraclete. She wants Peter to exercise the same spirit of discernment as had Benedict and other authorities in the tradition: "I would like to see the same dispensation granted in our own times, with a similar modification regarding matters which fall between good and evil and are called indifferent, so that vows would not compel what cannot now be gained through persuasion" (248.20–23; R 170). And finally: "If concession were made without scandal on neutral points, it would be enough to forbid only what is sinful" (248.23–24; R 170).

In sum, Heloise offers Peter what she considers to be indisputable guidelines to resolve the problem she has put forward. She then presents her case within these ground rules: women are not equal to men; the fathers do not impose a rule on them; only the Gospel is the norm. But if women follow the Gospel, they are equal to men. The only problem that remains for Heloise is how to deal with the existing legislation of the Rule. And her answer to that is to employ the practice of dispensation or concession.

At this point, we can see that Heloise has tied it all together: the text itself, a critique from Scripture and the Fathers, arguments from reason, and the practice of concession in history. Now, she can move forward to the theological insight that is at the heart of her exegesis of the Rule: in the end, all prescriptions, all directives, all practices are merely the exterior frame and an external work. These, she tells Peter, are common to the elect and to the damned (248.27–29; R 170). It is not observance that matters before God. It is only love.

The Development of Doctrine

As a theologian, Heloise does not merely write to complain to Peter about the problem of implementing the Benedictine Rule for a community of women. Nor does she quietly wait for his response to her request to authorize a modification of the Rule. She moves forward in a discussion of issues that is characterized by a logical progression of ideas that tries to leave no stone unturned. Such inquiry leads her to a reformulation of doctrine that sheds new light on its significance. In the final pages of her letter, Heloise takes a stand on the Rule that is dependent upon her conviction about what is essential to Christian life: "For the things which do not prepare us for the kingdom of God or commend us least to God call for no special attention. These are all outward works which are common to the damned and the elect alike, as much to hypocrites as to the religious" (248.26–29; R 170). Heloise continues that love alone (*sola caritas discernat*) distinguishes the children of God from those of the devil (248.31; R 170). Ultimately, love is the issue.

These reflections immediately precede Heloise's citation of Pauline teaching regarding the ineffectiveness of observance noted previously. She adds the citations and scriptural allusions that record the words of Christ dispensing the Apostles from the Law when preaching (249.26–29; R 172). She also cites Augustine's text *On the Good of Marriage* to enhance her insistence on the interiority of love, since he taught that even "continence is a virtue of the soul and not of the body" (250.3; R 173). Heloise continues to develop these ideas. Virtue alone merits in the eyes of God, and in virtue all—men, women, monk, cleric—can merit equally (250.30–32; R 174). The true Christian is concerned with the inner person, and there is no real interest in the external (250.32–34; R 174).

Heloise has already effectively demonstrated that dispensation or concession is perfectly acceptable. However, she furthers this claim by continuing to probe other aspects of the issue. From the Matthean account of the Sermon on the Mount, she reconstructs the main aspects of Christ's teaching that support her concerns: "The soul is not defiled by any external thing," she notes, "but only what proceeds from the heart" (250.40–251.1; R 174).[21] She even indicates her approval of the teaching of the Lord: "He [Christ] also rightly says that even adultery or murder proceed from the heart, and can be perpetrated without bodily contact" (251.3–4; R 174). Heloise can therefore claim that "unless the spirit is first corrupted by evil intention, whatever is done outwardly in the body cannot be a sin" (251.2–3; R 174). Finally, her last statement about purity of intention summarizes her theological stance:

> Such devotion of spirit is more highly valued by God the less it is concerned with outward things, and we serve God with greater humility and think more of our duty to God the less we put our trust in outward things. . . . For the pious devotion of the mind to God wins from God both what is necessary in this life and things eternal in the life to come. (251.18–21 and 25–26; R 175)[22]

It is simple indeed. We have no need for any prescriptions beyond the Gospel; and in all things, it is the intention that counts.

Heloise reminds Peter to imitate his patron, the Apostle Peter, not only in name but in discernment: "Modify your instructions," she urges, "so that we can be free to devote ourselves to the offices of praising God" (252.3–6; R 176). Later, she repeats the same request: "It is chiefly in connection with the offices of the Church . . . that provision is needed" (252.45–253.6; R 178). This is no attempt to avoid rigor, however. Heloise says that whatever is needed and beneficial is to be maintained (252.12–16; R 176–177). What she wants is an authorized concession to what is necessary, fitting, and salvific for her community at the Paraclete.

The final lines of this letter seem to return to the moving eloquence of its initial statement (Dronke, "Heloise"). Heloise's confession of love and devotion to Peter is expressed in terms of his relationship to her as Founder, Creator, and Director of their Community at the Paraclete. It is his duty to respond and to "lay down a Rule" that they in turn can follow for all time. But Heloise has already made it quite clear what she wants to hear, and she has done so by a rigorous critique of the Rule and its tradition, by discursive analysis of the rationale for its prescriptions, and by singling out the primary theological category that lies at the heart of all religious practice.

This essay is meant only as a prolegomenon for any study of Heloise's role as a commentator on the *sacra pagina*. In a more detailed analysis it would be important to probe more deeply into the content of her comments, some of which raise questions concerning the unity of her thought. For example, Heloise formally accepts the idea that women are frail, yet she spends most of this letter struggling to establish a norm by which women and men can be counted as equals. Having successfully done this by shifting the question of equality away from physical standards and social expectations to the simplicity of the Gospel, however, she still seems to see the "new" Rule that Abelard will write for them as an accommodation in view of the weakness of the female sex. While this ambivalence is not unusual (McLaughlin, "Peter Abelard"), the force of her argument could have led to a different conclusion, that is, a request to write a Rule whose intent would be to focus on the religious profession of women in terms of love or Gospel simplicity. Had this been the outcome, the need for a dispensation from or an accommodation of the Rule would have disappeared entirely.

In addition to this concern for her insight into the development of doctrine, her comments on the Rule also need to be evaluated in relation to the work of her predecessors and her peers—in particular, Peter's own handling of the text in his reply to Heloise.[23] But even in this brief examination of the text we can already sense how Heloise shared in the spiritual and intellectual reformation of theology in the twelfth century. Here we find evidence that she embraced all of the new methods that were being practiced in the schools: the text is examined in detail; she compares and contrasts authors and teachings; she seeks out historical precedent; she skillfully interprets through discursive inquiry, moving her argument forward in a step-by-step fashion to lead the reader to precisely the point she wishes to establish. Heloise seems unafraid to overturn idols—with reason, with the needs of human nature, and with a realistic simplicity that understands the power of moderation in human endeavors. It is true that her doctrine is drawn from Scripture and the Fathers, but it is also related to precisely those points of Abelard's doctrine that set him apart from others: interiority and intentionality as the hallmark of the human spirit.[24]

We say so quickly that Heloise was Peter's pupil in all things. Indeed, from Peter she learned that commenting on Scripture was a skill that included not only a prayerful reading of that Word but also the kind of critical and systematic analysis of the text that would lead to a vigorous reappropriation of Christian doctrine in the West. Yet Heloise's letter on the Rule of Benedict clearly shows the power of her own intellect and insight. As a commentator on the *sacra pagina* Heloise brings freshness and vitality to the art of inquiry indicative of her own skill and of her place in the development of the theological tradition.

Notes

1. For more details on Heloise, consult Etienne Gilson's study *Heloise and Abelard* or that of Peter von Moos, *Mittelalterforschung*.

2. It is especially the research of the last fifteen years that is important. John Benton's initial essay, "Fraud," and subsequent developments are traced by David Luscombe in "The Letters" and by Benton's own reevaluation in "A Reconsideration." The most recent inquiry is that of Peter Dronke, *"Excursus."*

3. Beryl Smalley's pioneering studies are without equal, for example *The Study of the Bible*. Her last published essays explore how the Bible was studied from about 1150–1250 and open yet another horizon for our understanding of the development of exegesis and theology in the later twelfth and early thirteenth centuries. These essays have been collected and published posthumously in *The Gospels in the Schools, c. 1100–1280*. However, the most recent and comprehensive examination of medieval biblical studies is the major collaborative effort *Le Moyen Age*.

4. The work on the *Glossa ordinaria* at Laon and in Paris reflect this concern to provide a coherent synthesis of doctrine (Smalley, *The Gospels*). The most recent discussions of the historical difficulties involved in recovering the activities and accomplishments of the scholars associated with Laon are by Marcia Colish and Valerie Flint.

5. Abelard's *Sic et non* remains a most significant contribution for the use of dialectics within theology. The most thorough analysis of his theological method in relation to dialec-

tics is Jean Jolivet's study *Arts du langage*. Smalley's brief essay, *"Prima clavis,"* offers a clear precise illustration of one aspect of Abelard's innovative skill.

6. There are three letters written to Abelard that form part of the collected correspondence; in addition, Heloise wrote a long Letter-Preface and questions for the *Problemata Heloissae* and a Letter to Peter the Venerable after the death of Abelard.

7. No critical edition of the *Problemata Heloissae* is available yet. The Migne edition is in *Patrologia Latina* 178:677–730.

8. See Problems 5, 6, 8, 16, 18, 24, and 37–39.

9. Letter Six in the collected correspondence is Heloise's third letter. I have used the edition of J. T. Muckle in *Mediaeval Studies* for the Latin reading; for the English version consult Betty Radice's translation of *The Letters* (159–179). Information on the manuscript tradition can be found in Muckle's introductory essay (240–241); for a discussion of the dating of all the Paraclete literature, see Damien Van den Eynde's essay "Chronologie."

10. All references are included in the essay. For the most part I cite the text in English, but I include reference to both the Latin and English readings. The Latin is cited first by page and line, followed by the Radice translation with page number only (for example: 241.1– 242.15; R 159–160).

11. Heloise refers to the following chapters of the Rule: 2, 11 (twice), 18 (twice), 35– 41, 36, 40, 48, 55, 58, 64, and 73.

12. Thomas Waldman discusses some of these issues as they might have arisen in Abbot Suger's cause to gain possession of the convent of Argenteuil where Heloise resided, "Abbot Suger," pp. 245–249. It was this incident that led Heloise to begin her life as Abbess of the Paraclete. When expelled from Argenteuil by Suger, Heloise and some of her companions, invited by Abelard, founded the monastery of the Paraclete in 1130.

13. The term dispensation refers to an official granting of a licence to do something that would otherwise be considered canonically illegal. At the time of Heloise's writing one could read about dispensation in the *Decretum* of Ivo of Chartres and in the *De sacramentis* of Hugh of St. Victor (Villien, "Dispenses," 1428–1440).

14. The following are explicitly mentioned by Heloise: Chrysostom, "Sermon 7" in his Commentary on Paul's *Letter to the Hebrews* and the *Letter to Timothy;* Augustine, *On the Good of Marriage* and *On the Good of Widowhood;* Jerome, Letters 22, 52, 117, and 130 as well as the *Vita patrum;* and Canon Law, that is, a decree from the Council of Chalcedon, 451.

15. There are about sixty explicit biblical citations from both Christian and Hebrew Scriptures.

16. For example, Heloise writes: Unless I am mistaken (*ni fallor,* 245.11), I think (*arbitror,* 244.28) and I ask (*quaeso,* 248.17). Also, Heloise often used the technical terms and phrases that we associate with textual analysis and criticism: *inquam* (244.19), *scimus* (252.25), *arguerentur* (250.39), *ex his liquide verbis colligitur* (250.30), *ex quibus quidem verbis aperte colligitur* (245.7). I omit reference to the English text in these instances since the translation does not always indicate the more technical term she used.

17. Mary McLaughlin's analysis of Abelard's teaching in this regard provides many examples that compare Abelard and Heloise with their contemporaries ("Peter Abelard").

18. A most interesting development in light of this general trend is Abelard's Letter to Heloise *On the Origin of Nuns.* In this work Peter explicitly considers the history of religious life through an analysis of the life and work of the feminine leaders of the tradition. There is no English translation as of yet; the Latin is edited by J. T. Muckle in *Mediaeval Studies.*

19. Heloise uses a variety of terms in this letter in relation to the idea of dispensation: *concessus* (244.24), *dispensatio* (248.21), *indulgentia* (244.14), and *indultum sit* (252.15).

20. She mentions the teaching of Gregory from Chapter 24 of the *Liber Regulae Pastoralis* where he counsels pastors to be lenient with women (243.35–39; R 162) and various dispensations from the Rule authorized by Benedict, for example, on the concession for drinking wine (248.1–4; R 169) and on the modification of the laws of abstinence (248.17–20; R 170).

21. Consult Abelard's exegesis of this scriptural passage in the *Problemata Heloissae* (*Patrologia Latina* 178:709D–711A). This exegesis is, in fact, the biblical foundation for his ethical stance. As previously noted, the *Problemata* were written at the same time as the Letters, whereas the earliest date for the *Ethics* is 1135, just after the Paraclete material. For a discussion of the *Ethics,* see the edition by Luscombe.

22. I have emended the English reading here; for example, Radice translates *animi devotio* and *pia mentis . . . devotio* as "devotion of the heart" and "devotion of the mind" respectively. The Latin for heart, *cor,* is used by Heloise several times in this letter, especially in a biblical context. Her shift here to *animi* and *mentis* is, I think, deliberate and significant, paralleling the same kind of movement from biblical to discursive language that we find in Abelard's work. Another change I have made throughout my essay is to translate *discretio* as discernment rather than discretion since I think this renders Heloise's meaning more clearly.

23. Heloise's work on the Rule is original when compared with most commentaries, for example Rupert of Deutz; however, her ethical doctrine, with its perspectives on the primacy of intentionality, is Abelardian. Rudolph Mohr's essay examines both Heloise and Abelard's letters on the Rule of Benedict; however, Mohr only offers a summary of the contents of each letter ("Der Gedenkenaustausch").

24. In particular, Abelard's *Ethics* delineates the precision with which he understood the notion of sin (or innocence) in relation to consent or right intention.

Works Cited

"Abelard's Rule for Religious Women." Edited by T. P. McLaughlin. *Mediaeval Studies* 18 (1956): 241–292.

Benton, John. "Fraud, Fiction and Borrowing in the Correspondence of Abelard and Heloise." In *Pierre Abélard, Pierre le Vénérable. Les Courants philosophiques, litteraires et artistiques en occident au milieu du XIIe siècle.* Colloques Internationaux du Centre National de la Recherche Scientifique, 546. Paris: Editions du Centre National de la Recherche Scientifique, 1969.

————. "A Reconsideration of the Authenticity of the Correspondence of Abelard and Heloise." In *Petrus Abaelardus (1079–1142). Person, Werk und Wirkung.* Trier Theologische Studien, 38. Edited by R. Thomas et al. Trier: Paulinus Verlag, 1980.

Bourgain, Paschale. "Héloïse." In *Abélard en son temps.* Actes du colloque international organisé à l'occasion du 9e centenaire de la naissance de Pierre Abélard (14–19 Mai 1979). Paris: Les Belles Lettres, 1981.

Cartulaire de l'Abbaye du Paraclet. Edited by C. Lalore. *Collection des principaux cartulaires du diocèse de Troyes.* 7 vols. Paris: Ernest Thorin, 1878.

Colish, Marcia L. "Another Look at the School of Laon." Forthcoming, *Traditio* 43 (1987).

Dronke, Peter. *Abelard and Heloise in Medieval Testimonies.* W. P. Ker Memorial Lecture, 26. Glasgow: University of Glasgow Press, 1976.

————. "*Excursus:* Did Abelard Write Heloise's Third Letter?" In *Women Writers of the Middle Ages. A Critical Study of Texts from Perpetua (+203) to Marguerite Porete (+1310).* Cambridge: Cambridge University Press, 1984.

————. "Heloise." In *Women Writers of the Middle Ages. A Critical Study of Texts from Perpetua (+203) to Marguerite Porete (+1310)*. Cambridge: Cambridge University Press, 1904.

————. "Heloise's *Problemata* and *Letters:* Some Questions of Form and Content." In *Petrus Abaelardus (1079–1142). Person, Werk und Wirkung*. Trier Theologische Studien, 38. Edited by R. Thomas et al. Trier: Paulinus Verlag, 1980.

Flint, Valerie. "The 'School of Laon': A Reconsideration." *Recherches de théologie ancienne et médiévale* 43 (1976): 89–110.

Georgianna, Linda. "'Any Corner of Heaven': Heloise's Critique of Monasticism." Forthcoming, *Mediaeval Studies* 49 (1987).

Gilson, Etienne. "Abélard." In *La Théologie mystique de saint Bernard*. Etudes de philosophie médiévale, 20. Paris: Librairie J. Vrin, 1947.

————. *Heloise and Abelard*. Ann Arbor: University of Michigan Press, 1972.

Jolivet, Jean. *Arts du langage et théologie chez Abélard*. Etudes de philosophie médiévale, 57. Paris: Librairie Philosophique J. Vrin, 1969.

Landgraf, A. "Quelques collections de 'Quaestiones' de la second moitié du XIIe siècle." *Recherches de théologie ancienne et médiévale* 66 (1934): 368–393; and 67 (1935): 113–128.

"The Letter of Heloise on Religious Life and Abelard's First Reply." Edited by J. T. Muckle. *Mediaeval Studies* 17 (1955): 240–281.

The Letters of Heloise and Abelard. Translated by Betty Radice. New York: Penquin, 1974.

Luscombe, David E. "The Letters of Heloise and Abelard since 'Cluny 1972.'" In *Petrus Abaelardus (1079–1142). Person, Werk und Wirkung*. Trier Theologische Studien, 38. Edited by R. Thomas et al. Trier: Paulinus Verlag, 1980.

McLaughlin, Mary. "Peter Abelard and the Dignity of Women: Twelfth Century Feminism in Theory and in Practice." In *Pierre Abélard, Pierre le Vénérable. Les Courants philosophiques, litteraires et artistiques en occident au milieu du XIIe siècle*. Colloques Internationaux de Centre National de la Recherche Scientifique, 1969.

Mohr, Rudolf. "Der Gedenkenaustausch zwischen Heloise und Abaelard über eine Modifizierung der *Regula Benedicti* für Frauen." *Regulae Benedicti Studia* 5 (1976): 307–333.

Le Moyen Age et La Bible. Bible de Tous les Temps, 4. Edited by Pierre Riché et Guy Lobrichon. Paris: Editions Beauchesne, 1984.

Peter Abelard. Sic et non. A Critical Edition. Edited by Blanche B. Boyer and Richard McKeon. Chicago: University of Chicago Press, 1974.

Peter Abelard's Ethics. Edited by David E. Luscombe. Oxford: Clarendon Press, 1971.

Problemata Heloissae. Edited by J. P. Migne. Vol. 178. *Patrologia Latina*. Paris, 1855.

Radice, Betty. "The French Scholar-Lover: Heloise." In *Medieval Women Writers*, edited by Katherine N. Wilson. Athens: University of Georgia Press, 1984.

Smalley, Beryl. *The Gospels in the Schools, c. 1100–1280*. London: The Hambledon Press, 1985.

————. "*Prima clavis sapientiae:* Augustine and Abelard." In *Fritz Saxl, 1890–1940. A Volume of Memorial Essays from His Friends in England*. New York: T. Nelson & Sons, 1957.

————. *The Study of the Bible in the Middle Ages*. 2d ed. Notre Dame, Ind.: University Of Notre Dame Press, 1970.

Van den Eynde, Damien. "Chronologie des écrits d'Abélard à Héloise." *Antonianum* 37 (1962): 337–349.

Villien, A. "Dispenses," cols. 1428–1440. In *Dictionnaire de théologie catholique*. 15 vols. Paris, 1909–1950.

von Moos, Peter. *Mittelalterforschung und Ideologiekritik der Gelehrtenstreit üm Héloise*. Kritische Information, 15. Munich: Wilhelm Fink Verlag, 1974.

Waddell, Chrysogonus. "Peter Abelard as a Creator of Liturgical Texts." In *Petrus Abaelardus (1079–1142). Person, Werk und Wirkung*. Trier Theologische Studien, 38. Edited by R. Thomas et al. Trier: Paulinus Verlag, 1980.

————. *The Twelfth Century Cistercian Hymnal*. Cistercian Liturgy Series, 1–7. Kalamazoo, Mich.: Cistercian Publications, 1984.

Waldman, Thomas G. "Abbot Suger and the Nuns of Argenteuil." *Traditio* 41 (1985): 239–272.

The Frivolities of Courtiers Follow the Footprints of Women: Public Women and the Crisis of Virility in John of Salisbury

Cary J. Nederman and N. Elaine Lawson

istorians of social ideas and cultural practices are well aware that the identity of women during antiquity was an essentially domestic one.[1] Already Penelope had revealed the traits of the ideal woman—devotion to the maintenance of home, family, and *oikos*—and these were only confirmed by Antigone's stand on behalf of her brother against the public needs proclaimed by Creon. Aristotle thus appears typical, not only of classical Athens but of the whole ancient period,[2] in his characterization of women as creatures whose completely rational souls suit them only to be ruled by the head of a household on the basis of his marital or paternal authority (Aristotle, 1259a–1260a). By contrast, men are deemed to be equipped for citizenship and public affairs, which require the art of statesmanship in contradistinction to that of household management, according to Aristotle (Aristotle, 1252a–1253a). Historically, the Greek *oikos* and the Roman *familias* both rested on a "division of labour between men and women" rooted in the difference "between the woman's domestic functions" and the "political life of her male compatriot" (Wood and Wood, 51). Of course, the operative premise of such a nonpolitical conception of women is that it is possible to distinguish meaningfully between political rights and powers, on the one hand, and the private realm of domesticity, on the other. And, indeed, the evidence from ancient sources overwhelmingly suggests that Greeks and Romans alike understood and accepted a clear separation between public and private realms.

In the Latin Middle Ages, however, this distinction between public and private was substantially blurred because of the fragmented distribution of political power in the hands of an aristocracy of mounted warriors whose connection with one another remained tenuous at best.[3] In other words, it was no longer possible to use women's domesticity as the basis for their exclusion from the political arena. Rather, the structure of the household and the family largely formed the political arena, at least so far as the aristocratic elite of the Middle Ages was concerned. Political rights and jurisdiction were ordinarily determined by patterns of inheritance and marriage; and the social and political locus of noble intercourse, the court, was coextensive with the household of some greater or lesser feudal lord. In this context, the historical role of medieval women (or at least those of aristocratic origin, about whom we know most) was not strictly comparable to the circumstances of their classical Greek and Roman predecessors. Admittedly, because women were considered unsuited to military pursuits, they were excluded from knighthood and hence from a primary element of the identity that united the medieval ruling class. But within the confines of courtly society, women exercised a considerable measure of influence. This was especially true once the incessant warfare of the early Middle Ages had subsided and knights began to spend more time in their own castles or in the castles of their lords, partaking of the feasts, drinking sessions, and entertainments that a wealthy aristocracy in more peaceful times could enjoy. Indeed, by the twelfth century, openhandedness and hospitality were considered roughly as important to true nobility as military prowess.[4] At the core of courtly society, in turn, was the person traditionally responsible for organizing and managing the household, the woman. Not only were women of the court expected to costume themselves in a pleasing manner,[5] but they might also present gifts to favorites,[6] play chess and other games with courtiers,[7] and patronize the performers who

entertained at courtly functions.[8] If noblemen were the main bene-
ficiaries of a leisurely life at court, then it was their wives and female
relatives whose duty it was to provide courtly diversion. Women
thereby enjoyed access to the very center of aristocratic social and
political life during the Middle Ages.

Nor were medieval noblewomen ever completely relegated to
the still essentially domestic setting of the court. While no queen
inherited a kingdom or ruled on her own during the Middle Ages,[9]
many women exercised public powers through their inheritance of
lesser jurisdictions like fiefs, counties, and even entire provinces
(Ferrante, 9–10). It is not until quite late in the medieval period that
Salic law and similar legal tools of female exclusion were invoked
to prevent the transfer of political rights over lands to women.
Scholars have consequently concluded that some women of the
High Middle Ages cut a more public figure than at any other time in
Western history up to the present century.[10]

One of the primary examples that may be adduced to justify this
conclusion is Matilda, the daughter of English King and Norman
Duke Henry I.[11] From early life, Matilda was implicated in her
father's dynastic pretensions. In 1114, at the age of thirteen, she was
married to the German Emperor Henry V as the cement in an
Anglo-imperial alliance formed to combat papal intrigues. But the
death of Matilda's brother and stepbrother in an 1120 shipwreck,
coupled with Henry I's inability to father any further offspring,
made her once again valuable to her father. When Henry V pro-
pitiously died in 1125, Henry I immediately recalled Matilda and
compelled a large portion of his baronage to swear an oath of
allegiance to her as the royal successor. She was then betrothed a
second time, now to the Angevin Count Geoffrey, a marriage that
resulted in Anjou's inclusion within the Anglo-Norman sphere of
influence. When Henry I died in 1135, however, his barons rapidly
renounced their promise and transferred allegiance to Stephen of
Blois, a cadet grandson of William the Conqueror, and one of the
magnates who had previously sworn an oath to Matilda. The aspir-
ing queen was forced to rally her supporters, invade England, and
provoke civil war in order to regain the kingdom that was commit-

ted to her by her father. At the end of it, after nearly two decades of military action, she succeeded in acquiring Stephen's recognition of her son, the future Henry II, as his heir in return for her acceptance of the reigning king's legitimacy for the remainder of his life.

Scholars have sometimes suspected that Matilda's failure to retain the loyalty of the Anglo-Norman baronage after Henry I's death stemmed from the fact that she "was disliked . . . for her sex" (Douglas, 26). But the contemporary evidence does not substantiate this conclusion. English chronicles of the time and somewhat later are generally agreed in their admission that, whatever Matilda's quirks or flaws of personality, she possessed the most legitimate claim on the rule of England and Normandy and that Stephen was basically a usurper. Not once is Matilda's sex cited as a rationale for her exclusion from power.[12]

This interpretation of events is in all essentials confirmed by John of Salisbury's *Historia Pontificalis,* a chronicle of four years (1148–1152) in the pontificate of Eugenius III. John reports Stephen's attempt to legitimate his own usurpation of the English throne by obtaining a papal dispensation to crown his son, Eustace, as his successor.[13] John's account of Stephen's rationalization for this plan does not include any direct reference to Matilda's sex as an infirmity precluding her ability to rule. Rather, Stephen claimed that "the empress was not entitled to succeed her father, because she had been born of an incestuous union and was the daughter of a nun." While these constituted serious charges about Matilda's lineage, they cannot be construed as an assault upon her qualifications to reign based on her sex. Nor does Stephen assert that his oath to Matilda was somehow less legitimate because she was a woman. On the contrary, he "maintained that it had been extorted by force and was conditional only: namely, that he would uphold the empress's right to succeed to the best of his ability unless her father changed his mind." Stephen then proceeds to claim that Henry, on his deathbed, transferred his preference from his daughter to his sister's son, the selfsame Stephen. Finally, Stephen appeals to the fact that his ascension to the throne was a *fait accompli,* confirmed by the appropriate political procedures: "Stephen's claim to the crown" had been authorized "with the unanimous consent and approval of the bishops and nobles. What had been done with such ceremony could not, he concluded, be undone."

In short, nowhere in John of Salisbury's lengthy account of Stephen's defense of his own royal legitimacy do we encounter any element of the misogynistic attack upon Matilda that we would expect. It might be objected, of course, that Stephen was in no position to cast aspersions upon the female sex too strenuously, since his own claim to the rule of the Anglo-Norman realm was through his mother. But while such maternal inheritances were common enough during the Middle Ages,[14] the notion of a woman reigning as queen in her own right was utterly without precedent. It seems instead that Matilda's sex was simply not a relevant factor in the political discourse of the mid-twelfth century. Stephen's case was presented (and, by the way, defeated) on its own merits as a dynastic and feudal dispute.

What makes the report of the *Historia Pontificalis* particularly interesting is that its author is widely known today for the misogynistic views which he expressed elsewhere, notably in his *Policraticus* (1159).[15] The *Policraticus* is a scathing critique of the manners and mores that John of Salisbury took to be prevalent among Western European aristocrats of his day.[16] John preaches against an array of courtly practices, which he collectively labels "nugis curialium" ("frivolities of courtiers") and contrasts with "vestigiis philosophorum" ("footprints of philosophers"). It is mainly as an element of his critique of contemporary court life that John sprinkles his text with remarks about the vicious traits of the female gender and about the "effeminacy" of men who fall prey to the influences of women. Yet this is the same John of Salisbury who was clearly a partisan of Matilda's cause,[17] if only because he strongly opposed Stephen's usurpation,[18] and who declined the opportunity to direct misogynistic barbs towards her in the *Historia Pontificalis*. Was John a hypocrite? Or a blockhead? Or is there some more interesting explanation for his apparently ambivalent attitude towards women?

In order to resolve this dilemma, we need first of all to afford attention to John's rhetorical purposes in the *Policraticus*. One of his main themes throughout the work is that knighthood, which he takes to be the primary function of the feudal aristocracy, has come to be replaced and redefined by the other roles of the medieval warrior, namely, as ruler and especially as courtier. John is ordinarily regarded as an exponent of "religious chivalry," that is, the doctrine that military and political power should be placed at the disposal of the Church and its rights.[19] Hence, it is his view that any activities which detract from knightly service to God and His earthly representatives—which are, in effect, purely secular—ought to be banished. While John acknowledges that courtly and political activities are necessary aspects of lordship, he believes that the noble's crucial role as *bellatore* has been undermined. It is precisely in this regard that the female gender becomes significant to the central argument of the *Policraticus*. John in effect accepts that women cannot be excluded from the public life of the feudal aristocracy, that is, at court and in politics. But he fears that this intractable female participation has resulted in the weakening of men's military abilities, creating a crisis of virility in which the male sex becomes enmeshed in feminine preserves and concerns. The prevalence of feminine traits and behavior among feudal warriors is a sure sign to the author of the degeneration and dissipation of a thoroughly secularized military.

John is quite forthcoming in his depiction of the normative position of women, although he tends to cloak conventional attitudes in classical references. Each woman ought to be like Aeneas' wife Creusa, "who clings to her husband, tracking the footsteps of others because of the weakness of her sex" (*S* 51; *P* 534d). In general, John approves of marriage as a remedy for fornication (*S* 355; *P* 749a), although he doubts that marriage is compatible with a contemplative life. He warns against the wily, deceptive, and demanding ways of wives (*F* 356–360; *P* 749c–752d), even describing them as "domestic tyrants" (*F* 197; *P* 503d). John is particularly concerned that the orderly "natural" relationship between man and woman—man leading, woman following—has in his own day become inverted so that the "frivolities of the [female] sex" (*F* 360; *P* 753a) have come to dominate men. This "inversion" of characteristics in which women "rule" men occurs whenever the latter allow their "virile" military prowess to be placed at the disposal of or to be sapped by the female sex. In other words, John fears that women, excluded from participation in the chivalric order, may still threaten male hegemony over warfare by tempting knights with less honorable and spiritual pursuits at court. As a consequence of succumbing to such temptation, the warrior becomes merely a creation or creature of secular aims and goals, stripped of his higher and more noble calling.

It is easy enough to recognize that John's argument depends upon a conception of women that is deeply imbedded within the theological, literary, and philosophical traditions known both to him and to his audience.[20] This view holds that woman's nature, unlike man's, is rooted in her body and hence is of a sensuous rather than rational quality. Women are conceived as the agents and symbols of sexuality, of pleasure seeking, of physical gratification— the qualities that are most "typical" of feminine nature. Thus women are naturally akin to all manner of luxury as creatures of their passions. John's repeated insistence throughout the *Policraticus* that luxury and vice make men effeminate intimates his notion of the feminine essence as a bodily one. All of the temptations and vices of the flesh, which John denotes by the term "luxury," flow from that nature which is distinctively feminine. It is true that the *Policraticus* does not deny that women, even public women, can be virtuous insofar as they renounce the passionate aspect of their nature. John admits that Dido, the Carthaginian queen of Vergil's imagination, began her reign as a virtuous ruler. Only when she allowed her desire for Aeneas to color her judgment—once, that is, her repressed nature issued forth—did she permit and promote the hunting, feasting, and fornication that was the moral and political downfall of Carthage.[21] The female ruler must be especially careful not to indulge her characteristic vices, but John does not exclude her from governing on principle.

John's main concern, instead, is with the direct effects of courtly life upon those men who are exposed to its typical temptations. He fears that court, as a public realm from which women cannot properly be excluded, is not conducive to the maintenance of virility and its highest expression, warfare. In a notably graphic passage of the *Policraticus,* John compares the court to the "enervating" Fountain of Salmacis described by Ovid in the *Metamorphoses:*

> Its waters, according to the tale, were fair to the sight, sweet to the taste, pleasant to the touch and most agreeable to every sense, but so enervated all men who entered therein that they made them effeminate and deprived them of their nobler sex; and no man came forth therefrom without perceiving to his amazement and sorrow that he had been changed into a woman. For either his sex was totally destroyed and converted into the weaker counterpart, or else, some trace of his dignity remaining, he became a hermaphrodite . . . This poetic fiction represents the nature of life at court which enfeebles men by the loss of their manhood or perverts them while they yet retain its semblance. (*S* 121–122; *P* 566d–567b)

The significance of John's depiction of the court as a "feminizing" agency should not be lost on us. The court as seen through John's eyes was the center of pleasure-seeking and sensual gratification, in short, of "womanish" conduct which reflected preoccupation with physical rather than spiritual concerns. When John says that courtiers "sink down into the weaker sex, effeminate as the result of vice and the corruption of morals" (*F* 200; *P* 505b–c), he is illustrating the transmutation of man's nature (spirit or reason) into woman's nature (flesh) occasioned by exposure to courtly luxury. How could a courtier possibly behave with virtuous moderation when at each turn he was tempted with food, drink, sex and every imaginable form of diversion? "The best man" at court "is he who resists longest and most effectively, and is corrupted least" (*S* 121; *P* 566c). Court life emanates from and radiates feminine nature: it encourages all the typically female vices of "vanity, pride, greed, promiscuity, gluttony, drunkenness, bad temper, fickleness and more" (Shahar, 3). Women are characteristically court creatures; perhaps the court can do them no further harm. But the lure of court is so strong that any man who sets foot there, no matter how great his virtue, will inevitably succumb to the wiles and temptations of feminine delights.

John is equally insistent that many activities typical of the twelfth-century court are also to be reproved on the grounds that they place men under the guidance of women. The opening books of the *Policraticus* contain a critical roster of the various courtly frivolities, and it is here that John's assault on women is particularly virulent. For instance, hunting—a favored pastime of the Anglo-Norman aristocracy—is said to originate with "effeminate, spineless people" (*F* 13–14; *P* 340c–d). According to ancient mythology, John speculates, "a goddess was chosen to preside over hunting because the people did not wish to degrade their gods by making them preside over an activity characterized by self-indulgence and vice" (*F* 14; *P* 391a). On similar grounds, whatever virtue had previously been found in music is debased "by the fact that a harlot's appearance is given to that which was wont to inspire virile minds with manly ideas" (*F* 32; *P* 402b–c). What John means by "a harlot's appearance," of course, is the secularization of music through love lyrics and melodies which render "males effeminate" (*F* 33; *P* 403b). In both theme and style, love songs represent a danger that John describes as the "effeminate dalliance of wanton tones and musical phrasing" (*F* 32; *P* 402c).

Analogous considerations pertain to the theater, which at medieval court "descends to romances and similar folly, prostitutes not only the ear and the heart to vanity, but also delights its idleness with the pleasures of the eye and ear. It inflames its own wantonness, seeking everywhere incentives to vice" (*F* 37; *P* 405b–c). Even gambling and gaming, John declares, "tone down the manly voice into dulcet, effeminate strains" insofar as they constitute "lustful pleasures whence vices spring" (*F* 20; *P* 400c). From such harmful entertainments it is not far, according to John, to the more serious vices of drunkenness, gluttony, and, eventually, fornication.[22] "Lust is a child and connection of luxury," he remarks at one point; elsewhere he insists that "pleasure is not perfect without satisfaction of lust" (*F* 314, 354; *P* 723c, 739a). The logical and irredeemable consequence of all the courtly pursuits John catalogues in the *Policraticus* is the commission of illicit sexual union. Since women from the time of Eve have been particularly prone to sexual temptation, all the forms of courtly machination, culminating in the carnal act, must be credited to the feminine gender. The delights of the court, like that "poisonous courtesan" Cleopatra, are "created to corrupt character and assault the virtue of noble men" (*F* 182; *P* 495a). Seduction by this Cleopatran court is nearly impossible to avoid; withdrawal from its pleasures alone assures the retention of virtue and the salvation of the soul (*S* 14; *P* 518c).

John's exercise in misogyny should not be construed, however, as mere moralizing. Instead, he saw practical value in his teachings about the "feminization" of the aristocratic lifestyle. Feminine dominance over rulership and the court has the effect of destablizing the institution of knighthood, upon which medieval society was built. John's primary concern is with the military implications of the "womanish luxury" that has infiltrated chivalric society. In general, his view is that excessive luxury creates a "crisis of virility" characterized by the disintegration of the primary military functions of the polity and the erosion of the nobility as a warrior class. Luxury, John declares, "leads of necessity to dishonour. What can a man do bravely whom luxury and intemperance have not so much disarmed as completely sapped of life?" (*S* 206; *P* 603a). A luxurious lifestyle means succumbing to pleasure, a trait of womanish nature; and pleasure during times of peace wounds a soldier irreparably just as "in war men's bodies are wounded with swords" (*S* 14; *P* 518c). John elsewhere speaks of the ills of prolonged peace, which are often harder to combat and more insidious than an armed foe (*S* 193; *P* 597d–598a). Without experience of combat knights suppose that "military glory consists in cutting a fine figure with clothes of a brighter hue than others . . . and in being more proficient in the arts of pleasure than notable for valor" (*S* 184; *P* 594c). The sorts of behavior typical of court chivalry are consequently thought to be sufficient qualifications for the rigors of armed battle:

> The gamester, the fowler, and . . . makers of foolish songs and men who have never dealt in manly deeds nor have the marks of duty on them (for bristling beard and hardened skin are now in disrepute as being unmeet for works of wantonness) today put on the soldier, aspire to command and authority, and hold themselves out as leaders and teachers of a calling which they themselves have never learned. (*S* 226; *P* 661c)

Conspicuous consumption and fornication, sensual pleasure, and courtly entertainment hardly instill the moral and physical qualities necessary in a trustworthy and courageous soldier (*S* 194; *P* 598b).

By way of contrast, the *Policraticus* depicts the ideal knight as one "brought up under the open sky and in the habits of work, trained to endure the sun's heat, caring nothing for the shade, ignorant of the pleasures of the bath and other luxuries, simple-minded, content with little food, limbs hardened to endure all manner of toil" (*S* 181; *P* 593a–b). Such attributes of character and habit reflect true "virility," that is, dissociation from bodily satisfaction, the practice of self-denial, and the absence of "feminine" influences. In a sense, John's ideal warrior is a monk on horseback; steeped in abstinence he fights for the spiritual principles of God and justice,[23] associates only with like-minded individuals, and avoids temptations of the flesh. John's belief that completely virile knights on this order are virtually extinct in his own day, in turn, stems from his perception that their mode of conduct is shaped and fashioned by a necessarily feminine court. When women become attached to courtly and public life, the code of the mounted warrior loses its virility; knights follow wherever their "womanish passion" leads them, in disregard of the rigor which their military calling imposes upon them.

Other evaluations aside, John of Salisbury was neither a hypocrite nor a blockhead in espousing his attitude towards women. He was prepared in principle to accept the rule of a woman as monarch, provided that she maintained her virtue and did not (like Dido) succumb to her desires.[24] John also realized that the twelfth-century organization of noble social and political relations inevitably and unavoidably meant that women could not be detached from court life. At least within the exalted circles in which John moved, women played a public role. As a consequence, John's misogyny was addressed to a more specific problem. He supposed that the pleasures of a staid courtly existence, the physical gratification associated with luxury, resulted in the feminization and depletion of the manly clash of arms. Thus, as both a rhetorical device and a historical observation, the *Policraticus* treats the courts and the female sex as coextensive (or really, identical) factors in the dissipation of military valor. In consequence, John's remedy for the revival of a virile warrior class is withdrawal from women and from court, retreat into the armed encampment far away from all luxuries and feminine influences. Without the temptations of worldly goods or desires, noblemen can practice and refine the skills and qualities that they require for the conduct of warfare. This misogynistic view reconciles perfectly and completely with John's refusal in his writings to condemn or excuse the Anglo-Norman obligation to obey the rule of Matilda on the grounds of her sex. He is quite willing to let a woman govern so long as she does not interfere with that proper and exclusive realm of masculine identity, warfare. And while he may not be an admirer of the female sex, he is sufficiently realistic to recognize that women cannot reasonably be prohibited from involvement in the public affairs of the twelfth century.

More broadly, the case of John of Salisbury illustrates some reasons why historians of political thought (and intellectual historians on the whole) ought to beware of a complacent notion that medieval authors were uncritical inheritors of classical traditions and prejudices.[25] John certainly revels in the misogyny of his pagan and Christian sources. But we must never forget that he is putting those ancient authorities to work for his own rhetorical purposes, in relation to the very basic changes that had occurred in the historical position of women during the Middle Ages. In this sense, it is virtually as deceptive for the medieval segment of a survey of women in the history of political thought to concentrate exclusively upon St. Thomas's Christian-Aristotelian synthesis as it is to ignore the Middle Ages altogether.[26] For the typical medieval fusion of the private and the public, of household and political rights, meant that the role of women within a theoretical scheme of society was bound to differ significantly from antiquity. Just as Aristotle could confidently expect his division between the domestic female and the political male to be comprehensible to his audience, so John of Salisbury (or any author of that era) had to conform his thought to the general features of contemporary feudal society and thus had to admit women's public personae. It ought not be forgotten that no matter how bookish the medieval political theorist appears, his ideas were ordinarily rooted in a range of historically relevant concerns and assumptions about society and politics. For John this is perhaps especially true because of the political nature of his career, as well as his repeated insistence that philosophy was never to be separated from practical matters.[27] When it comes to John of Salisbury's remarks about women and their essential traits, likewise, we are confronted with ideas that are far more complex and historically rich than scholars have previously allowed.

Notes

Research for this paper was supported by the Women's Studies Programme of Glendon College, the Graduate Development Fund of York University, and the Mactaggert Fellowship of the University of Alberta. An earlier version was read at the 1983 annual meeting of the Popular Culture Association.

1. The best general introduction to women in the ancient world is Pomeroy.

2. Aristotle's representativeness is defended by Pomeroy, 230.

3. These general features of the medieval social and political structure are explored by Duby, *The Early Growth,* and Anderson, 147–172.

4. Painter, 30–32.

5. Holmes, 163–164.

6. Map, 212–213 and 378–379.

7. Map, 384–387.

8. Shahar, 160–164.

9. But see Hamilton's review of female involvement in the Latin realms of the Near East.

10. This is a central thesis of both Power and Shahar, 12–13 and 171–172.

11. We have been unable to discover any survey of Matilda's career: for an introduction to the period, see Davis.

12. Chroniclers' remarks about Matilda have been summarized by Bandel, 117–118.

13. John of Salisbury, *Historia Pontificalis,* 183–184; quotations in the following paragraph are drawn entirely from this passage.

14. See Duby, *The Chivalrous Society,* 134–148.

15. As noted by Bullough, 186–187 and Shahar, 152.

16. The *Policraticus* has been translated into English in two separate volumes, one containing the "political" chapters (*The Statesman's Book*), the other the "courtly" material (*Frivolities of Courtiers and Footprints of Philosophers*). For the sake of nonspecialists, references will be given to the translated versions, as well as to the marginal numeration of Webb's critical edition. In subsequent citations the Latin edition of the *Policraticus* will be abbreviated as *P, The Statesman's Book* as *S,* and *The Frivolities of Courtiers* as *F.*

17. *S* 234; *P* 614d–615c argues for Matilda's legitimacy.

18. John's attitude towards Stephen and its significance for his political theory are matters that have not previously been explored in great detail, a lacuna that Dr. Nederman intends to address in a projected essay.

19. This interpretation is defended at length by Painter 68–72 and passim.

20. The sources to which John had access are surveyed by Ruether, McLaughlin, Gies and Gies, 13–18 and 48–50, Tavard, 3–120, and Ferrante, 153–160.

21. For John's account of Dido, see *S* 248 and 251; *P* 621c–d and 623a.

22. The interconnections between these various activities are discussed by John at, for instance, *F* 37, 316, and 323; *S* 249; *P* 405c, 725a–d, 729b, 622a–b.

23. On the importance of the warrior's devotion to justice, see Nederman, "The Physiological Significance."

24. This is in line with John's general emphasis on the moral qualifications necessary for rulership; see Nederman and Brückmann, 224–227, and Nederman, "The Aristotelian Doctrine."

25. For an attempt to address a similar problem in the later Middle Ages, see Nederman, "Aristotle as Authority."

26. This charge is applicable to the range of recent work on women in social and political thought, including Clark and Lange, Okin, Elshtain, Saxonhouse, and Cole.

27. By far the best appraisal of John's intellectual and political circumstances is Guth. On John's practical approach to philosophy, see Nederman, "Aristotelian Ethics."

Works Cited

Anderson, Perry. *Passages from Antiquity to Feudalism.* London: New Left Books, 1974.

Aristotle. *The Politics.* Translated by E. Barker. Oxford: Oxford University Press, 1946.

Bandel, Betty. "The English Chroniclers' Attitude towards Women." *Journal of the History of Ideas* 16 (1955): 113–118.

Bullough, Vern. *The Subordinate Sex.* Urbana: University of Illinois Press, 1973.

Clark, Lorenne M. G., and Lynda Lange, eds. *The Sexism of Social and Political Theory.* Toronto: University of Toronto Press, 1979.

Cole, Diana. "Re-reading Political Theory from a Woman's Perspective." *Political Studies* 34 (March 1980): 129–148.

Davis, R. H. C. *King Stephen.* London: Longman, 1967.

Douglas, David C. *The Norman Fate, 1100–1154.* Berkeley: University of California Press, 1976.

Duby, Georges. *The Early Growth of the European Economy: Warriors and Peasants from the Seventh to the Twelfth Centuries.* Translated by H. B. Clarke. London: Weidenfeld and Nicolson, 1974.

———. *The Chivalrous Society.* Translated by C. Postan. Berkeley: University of California Press, 1977.

Elshtain, Jean Bethke. *Public Man, Private Woman: Women in Social and Political Thought.* Princeton, N.J.: Princeton University Press, 1981.

Ferrante, Joan M. *Woman as Image in Medieval Literature.* New York: Columbia University Press, 1975.

Gies, Frances, and Joseph Gies. *Women in the Middle Ages.* New York: Barnes and Noble, 1978.

Guth, Klaus. *Johannes von Salisbury (1115/20–1180): Studien zur Kirchen-, Kultur- und Sozialgeschichte Westeuropas im 12. Jahrhunderts.* St. Ottilien: Eos Verlag, 1978.

Hamilton, Bernard. "Women in the Crusader States: The Queens of Jerusalem (1100–1190)." In *Medieval Women,* edited by D. Baker. Oxford: Blackwell, 1978.

John of Salisbury. *Frivolities of Courtiers and Footprints of Philosophers.* Translated by J. B. Pike. Minneapolis: University of Minnesota Press, 1938.

———. *Historia Pontificalis.* Edited by M. Chibnall. London: Nelson, 1956.

_____. *Policraticus.* Edited by C. C. J. Webb. Frankfurt a. M.: Unveränderter Nachdruck, 1965.

_____. *The Statesman's Book.* Translated by J. Dickinson. New York: Knopf, 1927.

Map, Walter. *De nugis curialium.* Edited and translated by M. R. James. Revised by C. N. L. Brooke and R. A. B. Mynors. Oxford: Oxford University Press, 1983.

McLaughlin, Eleanor C. "Equality of Souls, Inequality of Sexes: Women in Medieval Theology." In *Religion and Sexism,* edited by R. R. Ruether. New York: Simon and Schuster, 1974.

Nederman, Cary J. "The Aristotelian Doctrine of the Mean and John of Salisbury's Concept of Liberty." *Vivarium* (forthcoming).

_____. "Aristotelian Ethics and John of Salisbury's Letters." *Viator* (forthcoming).

_____. "Aristotle as Authority: Alternative Aristotelian Sources of Late Medieval Political Thought." *History of European Ideas* (forthcoming).

_____. "The Physiological Significance of the Organic Metaphor in John of Salisbury." *History of Political Thought* (forthcoming).

Nederman, Cary J., and J. Brückmann. "Aristotelianism in John of Salisbury's *Policraticus.*" *Journal of the History of Philosophy* 21 (April 1983): 203–229.

Okin, Susan Moller. *Women in Western Political Thought.* Princeton, N.J.: Princeton University Press, 1979.

Painter, Sidney. *French Chivalry.* Baltimore: Johns Hopkins University Press, 1940.

Pomeroy, Sarah B. *Goddesses, Whores, Wives and Saints.* New York: Schocken Books, 1975.

Power, Eileen. *Medieval Women.* Edited by M. M. Postan. Cambridge: Cambridge University Press, 1975.

Ruether, Rosemary R. "Misogynism and Virginal Feminism in the Fathers of the Church." In *Religion and Sexism,* edited by R. R. Ruether. New York: Simon and Schuster, 1974.

Saxonhouse, Arlene W. *Women in the History of Political Thought.* New York: Praeger, 1985.

Shahar, Shulamith. *The Fourth Estate: A History of Women in the Middle Ages.* Translated by C. Galai. London: Methuen, 1983.

Tavard, George H. *Women in Christian Tradition.* Notre Dame, Ind.: University of Notre Dame Press, 1973.

Wood, Ellen Meiksins, and Neal Wood. *Class Ideology and Ancient Political Theory.* Oxford: Blackwell, 1978.

TWO

ereadings of Medieval
and Renaissance
Literary Texts

Domestic Treachery in the *Clerk's Tale*

Deborah S. Ellis

he characterization of Griselda used in Chaucer's *Clerk's Tale* and in its sources has befuddled both medieval and modern audiences (Allen; Carruthers). The tale's key position in the *Decameron* and its obvious attraction for Petrarch are problematic enough without Chaucer's intensification of the demon-saint relationship enacted by Walter and his wife. Yet, as Carruthers, following Severs' study, points out, the changes Chaucer makes are "the central critical problem of the *Clerk's Tale*": "Why, having elected to tell such an unappealing story in the first place, make it emphatically less attractive than it was to begin with? Why make a problematic story even more difficult?" (222). Among the many valid answers to this question lies one that has been previously unexplored: Griselda as not only a victim of her own docility, her husband's abuse, or the conditions of medieval marriage, but also as an emblem of the domestic treachery that forms an important motif in many of Chaucer's works.[1] The story of patient Griselda, whose husband tests her by his pretense of killing her children, casting her away, and calling her back only to prepare the house for his new wife, expresses a pervasive conflict in Chaucer's portrayal of medieval life.

Chaucer's concern with the problems of human relationships, especially those involving conflicts between men and women, is often focused through his attention to the illusory security of the home and its potential for abuses of power. Griselda's problems in Walter's palace only exaggerate those of her literary sisters. The extent of this motif of domestic insecurity is enormous in Chaucer's works, ranging from the frequent casual but telling figure of speech—"Youre wommen slepen alle, I undertake, / So that, for hem, the hous men myghte myne" (*Troilus* 3.766–767)—to the heavy-handed symbolism of the insecure home in the *Melibee*.[2] The latter story, as we might expect, associates domestic insecurity with the plight of women: "His wyf and eek his doghter hath he left inwith his hous, of which the dores were faste yshette. / Thre of his olde foes han it espyed, and setten laddres to the walles of his hous, and by wyndowes been entred, / and betten his wyf, and wounded his doghter" (VII, 969–971). Even the Wife of Bath, in consciously spurning this identification of woman's home and vulnerability, emphasizes its pervasiveness with her rebuttal:

> I holde a mouses herte nat worth a leek
> That hath but oon hole for to sterte to,
> And if that faille, thanne is al ydo.
>
> (572–574)

Female characters in literature, as well as historical women who resist this stereotype of domestic vulnerability, end by being characterized as powerless or captive. Resistance gives rise both to the occasional literal imprisonment of women—as in the Paston family—and to the literary wish fulfillment of works such as Caxton's translation of *The Book of the Knight of the Tower,* where a queen who insisted on staying within the walls of her own room is later immured between them (for example, Davis, 2:32; Caxton, 95). Such male responses are a standard joke in Chaucer. The jealous older husband of the *Miller's Tale,* who "heeld [his wife] narwe in cage" (3224) and his counterpart in the *Merchant's Tale,* who

> . . . neither in halle, n'yn noon oother hous,
> Ne is noon other place, neverthemo,
> . . . nolde suffre hire for to ryde or go . . .
>
> (2088–2090)

both delude themselves into thinking that they have complete control over their houses and, by extension, their wives. The Wife of Bath could have told them differently, for, as we hear in the *Manciple's Tale,*

> A good wyf that is clene of werk and thoght
> Sholde nat been kept in noon awayt, certayn;
> And trewely, the labour is in vayn
> To kepe a shrewe, for it wol nat bee.
>
> (148–151)

Associations of the home with ambiguity, insecurity, and women's vulnerability merge most effectively, however, in the *Troilus* and in the *Clerk's Tale*. Pandarus, for instance, the classic manipulator of domestic terrain, is compared to a master carpenter/builder/architect and by extension, using Geoffrey of Vinsauf's metaphor, to a poet and creator (*Troilus* 1.1058–1071). His double "role" as creator of space and of words allows him to exploit the home's dramatic potential to express intrigue and insecurity (Ellis, 5–10). He is more conscious than most of the other characters of the intrinsic precariousness of the home, and his using an image of domestic insecurity to persuade Criseyde into loving Troilus foreshadows the whole nature of the treacherous love between herself and Troilus:

> "Nece, alle thyng hath tyme, I dar avowe,
> For whan a chaumbre afire is, or an halle,
> Wel more nede is, it sodeynly rescowe
> Than to dispute and axe amonges alle
> How this candele in the straw is falle."
>
> (3.855–859)

Similarly, the treacherous nature of Griselda's married life is adumbrated by the background of her insecure home, a world in which all reversals are possible: servants can become monsters, wives become servants, children become wives, and husbands become Walter.

The *Clerk's Tale* and *Troilus and Criseyde* have, in fact, a great deal more in common than their verse form; both emphasize the vulnerability of women, and both draw on images of potential homelessness to express that vulnerability. Criseyde in particular, faced with exile from her town and her people as well as from her house and her lover, magnifies this association of loss of security. All the salient events of her insecure life interrelate love and bargaining; all values are relative, especially to that master of love-bargaining, Pandarus. The contextual irony of Hector's innocent "We usen here no wommen for to selle" (*Troilus* 4.182), undercut as it is by references to Helen and to negotiable sisters (e.g., 1.860–861, 3.409–413), also has a wider significance in Chaucer's writings. His fictional world depends on ethical and social ambiguities. Not just love but safety and security as well are presented as relative values, subject to encroachment through direct attack or—more frequently—through negotiation and subtle treachery. When the townspeople tell Walter, "Delivere us out of al this bisy drede, / And taak a wyf, for hye Goddes sake!" (134–135), we get our first such intimation in the *Clerk's Tale:* a sense of security is negotiable. The town wins this bargain, and since Walter loses nothing in exchange—lines 162 to 168 clearly revoke the rhetoric of lines 145 to 147—it must be Griselda who pays. Ideas of exchange or negotiation persist throughout the tale and are often associated with the security or insecurity of Griselda's home. Walter, for instance, suggests to her that her entry into the house has cost him popularity that must be paid for with the sacrifice of their daughter:

> "Ye woot youreself wel how that ye cam heere
> Into this hous, it is nat longe ago;
> And though to me that ye be lief and deere,
> Unto my gentils ye be no thyng so.
> . . . .

But I desire, as I have doon bifore,
To lyve my lyf with hem in reste and pees.
I may nat in this case be recchelees;
I moot doon with thy doghter for the beste."

(477–480, 486–489)

Even his use of the pronoun—"*thy* doghter"—signals to us that it is Griselda who is expected to pay the price of her husband's "reste and pees." Walter, in fact, is expert at stabbing with pronouns that casually signal dispossession and exile: "My newe wyf is comynge by the weye. / Be strong of herte, and voyde anon *hir* place" (805–806; my emphasis). Griselda understands that her security in her home, indicated by Walter's transitory possessive pronouns, is an unstable product of whatever bargain Walter is making at the time, and this is true even in their initial "bargain," the betrothal at Griselda's cottage.

Griselda's identification with Walter's home and her consequent problems with that home are perhaps more obvious but no less binding than is her earlier, similar identification with her father's hovel. She transcends her setting, of course, by her innate nobility and talents (Carruthers).

. . . it ne semed nat by liklynesse
That she was born and fed in rudenesse,
As in a cote or in an oxe-stalle,
But norissed in an emperoures halle.

(396–399)

Nevertheless, she is also limited and defined by the very rudeness of that home: the fact that she is the perfect daughter, for instance, is proven rather than represented by the fact that she "made hir bed ful hard and nothyng softe" (228). Walter's approach to Griselda implies a need to remove these limits, and his betrothal "ceremony" in the *Clerk's Tale* is marked by a constant recognition of doors, thresholds, and barriers, in a way more emphatic than Petrarch's and far distinct from Boccaccio's.[3] With innocent irony, Griselda, having completed her housework to free herself for the spectacle, plans to watch the marquis' intended from her doorway, along with the other curious maidens (281–287). Just as she is about to cross the threshold, however, Walter comes and summons her (288–289); at this key moment of transition, she kneels by her water jug "biside the thresshfold" (290–292). Walter sends her in to fetch her father, and they make their marriage agreement outside the hovel, the only suitable setting in which to remove Griselda from the constraints of her current domestic life. Yet Walter then insists on confirming their agreement by a meal inside the house; apparently Griselda can offer her body outside the house but can commit her free will only within-doors.[4]

> "Yet wol I," quod this markys softely,
> "That in thy chambre I and thou and she
> Have a collacioun, and wostow why?
> For I wol axe if it hire wille be
> To be my wyf, and reule hire after me."
>
> (323–327)

The separation of her submission and her will, with the latter invoked by her home, becomes blurred in her subsequent outer transformation, where, in the best fairy tale tradition, she becomes a princess at the threshold of her home and of her consent:

> And for that no thyng of hir olde geere
> She sholde brynge into his hous, he bad
> That wommen sholde dispoillen hire right theere.
> . . . .
> Unnethe the peple hir knew for hire fairnesse,
> Whan she translated was in swich richesse.
>
> (372–374, 384–385)

Griselda herself, for all that she appears almost unconscious in this scene, comes close to recognizing that her own will is only operative in a place where she is truly at home, and her later reproach to Walter implies that she has been taken out of herself as well as out of her father's home: "Lefte I my wyl and al my libertee, / And took youre clothyng" (656–657). Unfortunately for Griselda, she had been translated not into heaven—or at least not yet—but rather into Walter's palace, the unbending emblem of *his* will.

Griselda's vulnerability to her husband's power within her husband's home is an exaggerated version of a common medieval perception of marriage. Although it was a commonplace in the Middle Ages that nagging wives drove their husbands out of their homes, for instance—"thre thynges dryven a man out of his hous . . . smoke, droppynge of reyn, and wikked wyves" (*Melibee* VII, 1086; compare *Wife of Bath's Tale* 278)—it was the woman far more often than the man who was the real victim of an unstable home. Griselda's dispossession from her own home by her own husband resonates with the tensions intrinsic to medieval domestic life.

The conflict between the promise of marital security and this threat of a Griseldian exile is reflected by architectural inconsistencies, among other expressions of domestic unease. The medieval English house in all its varieties, from Griselda's hut to Walter's palace, was essentially a combination of a hall and chamber (Faulkner; Mercer; Wood). Generally speaking, the hall was the public room and the chamber was more private. But although these units merged to form a single house, they had a surprising autonomy, forming a functional spousal metaphor of cooperative but sex-defined independence. They were, for instance, often bequeathed separately in wills, and each had the potential to subdivide or to expand in order to take on the characteristics of the other (Sheehan; Kittel). The hall was consistently associated with the knight and lord, while the chamber was the woman's province. As the representative refrain from *Guy of Warwick* tells us: "Knights sat in the hall / Ladies in the chamber all" (Zupitza, 87). The house is thus intrinsically ambivalent and can be characterized in terms of a sort of shifting polarity between chamber and hall, man and woman, and privacy and public life, as well as between inner and outer.

Such tensions are profoundly important in the *Clerk's Tale,* where Walter takes over Griselda's will so completely that she loses even her autonomy over the chamber. At her moment of exile, for instance, the poignancy of her speech depends at least partly on an architectural awareness of her dispossession. The chamber, and the palace as a whole, belong only to Walter and cannot offer the slightest protection: her nakedness and lack of shelter are equated emotionally and physically.

> "The remenant of *youre jueles* redy be
> Inwith *youre chambre,* dar I saufly sayn.
> Naked out of *my fadres hous,*" quod she,
> "I cam, and naked moot I turne agayn.
> Al *youre plesance* wol I folwen fayn;
> But yet I hope it be nat *youre entente*
> That I smoklees out of *youre paleys* wente."
>
> (869–875; my emphases)

Walter's further attempts to humiliate Griselda, as well as her response to those attempts, recognize in perverted form the distinctions between "her" chambers (now totally alienated from her) and "his" hall, which will be the scene of her mortification. Walter calls Griselda in to prepare the palace for his new bride, since, as he says, "I have no wommen suffisaunt, certayn, / The chambres for t'arraye in ordinaunce / After my lust" (960–962). In response, Griselda assumes the role of head "chamberere":

> And with that word she gan the hous to dighte,
> And tables for to sette, and beddes make;
> And peyned hire to doon al that she myghte,
> Preyynge the chambereres, for Goddes sake,
> To hasten hem, and feste swepe and shake;
> And she, the mooste servysable of alle,
> Hath every chambre arrayed and *his* halle.
>
> (974–980; my emphasis)[5]

Walter's home is an extension of his power over his wife, since within that home he can cast her in any role she will accept. His power is socially absolute and psychologically as absolute as her abnegation of will and her saintly stoicism will allow. Her security thus becomes defined in terms of his sovereignty, and his misuse of the latter (through excesses frequently criticized by the Clerk) necessarily distorts the delicate balance of his home, which can no longer accommodate the needs of both spouses. The home is a natural expression of power struggles, as Georges Duby has indicated for an earlier period, and thus serves as a natural setting, and metaphor, for the abuse of that power.[6] Chaucer's alertness in exploiting this image gives the *Clerk's Tale* much of its strength; domestic power at its most extreme, expressed as Walter's betrayal of Griselda's trust, provides the plot as well as the mood of the *Clerk's Tale.*

Chaucer carries these questions of domestic power and its abuse one step further, for domestic treachery is at the heart of his literary home. The *Merchant's Tale* pokes fun at what is the serious core of the *Clerk's Tale,* but both ultimately work within the same set of assumptions.

> O perilous fyr, that in the bedstraw bredeth!
> O famulier foo, that his servyce bedeth!
> O servant traytour, false hoomly hewe,
> Lyk to the naddre in bosom sly untrewe.
> (Merchant's Tale 1783–1786)

Certainly the idea of servants turning on their masters is as old as the first master-servant relationship, but the paranoia attendant on power seems to have been especially strong in the Middle Ages and Renaissance.[7] The fifteenth-century household rules attributed to Bishop Grosseteste, for instance, are filled with warnings about not allowing servants to assemble in groups of more than three or four, not allowing them to visit their homes, and a host of other proscriptions (Furnivall, for example, 218, 249, 269).[8] Chaucer is always ready to recognize the potential, often ironic, treachery of the household: "And som man wolde out of his prisoun fayn, / That in his hous is of his meynee slayn" (*Knight's Tale* 1257–1258). Sometimes this ironic recognition takes the form of conflating expectations of household betrayal with literary conventions of women's treachery. Just as male lovers are always ready to deceive their ladies,[9] so women are "ay as bisy as bees . . . us sely men for to deceyve" (*Merchant's Tale* 2422–2423). The ending of the excursus in the *Merchant's Tale,* quoted

above, plays with the notion of treachery ambiguously attributed to
household or to spouse: "For in this world nys worse pestilence /
Than hoomly foo al day in thy presence" (1793–1794). Similarly, the
temple of Mars in the *Knight's Tale* shows images of warfare and
death that link town, farm, and bedroom:

> The smylere with the knyf under the cloke;
> The shepne brennynge with the blake smoke;
> The tresoun of the mordrynge in the bedde . . .
>
> (1999–20001)

No one is safe from such domestic treason, not even small
children. The seven-year-old St. Kenelm is too young to understand
his vision of his murder (*Nun's Priest's Tale* 3114–3119), but more
wisdom could not have helped him much; he lives in a world where
his elders corrupt the young more or less routinely, despite warnings: "Of alle tresons sovereyn pestilence / Is whan a wight bitray-
eth innocence" (*Physician's Tale* 91–92; compare 93–100). And, of
course, spousal murder, particularly of husbands by their wives, is a
literary commonplace, as the Wife of Bath must learn to her
exasperation.

> Of latter date, of wyves hath he red
> That somme han slayn hir housbondes in hir bed,
> And lete hir lecchour dighte hire al the nyght.
> ·
> And somme han dryve nayles in hir brayn,
> Whil that they slepte, and thus they had hem slayn.
> Somme han hem yeve poysoun in hire drynke.
>
> (765–767, 769–771)

As Sledd says, "We need not write a history of medieval taste . . . to
discover the narrative values of the *Clerk's Tale,* which other means
makes clear enough" (168). By putting Griselda's story into the
context of Chaucer's attitudes towards domestic harmony—or,
more often, its absence—we may seek to extend rather than ignore
our understanding of "the rules of [Chaucer's] fictional world"

(Sledd, 169). In such contexts, both generally medieval and specifically Chaucerian, Griselda's resignation to her inevitable fate becomes more understandable.

In a world of treacherous households, the confusion between Griselda's two domestic roles makes each one seem more threatening. Her equation of the roles of wife and servant indicates her humility and even more importantly reinforces our sense of the domestic insecurity and ambiguities of her life:

> "I ne heeld me nevere digne in no manere
> To be youre wyf, no, ne youre chamberere.
> And in this hous, ther ye me lady maade.
> . . . .
> I nevere heeld me lady ne mistresse . . ."
>
> (818–820, 823)

Similarly, though Griselda's will—like Dame Prudence's in *Melibee*—had earlier been identified with her father's home, it becomes centered in her heart as she is increasingly dispossessed from her husband's home. This turning inward signals not an increasing strength of character, however, but rather an increasing alienation from any sense of self:

> "Ther may no thyng, God so my soule save,
> Liken to yow that may displese me;
> Ne I desire no thyng for to have,
> Ne drede for to leese, save oonly yee.
> This wyl is in myn herte, and ay shal be."
>
> (505–509)[10]

It is the narrator's dryness of tone that alerts us to the dangers of this self-abnegation of will:

> For which it semed thus, that of hem two
> Ther nas but o wyl; for, as Walter leste,
> The same lust was hire plesance also.
> And, God be thanked, al fil for the beste.
>
> (715–718)

As Richmond (337) points out, "Since she is self-contained neither material nor emotional loss can destroy her"; nonetheless, such losses are both provoked and intensified by her self-contained quality, and though they do not destroy, they do considerable damage. She loses her children, for instance, and her recovery of them ten years later cannot compensate for her bereavement: "I have noght had no part of children tweyne/But first siknesse, and after, wo and peyne" (650–651). Because of her first exile from her home, she is exiled from her children, from her own sense of purpose, and from any security or satisfaction she might have found in her role as wife. Though she is never physically far from her first home, and indeed "gladly" returns there at Walter's wish (832–835), her marriage is a spiritual and emotional exile parallel to Constance's longer journey:

> Allas! what wonder is it thogh she wepte,
> That shal be sent to strange nacioun
> Fro freendes that so tendrely hire kepte,
> And to be bounden under subjeccioun
> Of oon, she knoweth nat his condicioun?
> Housbondes been alle goode, and han ben yoore;
> That knowen wyves; I dar sey yow na moore.
>
> (*Man of Law's Tale* 267–273)

One marriage is much like another, Chaucer tells us, since women must suffer patiently: "Therto we wrecched wommen nothing konne, / Whan us is wo, but wepe and sitte and thinke; / Our wrecche is this, our owen wo to drynke" (*Troilus* 2.782–784).

It is undoubtedly true, as many critics have pointed out, that the *Clerk's Tale* is an attack on Walter and the overmastering husbands he represents, since "wedded men ne knowe no mesure / Whan that they fynde a pacient creature" (622–623). Yet ultimately, since there is no refuge in the medieval home for either men or women, Walter proves to be not all that much worse than, say, Troilus. Chaucer's perspective on the home is one facet of the overwhelmingly medieval nature of the *Clerk's Tale*. In Boccaccio's original story, on the other hand,

Dioneo's *reductio ad absurdum* of the traditional concept of marriage undermines absolute standards and provides the opening wedge for relative morality. . . . [T]he whole thrust of the *Decameron* is an assertion of the individual's capacity to achieve his own well being in spite of obstacles imposed by human agency or by fortune—a doctrine that marks the change from the medieval to the modern world. (Allen 6, 8)

Relying on Petrarch rather than Boccaccio and on his own world view rather than that of either writer, Chaucer fills his version of the Griselda story with bleak references to the insecurity and treachery of daily domestic life. Morality is not relative, and Griselda has no way of asserting her integrity except by suffering in a house within which she is exiled. The ultimate failure of the home to protect its inhabitants is exaggerated in Griselda's case until the failure itself becomes invested with Chaucer's ironic view of human relationships and human possibilities. Griselda is the perfect Christian heroine precisely because she understands that life on earth is such an imperfect mirror of the rewards of heaven, and the Clerk's ironic approach to her story measures his understanding of the same distance.

Notes

I wish to thank Professor Janis Lull for her very helpful comments on this paper.

1. At least one article (Bolton) has focused on the theme of betrayal in Chaucer, specifically on the parallels between treason within Troy and treason within the love affair of Troilus and Criseyde. However, neither this article nor anything else I have been able to find isolates the idea of domestic treachery in Chaucer's works.

2. All references to Chaucer's writings are taken from Robinson. Individual works, where not identified by the text, are identified in parentheses following the quotation.

3. In Boccaccio's story, Gualtieri and his companions meet Griselda as she is returning home with water from the fountain rather than encountering her at the threshold of her own home: "E giunti a casa del padre della fanciulla, e lei trovata che con acqua tornava dalla fonte in gran fretta per andar poi con altre femine a veder venire la sposa di Gualtieri" (Boccaccio, 540). In Petrarch's version, Griselda is coming home with the water and just crossing the threshold when Walter comes; she has no plans to watch the procession from her doorway. I use R. D. French's translation of the *De obedientia ac fide uxoria mythologia* (Miller, 140–151).

4. Velma Richmond seems to recognize an implicit connection between the fact that Walter "is careful not to be alone with [Griselda] before their marriage" and the fact that "he

is careful to recognize her integrity," but she associates this wariness with no particular setting (337).

5. The last line, an especially significant one, is Chaucer's addition to Petrarch (French, in Miller, 150).

6. "[E]very structure that sought to express power relationships—whether between feudal lord and vassal, within the seigneury, the principality, or the kingdom—in some way made use of the image of the house" (Duby, 4).

7. Part of this endemic distrust is due to the conditions of "bastard feudalism"; see, for example, Myers' discussion of a magnate's need to employ "men who might desert him if some other lord could pay them better or help them more effectively" (155–156). Letters written by the Pastons and their peers frequently blame their servants even while fearing to treat them badly, "lyek masterles hondys" (Davis 1:547). An interesting extension of these household fears to Renaissance families can be found in Greenblatt.

8. Compare this warning from Chaucer's *Parson's Tale:* "Murmure eek is ofte amonges servauntz that grucchen whan hir sovereyns bidden hem doon leveful thynges; / and forasmuche as they dar nat openly withseye the comaundementz of hir sovereyns, yet wol they seyn harm, and grucche, and murmure prively for verray despit" (505–506).

9. For example, *House of Fame* 279–285, *Legend of Good Women* 1254–1263, *Troilus* 5.1779–1785, etc. See also Diamond.

10. Diamond takes this passage as evidence of "the embrace of degradation" characteristic of "the murky realm of *The Story of O*" (74).

Works Cited

Allen, Shirley S. "The Griselda Tale and the Portrayal of Women in the *Decameron.*" *Philological Quarterly* 56, no. 1 (1977): 1–13.

Boccaccio, Giovanni. *Decameron.* Edited by Domenico Consoli. Rome: Bietti, 1978.

Bolton, W. F. "Treason in *Troilus.*" *Archiv* 203 (1967): 255–262.

Carruthers, Mary J. "The Lady, the Swineherd, and Chaucer's Clerk." *Chaucer Review* 17, no. 3 (1983): 221–234.

Caxton, William, trans. *The Book of the Knight of the Tower.* Edited by M. Y. Offord. Early English Text Society, supplementary series 2. London: Oxford University Press, 1971.

Davis, Norman, ed. *Paston Letters and Papers of the Fifteenth Century.* 2 vols. Oxford: Clarendon Press, 1971, 1976.

Diamond, Arlyn. "Chaucer's Women and Women's Chaucer." In *The Authority of Experience: Essays in Feminist Criticism,* edited by Arlyn Diamond et al. Amherst: University of Massachusetts Press, 1977.

Duby, Georges. *Medieval Marriage: Two Models from Twelfth-Century France.* Translated by Elborg Forster. The Johns Hopkins Symposia in Comparative History, no. 11. Baltimore, 1978.

Ellis, Deborah S. " 'Calle It Gentilesse': A Comparative Study of Two Medieval Go-Betweens." *Comitatus* 8 (1977): 1–13.

Faulkner, P. A. "Domestic Planning from the 12th to the 14th Centuries." *Archaeological Journal* 115 (1958): 150–183.

Furnivall, F. J., ed. *Early English Manners and Meals.* Early English Text Society, original series 32. 1868. Reprint. London, 1894.

Greenblatt, Stephen. "The Cultivation of Anxiety: King Lear and His Heirs." *Raritan* 2, no. 1 (1982): 92–114.

Kittel, Margaret R. "Married Women in Thirteenth-Century England: A Study in Common Law." Ph.D. dissertation, University of California, 1973.

Mercer, Eric. *English Vernacular Houses.* London: Her Majesty's Stationery Office, 1975.

Miller, Robert P., ed. *Chaucer: Sources and Backgrounds.* New York: Oxford University Press, 1977.

Myers, A. R. *England in the Late Middle Ages.* 8th ed. The Pelican History of England, no. 4. Harmondsworth: Penguin, 1971.

Richmond, Velma B. "Pacience in Adversitee: Chaucer's Presentation of Marriage." *Viator* 10 (1979): 323–354.

Robinson, F. N., ed. *The Works of Geoffrey Chaucer.* 2d ed. Boston: Houghton Mifflin, 1957.

Sheehan, Michael. *The Will in Medieval England.* Toronto: Pontifical Institute of Medieval Studies, 1963.

Sledd, James. *"The Clerk's Tale:* The Monsters and the Critics." *Modern Philology* 51 (1953–54): 73–82. Reprinted in *Chaucer Criticism,* vol. 1, *The Canterbury Tales,* edited by Richard J. Schoeck and Jerome Taylor. Notre Dame, Ind.: University of Notre Dame Press, 1960.

Wood, Margaret. *The English Mediaeval House.* London: Phoenix House, 1965.

Zupitza, J., ed. *Guy of Warwick.* Early English Text Society, extra series 42, 49, 59. 1883. Reprinted in one volume, 1966.

Enid the Disobedient:
The *Mabinogion's Gereint and Enid*

Jeanie Watson

he purpose of this essay is to examine in detail *Gereint and Enid,* [1] one of the last-written stories of the Celtic *Mabinogion,* to show that the narrator uses a single disobedient wife as a model for a broadly subversive statement about the relationship between men and women in medieval society as a whole. Much of what has been written about the romance tales of the *Mabinogion—Peredur Son of Evrawg, Owein* or *The Countess of the Fountain,* and *Gereint and Enid*—has concentrated on the relationship between the Welsh tales and those of Chrétien de Troyes.[2] Since it is not the purpose of this paper to review this discussion, it should be sufficient to point out that there is general agreement that the heroes and stories of the *Mabinogion* romances "accept the topos of chivalric love and are concerned not only to describe successful wooing but to comment on the meaning of love" (Roberts, 224); they "exemplify the heroic, romantic, idealistic world of Celtic literature" (Gantz, 10). And *Gereint and Enid,* an Arthurian romance filled with knights and ladies, tournaments and jousts, does indeed portray the medieval heroic world of the aristocracy.

Critics also agree that the romances, like some of the other *Mabinogion* stories, have structural problems, that is, they are excessively "episodic and tend to ramble" (Gantz, 27); additionally, episodes are not always thematically integrated. Gantz comments, "'Maxen,' 'Owein,' and 'Gereint' all vitiate their climaxes with unintegrated afterthoughts, episodes which belong to the tradition but which found no place in the main body of the tale" (27); and Roberts agrees: "The author delays the reconciliation [of Gereint and Enid] so that he may introduce a number of loosely arranged combats set in the framework of a journey, and even after the reconciliation, a further irrelevant adventure at the Hedge of Mist is introduced" (228–229). Finally, given the loose, episodic *roman d'aventure* structure and the topos of chivalric love, most commentators are in agreement about the central characters of *Gereint and Enid*. Gereint is seen as a "distinctive personality," at the same time "sensible and courageous, but also uxorious and stubborn and sulky" (Gantz, 28). He is actively heroic, and he loves his wife, but he lacks balance. As Roberts notes: "Taken together, [Gereint and Owein] reflect two aspects of the knight's character as soldier and lover and are portrayals of the fault of immoderation, the overemphasizing of one virtue at the cost of another, which is, as Geoffrey of Monmouth had noted, the tension inherent in the topos of chivalric love" (224). Gereint's quest, then, in this view, is to achieve balance. Enid's task, on the other hand, is passively to endure; she undergoes the testing of the "patient Griselda" (Roberts, 229) that she may be reconciled with Gereint. Seen as less important than Gereint, Enid receives noticeably less critical treatment than Gereint. For example, Gantz summarizes:

> [Gereint] sports a fully realized fictional personality: cautious in approaching a better-armed opponent; generous in his terms to the same defeated opponent; reluctant to leave the tournament circuit for the responsibilities of home; doting on his wife; immediately suspicious of her; inordinately stubborn in his conviction of her infidelity; childish in his dejection over not being allowed to enter the hedge of mist. Through all this Enid is merely steadfast and enduring. (258)

It is the argument of this paper that if we take as true Roberts' statement that in the Welsh tales "the deeper significance is implied in the narrative" (224) and if we examine the narrative of *Gereint and Enid* closely to understand the significance implied therein, a very different reading of the story will emerge from the one commonly held. Specifically, the details of the text itself assert the imperative need for a revision of the traditional medieval view of women—and of men—and, further, a revision of the traditional concept of the marriage relationship. The tale, then, is about the meaning of love, but the meaning is not the expected one; rather, the tale argues for male and female equality of personhood, an equality that is carried over into marriage. Once Gereint's perception shifts and he comes to see Enid as a real and whole person and not some illusory mental construct, he himself becomes whole. When the story is viewed in this way, the structure falls into place and makes sense; even the Hedge of Mist episode becomes thematically relevant, an apt coda for the message of the tale.

At the very heart of this subversive story is the willed disobedience of Enid. Far from being a patient Griselda, obeying without question the demands of her husband, Enid deliberately goes against Gereint's wishes, not once but time and again. As Enid and Gereint set out on Gereint's journey, he sends her to ride ahead of him, demanding: "Whatever you see or hear about me, do not turn back, and say nothing to me unless I speak to you first" (279). But in this instance, as in subsequent ones, faced with the possibility of Gereint's being harmed, Enid rides back to warn him:

> Enid overheard this talk, but for fear of Gereint she did not know whether to speak or be silent. "God's vengeance on me," she said, "if I do not prefer death at Gereint's hand to death at another's. Though he may kill me, I will speak, lest he be killed without warning. (279)

Enid's dilemma throughout is the moral and emotional one of whether to speak or be silent; and, in each case, she disobeys Gereint out of love. He tells her, "Your concern means nothing to me," (279) but it is this very concern—rather than her subservient obedience—which must become significant to Gereint. His eventual change in perception signals a repudiation of the medieval view of the relationship between women and men.

As has been well documented,[3] the medieval attitude toward women was articulated by the Church and the aristocracy. In the Pauline tradition, women were at one and the same time viewed as Eve or Mary, deceiving temptress or holy mother, lustful whore or pure virgin. They were, therefore, in need of subjugation, while simultaneously serving as objects of worship. The aristocratic chilvalric code extended this dichotomy into the secular realm. Reason and action and speech rightly belonged to men; emotion and passivity and silence to women. An ideal wife was unquestioningly obedient to her husband; his will and word were law; sexual chastity and faithfulness to her husband were a wife's duty. Further, it is clear that obedience, chastity, and silence form an interlocking group of honorific female characteristics, on the one hand, while disobedience, sexual license, and a shrewish tongue comprise a pejorative grouping on the other. The two extremes find literary expression in admonitory patient Griselda stories and in satiric *fabliaux*. But that they *are* extremes is clearly indicated by the fact that both models of feminine character and conduct were so easily reduced to stereotypical types. The dichotymous extremes were mental constructs based more in the male imagination than in the daily experience of real men and women. These constructs— both of which distance women from men, make clear women's "otherness," and safely set her apart—formalize men's uncertainty and psychological uneasiness vis à vis women. In actual medieval life, women were required by the demands of ordinary existence to be quite capable, integrated members of society.[4] Women of the nobility had the responsibility of managing large households; in addition, they had to be able to assume their husband's responsibilities if he were absent. Actively making decisions and giving orders requires speech. Peasant women, sharing with their husbands in the struggle for subsistence, could hardly afford to be passive, shrinking violets. In both cases—as in the rising middle class also—communication and mutual effort and trust were necessary. While women were clearly at a disadvantage legally and educationally, the inequality was at odds with the lives they actually lived.

Gereint runs into trouble because he believes that the illusory imaginative constructs for female behavior, promulgated by Church and aristocracy, have validity in his real realtionship with Enid. Thus, he sees Enid as either Mary or Eve. When half-asleep (as indeed he is), he feels Enid's tears on his chest and hears her words, "Woe is me, if on my account these arms and chest are losing the fame and fighting ability they once possessed" (278); he instantly concludes that she loves another man. Speech and assumed unfaithfulness come together in his mind, and his immediate reaction is to close off communication and order Enid to submit to his will. He has "lost all peace of mind" (278); he is, in truth, disordered.

Gereint's disorder in relation to Enid is prepared for by his lack of order in his own person as a man. Abandoning wise activity out of arrogance and pride, he becomes passive, silent, and uxorious:

> When Gereint perceived how his fame had grown, he began to prefer comfort and leisure, for no one was worthy of combat with him. He loved his wife, and the routine of the court and songs and entertainment, so he dwelt in the court for a time; then he began to love being alone in his chamber with his wife, until that was pleasanter to him than anything else. (277)

In worshipping Enid, Gereint takes literally one-half of the societal view of women. Doing so excludes him from the real life going on around him, cuts him off from active knighthood, causes disharmony, and puts Enid into the predicament that results in his misunderstanding her words: "It was not easy to tell Gereint what was being said, and it was no easier to listen to it and not tell him" (278). Hearing her anxious words in bed, Gereint initiates their journey into the wilderness, refusing to speak or to be spoken to: "Enid rose and put on a simple dress and said, 'Lord, I know nothing of your thoughts.' 'Nor shall you yet,'" he replies. Gereint sets Enid apart from himself and makes her into the "other." Because of his own insecurity, he will not talk to her and physically separates her from himself by ordering her to ride a distance ahead of him, a distance as psychological as it is physical. Thinking her an Eve, he tries to force her into the role of patient Griselda, a role she finds impossible to play and therefore a role she refuses.

After Enid warns him about the first set of four knights, Gereint admonishes her: "Say nothing to me unless I speak to you first, for by my confession to God, if you disobey me you shall suffer for it." "My lord, I will do my best to obey you," she replies. But obedience is simply not as important to Enid as Gereint's life, so, once again, she warns him about a band of knights, explaining, "Lord, I spoke only lest you be taken by surprise." Gereint, however, determined to make her submit and thereby validate his manhood, responds, "Between me and God, I am less displeased by what these men say than I am by your talk and disobedience. . . . Be quiet, for your concern is worthless to me" (280). But even Gereint's harsh words cannot compel Enid to promise more than her heart will allow: "From now on, lord, I will be silent as long as I can" (281). Again and again, however, love will not be silenced, and Enid persists in disobedience. By the end of the story, the narrator makes it clear that societal constructs which falsify reality and negate the primacy of love ought to be disobeyed and abandoned.

Far from being a rambling series of loosely connected or thematically unrelated episodes, the narrative structure of *Gereint and Enid* is tightly and complexly organized to present over and over the message that the view of women and the relationship between women and men must change. The romance is divided into two major sections, with a summary coda at the end. The story is essentially about the education of Gereint, and the first section—which alternates between 1) Arthur's court and the hunt for the white hart and 2) Gereint's encounters with Edern, culminating in the hart's head's being given to Enid—presents three exemplums for Gereint's edification: the hunt for the hart, the defeat of Edern, and the relationship between Arthur and Gwenhwyvar. However, even though Gereint has himself participated in one of these, he has not seen the point of them, so in the second section his own journey becomes the exemplum, paralleling those in the first section.

The opening paragraph of *Gereint and Enid* introduces the reader to an orderly Arthurian world in which Church and court are interrelated and the authority of each is equitably divided. A sense of community and mutual celebration prevails. Into this communal atmosphere comes a lad with news of a white hart:

> "I saw in the forest a hart the like of which I have never seen before." "What is there about it for you never to have seen its like?" "Lord, it is pure white, and out of arrogance and pride in its lordliness it will travel with no other animal. I have come to you for advice on the matter." "I will do what is best," said Arthur. "Early tomorrow morning I will go and hunt it; tonight I will inform those in the guest houses, and Rhyverys [Arthur's Master of Hounds] and Elivri [Arthur's Head Groom] and everyone else." (260)[5]

The hart, while beautiful, is also arrogant and proud of its "lordliness." And because it is arrogant, the hart isolates itself, refusing to travel with others. Inappropriate lordliness must be vanquished, as Arthur knows; it is an action in which everyone at court wishes to participate and which Gwenhwyvar wishes to see. "Gwalchmei said, 'Lord, would it not be right to allow the hunter who succeeds in cutting off the head—whether he be mounted or on foot—to present it to his lover, or to a companion's lover?' 'I will gladly allow that,' said Arthur" (260). If the hart's loss of lordly arrogance is an appropriate gift for a lover, how much more so the knight's?

At Gwenhwyvar's suggestion, the hart's head is given finally to Enid, but Gereint, who needed to be the one to kill the hart, misses his chance through oversleeping. Thus, he participates in an alternative hunt, but one that parallels the hunt for the arrogant hart. Late for the hunt, Gereint and Gwenhwyvar are listening to the sounds of it at the edge of the forest when a dwarf, a lady, and a knight whose "strange heavy armour permits neither face nor countenance to be seen" (262) ride by:

> Then Gwenhwyvar said, "Woman, go ask the dwarf who the knight is." The girl went to meet the dwarf; he drew near when he saw her coming, and she said, "Who is the knight?" "I will not say." "As you are so discourteous, I will ask him myself." "By my

faith, you shall not." "Why not?" "Your rank does not entitle you to talk to my lord." The girl nonetheless turned her horse's head towards the knight, whereupon the dwarf struck her across the face and eyes with his whip, so that the blood welled forth. (262)

The pride of the knight—so heavily armed that his identity is lost and so arrogant that he thinks himself above being spoken to—is represented by the misshapen dwarf who, like Gereint in response to Enid later, refuses to answer the girl's question and orders her not to speak. When she disobeys, he strikes her, an action not uncommonly taken against wives and other inferior, disobedient creatures.[6] Gereint himself repeats the girl's experience when he confronts the dwarf and asks the knight's name, but the irony of the parallel is lost on him in his later confrontation with Enid.

Gereint follows the knight and the next day defeats him in a tournament. The knight then begs mercy, saying, "My wrongful arrogance has prevented my asking mercy until too late. Unless I am granted time to see a priest and confess my sins to God, I shall be none the better for mercy" (267). Once he has admitted "wrongful arrogance," the knight, Edern son of Nudd, gives his name, claims his identity, and can be granted mercy by Gereint and returned to fellowship with others at Arthur's court. Lordly arrogance, if not rejected in time, leads inevitably to death, as Gereint should be warned by both the hart and Edern.

Enid's circumstances when Gereint first sees her should also warn him against false and illusory views of her. Enid is, without question, noble; Gereint is "certain he had never seen a girl as full of abundant grace and beauty as she" (264). But she is also dressed in tattered clothing, and since there are no servants at the run-down castle where she lives with her parents, Enid performs those duties:

> The man said to the girl, "Tonight this gentleman has for his horse no groom but yourself." "I will wait upon him and his horse as best I can." She pulled off Gereint's boots and provided his horse with straw and grain, and then she made for the hall and returned to the chamber, where the man said, "Go to town, now, and have brought here the best supply of food and drink that you can get." "I will do that gladly, lord." (264)

Functioning both as aristocrat and peasant, Enid defies categorization. She is simply real and human; and Gereint, on quest to hunt down lordly arrogance, recognizes her beauty and grace and loves her. They ride together to the court of Arthur and Gwenhwyvar to be married.

The details of the wedding make it clear that the marriage of Enid and Gereint is meant to replicate that of Gwenhwyvar and Arthur. That the relationship between Gwenhwyvar and Arthur—which is one of mutual trust, communication, equality, and authority—is to serve as the third exemplum is illustrated throughout the story by the fact that the narrator gives Gwenhwyvar speech, authority, and attention equal to that given to Arthur. As he is the initiator of the hunt for the white hart, she is the initiator of Gereint's quest for Edern. Arthur cuts off the head of the hart; Gwenhwyvar proposes the solution for the debate over who should be given the head:

> As they reached the court Arthur and Gwenhwyvar heard their quarrelling, and the queen said, "Lord, my advice is that the hart's head should not be given until Gereint son of Erbin returns from his errand," and she told her husband the story of that errand. "Gladly, let that be done," said Arthur, and so it was agreed. (270)

On the look-out for Gereint Gwenhwyvar sees Edern approaching the city and goes out to greet him and hear his story; then Arthur comes out and the story is repeated:

> He related the entire adventure, whereupon Arthur said, "Well, Gwenhwyvar ought to show mercy, from what I hear." "Lord, I will show such mercy as you wish, for my disgrace is as much an insult to you as is your own." "Then this is the fairest thing," said Arthur. "Let physicians be called for this man until it is known whether he will live. If he lives, let him give such compensation as is ordered by the best men in the court, and let him give sureties: if he dies, the death of so good a lad as Edern is too much for the insult to the attendant." "I think that fair," said Gwenhwyvar. (271–272)

Arthur and Gwenhwyvar are both active in making Edern whole again. They arrive at decisions in concert, though each is obedient to his or her own sense of fairness. The insult done to one is shared by the other, and the mercy granted by one is granted by the other. When Gereint and Enid approach the castle, Gwenhwyvar goes outside to greet them. Coming inside, Gereint explains to Arthur: "It came of Edern's arrogance in refusing to identify himself" (273). Without arrogance, Gwenhwyvar and Arthur bring harmony and order.

At this point in the story, Enid and Gereint are worthy of each other and of the example of Arthur and Gwenhwyvar. When they marry, Enid "had her choice of Gwenhwyvar's clothing, and whoever saw her so dressed saw a radiant and beautiful sight" (273). Arthur gives her to Gereint in marriage. A celebration ensues, "and when it was time to sleep they went to bed; in the chamber of Arthur and Gwenhwyvar a bed was made up for Gereint and Enid, and that night they slept together for the first time" (273). The identification of the two couples is continued the next day as Arthur "satisfied the suppliants on Gereint's behalf, providing an abundance of gifts, while Enid became acquainted with the court, and won such companions that no lady on the island of Britain was better spoken of" (273). It is only right, then, that Enid be given the hart's head, taken by Arthur.

A revised view of the nature and role of women is cause for fame and celebration. Seeing an individual woman as an equal person allows a man to enter into an ideal marriage relationship; this marriage then effects changes in society as a whole. As Gereint and Enid begin a marriage that is like Arthur and Gwenhwyvar's, the next step is for them to become an exemplum themselves. Thus it is that as section two of *Gereint and Enid* begins and Arthur is holding court—as in the beginning of the tale—at Caer Llion, Gereint receives word from Erbin that it is time for him to return to his homeland and save it from invaders. Numbers of Arthur's companions accompany Gereint and Enid as they return to establish a court modeled on that of Arthur and Gwenhwyvar. The retinue remains at Gereint's court for a period of time, during which Gereint acts wisely in fulfilling the requests of suppliants and receiving their homage. Then they leave, and Gereint is on his own.

> At first, everything goes well, though not for very long: As had been his custom in Arthur's court he went to tournaments and encountered the boldest and strongest men, until he was as famous in that region as he had been before with Arthur, and had enriched his court and companions and noblemen with the best horses and arms and the best and rarest jewels. He did not leave off until his reputation had spread over the face of the land.
> When Gereint perceived how his fame had grown, he began to prefer comfort and leisure, for no one was worthy of combat with him. He loved his wife, and the routine of the court and songs and entertainment, so he dwelt in the court for a time; then he began to love being alone in his chamber with his wife, until that was pleasanter to him than anything else. (277)

Gereint becomes arrogant, prideful, and isolated, and "he began to lose the hearts of his noblemen" (277). To the dismay of the court—and also of Enid—Gereint has become the white hart. His wrongful arrogance causes a distorted perception in his relationship with others, and most especially with Enid whom he now mistakenly and harmfully views as Mary/Eve.

Because Gereint's perception is distorted, he is no longer rational, and he no longer sees the world as it really is. It is almost as though he moves in a state of enchantment, unable to escape the spell of his false notions. This state of illusion is emphasized in section two by the narrator's use of symbolic detail and symbolic landscape. The crucial "bed scene" at the beginning of the section parallels the wedding bed scene, except that this scene is given in much greater detail and whereas the first bed initiates union, the second becomes the source of separation. This is clearly not the couple's first night together, and the scene is quite sensual:

> One summer morning they were in bed. He was on the outer, protective side while she was awake in the glass chamber; the sun was shining down on the bed and the coverlet had slipped from over his chest and arms, and he was asleep. She gazed at the

magnificence of his good looks and said, "Woe is me, if on my account these arms and chest are losing the fame and fighting ability they once possessed," and at that the tears streamed down until they fell on his chest. That and the words she had spoken woke Gereint, and he was disturbed by the thought that she spoke not out of concern for him, but out of love for another man with whom she wished to be alone. (278)

It is a warm summer morning, and Enid, waking first, gazes at Gereint's naked body, from which the covers have slipped. The intimacy of the scene is intensified by the fact that the "glass chamber" belongs to Enid, while Gereint sleeps on the "outer, protective side." It is almost as though the warmth of the marriage bed subconsciously causes Gereint to hear something in Enid's words which might threaten his marital security and his ability to protect the glass chamber. The fact that he orders Enid to put on the shabby dress in which she rode to Arthur's court shows not only his desire to humble her as he fears he has been humbled but also his desire for Enid's return to a virgin state in which he could be sure of her purity and her obedience.

The journey itself is a journey into and through Gereint's disordered state of mind, symbolized by the forests in which he and Enid ride. Because he perceives the illusion to be the truth, he is no longer rational; nor will he listen to reason or heed warnings. In the beginning, Erbin warns him that the adventure is rash. Later the Little King tries to reason with him, but to no avail. Finally, when Enid and Gereint encounter Arthur and Gwenhwyvar and the knights late in the journey, Gereint has become the early Edern:

"Knight," Gwalchmei said . . . will you tell me who you are, or will you come to see Arthur, who is near by?" "I will not identify myself, nor will I go to see Arthur." He recognized Gwalchmei, but Gwalchmei did not recognize him. "It will never be said of me that I let you go without knowing who you are," said Gwalchmei, and he thrust his spear into Gereint's shield until the shaft splintered and the horses were head to head. At that he recognized his opponent. "Alas, Gereint, is it you?" "I am not Gereint." "Between me and God, Gereint, this is a wretched, ill-advised journey. . . . Come and see Arthur, your lord and first cousin." "I will not go—I am not in a condition to see anyone." (290)

Gereint denies his identity (and at this point, he truly has none), and, out of some residual shame or embarrassment, does not want to see Arthur and will not return with Gwalchmei. Enid's warnings anger Gereint throughout the journey. In fact, in all of section two, Gereint is consumed by strong emotion and irrationality.

In his own behavior, Gereint moves from an extreme state of uxoriousness to the opposite extreme of autocracy, extremes which are male responses to the Mary/Eve dichotomy and are, therefore, equally unrealistic and inappropriate. Disordered himself, he tries to make Enid into a Griselda by treating her as a servant, though he is actually more considerate of the servants than he is of his wife. She, on the contrary, assumes the real responsibility for the journey. She rides ahead as look-out; she drives the horses—as many as twelve at a time and representing unbridled emotion—ahead of her, thus controlling them; she stands watch while Gereint sleeps. In other words, she is the rational, active one, but acting always in love. Disobedience is her most reasonable action.

The rightness of her disobedience is emphasized by the repetitious encounters of the journey and by her overt disobedience to two men other than Gereint. In his effort to prove his physical prowess and his manhood, Gereint fights four knights, three knights, five knights, the Brown Earl and eighty knights, the Little King, and three giants—big ones, little ones, fat ones, skinny ones, kings and giants. The result is the same in every case, as is the fight formula: Enid, riding ahead, overhears the caitiffs planning to attack; she rides back to warn Gereint; he is angry because she will not obey him and be quiet—never mind the danger they are in; he defeats the opponents, but the victory is never enough. There is no artistic variation in the episodes because the lesson to be learned in each instance is the same. The lesson belongs to Gereint, and Gereint is a slow learner. The repetition also allows whatever sympathy the reader might have had for Gereint's view of things to evaporate. The deadliest responses to emotional excess are boredom and laughter on the part of the observer, and Gereint manages to elicit both. On the one hand, the reader says, "Not another set of knights, Gereint!" On the other hand, Gereint's obvious frustration at being unable to control Enid becomes funny:

"You are to do as you were told and be silent." (279)

"Say nothing to me unless I speak to you first, for by my confession to God, if you disobey me you shall suffer for it." (280)

"As you will not obey me, I am none the better for telling you to be silent." (281)

"Lord, had you heard the talk of those men as I did, you would be more anxious than you are." Gereint gave her a cool, bitter, mocking smile and said, "I hear you doing what I forbade you to." (281–282)

"I do not know what is the good of giving you orders, but this once, as a warning to you, I will do so." So Enid rode on to the forest, keeping well ahead as Gereint had commanded, and had it not been for his anger he would have been sorry to see the trouble so excellent a girl had with so many horses." (282)

"Lord," she said, "do you not see the man advancing toward you, and the other men with him?" "I see, and I see that despite my orders you will not be silent. Your warning means nothing to me—now be quiet." (286)

How are we to take seriously the view of a man who sounds petulant and ridiculous, especially toward a woman who keeps saving his life?

In addition to Gereint, Enid disobeys two other men: the Brown Earl and Earl Limwris. The earls, the second more violent than the first, are doubles for Gereint as he wanders into deeper and deeper forests of the mind. Both wish to marry Enid and control her. In both cases, it is Gereint's isolation from Enid that—except for her quick-wittedness and stubborn disobedience to the men—almost causes the event Gereint most fears, Enid's being with another man. As the guests of the Brown Earl, Gereint and Enid undress for bed, and Gereint says, "Go to the far end of the chamber and do not disturb me" (283–284). When the Brown Earl comes to visit later, he says to Gereint: "Have I your permission to go over to that girl and talk with her? . . . for I see that she is somewhat estranged from you" (284). Although the Earl tries to get Enid to stay with him, she tricks him (using "feminine deceit" in a good cause), so she and Gereint can escape.

Earl Limwris is a more serious matter. Severely wounded by one of the three giants he has killed, Gereint lies in a deathlike state as Limwris takes him and Enid to his castle. Limwris offers Enid his earldom and himself if she will agree and obey him; she, however, does not want to comply. When he asks her to change from her riding clothes, she replies, "Between me and God, I do not wish to." When he says, "Lady, do not be so sad," she responds, "It will be difficult to convince me why I should not be." "Take heart and cheer up," commands the earl; "By my confession to God, I will not be merry as long as I live," she counters. " 'Come and eat.' 'Between me and God, I will not.' 'Between me and God, you shall.' " The earl then drags her to the table and repeatedly asks her to eat, but she will not. Finally, echoing Gereint's earlier complaints, "I do not know what is the good of giving you orders" and "As you will not obey me, I am none the better for telling you to be silent," Earl Limwris, in total exasperation, escalates the confrontation from words to action: " 'Well,' said the earl, 'it is no better being kind to you than being unkind,' and he boxed her ears. She gave a loud piercing scream" (293). Limwris's physical abuse of Enid echoes the earlier abuse of Edern's dwarf and carries out the threat of violence Gereint made: "If you disobey me you shall suffer for it" (280), a threat Enid takes seriously: "Though he may kill me, I will speak, lest he be killed without warning" (279).

It is an extreme and desperate form of speech—Enid's scream —that finally penetrates Gereint's ensorceled brain: "With the reverberation of that scream Gereint came to his senses," and "risen from the dead," he kills Limwris, thereby killing the deceived man he himself once had been. Living in illusion is actively harmful to oneself and to others, and it can lead to death. Gereint has become a new man, and with his new, clear perception, he looks at Enid: "Then Gereint looked at Enid, and he felt two sorrows, one over her losing her colour and looks, and the other in knowing that she had been in the right" (293). Gereint has finally learned the lesson; his education is complete, and the two are united:

> "Lady, do you know where our horses are?" "I know where yours went, but not mine. Yours went to that house yonder." He went to the house and brought his horse out, and mounted it, and he lifted Enid up and set her in front of him, and so they rode out. (294)

As Gereint grants Enid her identity, he achieves his own, and all that remains of the story is the coda.

Riding home, Gereint and Enid, accompanied by the Little King, encounter the court of Earl Owein who requires that anyone staying at his court enter the Hedge of Mist. "Below there is a hedge of mist, and enchanted games within, and no man who has gone there has ever come back" (295), warns a man. Nonetheless, Gereint and the others go to Owein's court where Owein is so impressed with Gereint that

> he was sorry he had ever instituted these games, if only so as not to lose a man as excellent as this. If Gereint had asked him to call off the game he would have done so gladly. "Chieftain," he said, "what are you thinking of that you do not eat? If you are fearful of going to the game you will not have to go, and for your sake no one will ever have to go again." (295)

Gereint, however, wishes to enter the hedge, since even if no one were compelled to enter the game anymore, the game would still exist. The game is a deadly one, as the heads on the stakes in and through the hedge attest. The player of the enchanted game must play alone, and no one, even Owein, knows the way out of the hedge. Gereint, who has lived as though in a mist (since he could not see clearly), seeking a way through a hedge maze (wandering aimlessly and without guidance through forest) because he was playing a game of illusion and enchantment (his false, unrealistic notions of men and women and what it means to be human) has already been the solitary player in this game. By playing the game once more—but knowing it truly to be an enchanted game—Gereint is able to destroy it once and for all:

> Boldly and without hesitation Gereint entered the mist, and when he emerged he found a great orchard and a clearing within; there stood a brocade pavilion with a red canopy and the entrance open, and next to that an apple tree with a great hunting-horn hanging from a branch. He dismounted and entered the pavilion, and inside there was nothing but a girl sitting in a gold chair, with another chair opposite her vacant, so he sat in the vacant chair. "Chieftain, I advise you not to sit in that chair," said the girl. "Why?" "The man who owns it has never permitted anyone else to sit in it." "I do not care if he takes it badly that I sit here." (296)

Gereint enters the traditional enchanted orchard, which echoes the fairy orchard, but even more specifically here the Edenic orchard. The knight who guards the orchard, pavilion, chair, apple tree, and girl is isolated and prideful. Gereint sits in his chair and then defeats him, thereby symbolically defeating the false interpretation of the story of Eve and its dichotomous view of women, while also defeating his own false and enchanted self, for the mist cannot be lifted nor the game stopped except by someone who has overthrown within himself what the knight represents:

> "Alas, lord, mercy, and you shall have whatever you wish." "I wish only that these games cease, and that the hedge of mist and the magic and enchantment disappear." "Lord, you shall have that gladly." "Then disperse the mist." "Blow on that horn, for as soon as you sound it the mist will vanish. Until a knight who had overthrown me sounded the horn, the mist could not vanish." (297)[7]

Just as Arthur had blown the horn announcing the death of the white hart, Gereint now blows the horn hanging from a branch of the apple tree: "Enid, from where she was, worried and fretted, fearing for Gereint, but he came and blew the horn, and as soon as he did so the mist disappeared. Then the company gathered and peace was made among them all" (297). The tale of *Gereint and Enid* is indeed a subversive one, but the ending is one in which they live happily ever after.

Notes

1. For this paper, I have used the translation with an introduction by Jeffrey Gantz. While other translators have spelled the hero's name "Geraint," I have followed Gantz throughout with "Gereint."

2. In addition to Gantz's Introduction, several works examine in detail the issues of source and influence, for example: Bromwich, 83–136; Ford, 1–30; Frappier; Jackson; Loomis, *Arthurian Literature and Arthurian Tradition.*

3. See, for example: Ferrante; Gies and Gies; Power; and Shahar. For a good summary discussion of the position and role of women, specifically in Celtic society in the early Middle Ages, see Wendy Davies' essay "Celtic Women in the Early Middle Ages," 145–166.

4. See especially Powers and Shahar.

5. As Jean Frappier points out: "The hunt for the White Hart is the traditional white animal hunted by the hero or the knight in the 'forest of adventure' and sent by a fairy princess to lure her idol to herself in the otherworld" (68). The hunt for the white hart parallels and foreshadows, then, the Hedge of Mist encounter in which Gereint must overcome an illusory otherworld.

6. "Despite such pieties as the *Roman de la Rose*'s 'Serve and honor all women,' wife-beating was common. . . . The thirteenth-century French law code, *Customs of Beauvais,* stated: 'In a number of cases men may be excused for the injuries they inflict on their wives, nor should the law intervene. Provided he neither kills nor maims her, it is legal for a man to beat his wife when she wrongs him'" (Gies, 46).

7. The story, explains Frappier, "originally goes back to the one about the giant held prisoner by a fairy princess. Required to do battle with any who happened upon the forbidden scene, he, if victorious, would kill them, and, if vanquished, would himself be killed, then to be replaced by the victor who would take up with the fairy princess and play out the triple role of lover, captive, and guardian of a deadly custom" (69). In *Gereint and Enid,* the knight does perform the triple role, but it is a role that Gereint, the victor, does not want. Instead, he grants mercy to the defeated knight and wishes "only that these games cease, and that the hedge of mist and the magic and enchantment disappear" (297). Gereint has had enough of games of illusion.

Works Cited

Bromwich, Rachael. "The Character of Early Welsh Tradition." In *Studies in Early British History,* edited by H. M. Chadwick et al. Cambridge: Cambridge University Press, 1959.

Davies, Wendy. "Celtic Women in the Early Middle Ages." In *Images of Women in Antiquity,* edited by Averie Cameron and Amalie Kuhrt. Detroit: Wayne State University Press, 1983.

Ferrante, Joan M. *Woman as Image in Medieval Literature.* New York: Columbia University Press, 1975.

Ford, Patrick K., ed. "Introduction." In *The "Mabinogi" and Other Medieval Welsh Tales.* Berkeley: University of California Press, 1977.

Frappier, Jean. *Chrétien de Troyes: The Man and His Work.* Translated by Raymond J. Cormier. Athens: Ohio University Press, 1982.

Gantz, Jeffrey, ed. *The Mabinogion.* New York: Penguin, 1976.

Gies, Frances, and Joseph Gies. *Women in the Middle Ages.* New York: Thomas Y. Crowell, 1978.

Jackson, Kenneth H. *The International Popular Tale and Early Welsh Tradition.* Cardiff: University of Wales Press, 1961.

Loomis, Roger Sherman. *Arthurian Tradition and Chrétien de Troyes.* New York: Columbia University Press, 1949.

————. ed. *Arthurian Literature in the Middle Ages.* Oxford: Oxford University Press, 1959.

Power, Eileen. *Medieval Women.* Edited by M. M. Postan. Cambridge: Cambridge University Press, 1975.

Roberts, Brynley F. "Tales and Romances." In *A Guide to Welsh Literature,* edited by A. D. H. Jarman and Gwilym Rees Hughes, 1:203–243. Swansea: Christopher Davies, 1976.

Shahar, Shulamith. *The Fourth Estate: A History of Women in the Middle Ages.* Translated by Chaya Galai. London: Methuen, 1983.

Communication Short-Circuited: Ambiguity and Motivation in the *Heptaméron*

Karen F. Wiley

he theme of ambiguity so common in Renaissance writing finds ample expression in Marguerite de Navarre's *Heptaméron*,[1] the "French Decameron." The structure of this collection of tales resembles Boccaccio's masterpiece in many details: a calamity brings together ten noble persons who decide to pass their time in storytelling; each person contributes one story a day; and certain themes are treated over and over in various contexts.

Marguerite's work differs from her Italian model, however, in several significant aspects. One is her insistence that the tales are all "true."[2] Another is her expanded use of the discussions following each tale, conversations that very quickly lend a life of their own to the discussants. The *Decameron* has little of the serious-minded, philosophical, and pessimistic tone so prevalent in its French successor; although the tales sometimes seem destined to persuade (see the Introduction to the Fourth Day), they are characterized by their light-hearted nature and their light-handed approach. Marguerite's approach is to exploit each true story for its full moral value, using the tales as a means of communication not only between writer and reader but among the fictional tellers and listeners as well.

"Just what is communicated?" one could reasonably ask. Among frequently treated topics—love in its various permutations and perversions, religion and the spiritual life, the fragility of life and relationships—one that emerges as vital is the question of why people act the way they do. Coupled with Marguerite's insistence that the stories are all veritable, the emphasis on motivation might lead the unsuspecting reader to conclude that the *Heptaméron* would cast new light, would perhaps enable one to see more clearly the forces that move people to action. Not so. After close reading, we become ever more aware of the shadows clouding human vision, of the subtle misdirections, false starts, and obscurities, of all the obstacles to clear and straightforward communication. In Marguerite's fictional world ambiguity reigns supreme, apparently for good reason.

The reason may become clearer as we look at a particular technique employed by the writer, a technique I have named "short-circuited communication." As in all discourse, narrative meaning depends on a certain congruity or harmony between the message that is sent and the message received. Smooth communication assumes, if not consummate ability to match message and interpretation, at least the good will to try to do so. However, within a narrative framework it is often to the advantage of the author to see that this congruity is put off for a certain time. This forms the basis of much humorous writing; the French fabliaux offer various illustrations of such techniques. What we need to understand in reading Marguerite's tales is the difference between simple misunderstanding that is the basis of the standard farce and the willed miscommunication that is at the heart of her storytelling techniques. The latter is too easily overlooked in favor of the former. Yet its appearance in both the tales and the discussions that follow the tales is essential to an appreciation of the writer's view of human nature and of her world.

Short-circuited communication occurs on several levels and serves multiple narrative ends. To understand the advantages of such misleading discourse, we need only look at what happens when messages are clearly communicated. For instance, we find that as the discussants analyze the tales, they sometimes begin to understand each other's point of view more clearly than is desirable. Comprehension of each other's attitudes, particularly comprehension of each other's motives, inevitably leads to conflict. This conflict happily moves the reader on to the next story, but as a social phenomenon its value is questionable. The following are typical of this type of conversation:

> Nomerfide lui dit: Qui vous voudrait écouter, la Journée se passerait en querelles. Mais il me tarde tant d'ouir encore une histoire. (172)

> (Nomerfide said to him: If we wanted to listen to you, the day would be all quarrels. But I'm really eager to hear another story.)

> Parlamente, avec un peu de colère, lui dit "J'entends bien que vous estimez celles les moins mauvaises de qui la malice est découverte!"—"Or laissons ce propos là," dit Simontaut. . . . Mais venons à savoir à qui Parlamente donnera sa voix. . . . (223–224)

> (Parlamente, a little bit angry, said to him "I understand very well that you consider them the least bad whose malice is discovered!"—"Well, let's leave these words alone," said Simontaut. . . . But let's find out to whom Parlamente will give her voice. . . .)

These examples from the discussions prefigure the overall message that will emerge from the tales themselves: direct communication is dangerous; an unambiguous revelation of motives or attitudes leads inevitably to conflict, disturbance of the status quo, and frequently to tragedy; those who wish to preserve order and harmony would do well to protect themselves by deliberately sabotaging the signals that they send.

However, in Marguerite's complex fictional world nothing is quite so simple. For although protection of self and of the social order seems to dictate an obscuring of motivation through misleading discourse, the tales in the *Heptaméron* almost consistently lead one to a consideration of this very issue. The two themes— communication and motivation—seem inextricably linked by a relationship of paradox. The best way to unravel this mysterious tangle is to differentiate between various types of motivation found in the stories. We can then perhaps see that different levels of communication are appropriate in different types of situations.

Public Motivation

Three levels of motivation are illustrated in the *Heptaméron,* each with its own requisite manner of communication. The first is public motivation. Here we see reflected assumptions made about the state and its rulers as well as about their official reasons for acting as they do. When public motivation arises in the stories, the communication of reasons is relatively clear. The king, as king, must act according to certain official modes; that is, he is generous, fearless, decisive, justice-loving, and so forth. (He is also Marguerite's baby brother!) The social order is strengthened by an unmixed message on this point.

A well-known example is Tale 25, which recounts the amorous adventures of young Francis I, who stopped at church on his way home from each assignation to say his prayers. Although the king's motivation could be viewed as hypocritical to say the least, Marguerite takes care to establish a justification as well as an explanation for his activities. The lady in question is shown to be willing, if not eager, to receive the king's attentions, and the narrator emphasizes that the prayers were indeed sincere no matter what had preceded them.[3]

In another tale, the guile of an alien courtier contrasts amusingly with the subtle shrewdness of the king. Here, the storyteller merely suggests public motivation (rather than stating it outright) as we watch a little drama unfold. The king's faithful retainers discover that a visiting dignitary has accepted money in return for his promise to assassinate the ruler. Horrified, they reveal their suspicions to their master. The reader can have no doubt as to the motives prompting both their action and that of the deceiving courtier. However, the narrator does not immediately reveal the king's reasons for his actions. Rather, we watch the story develop.

The king seeks an occasion to be alone with the traitor, hints to him that he knows of the plot against him, and lets it be known cleverly and unequivocably that he is unafraid and capable of taking his vengeance should any plan against him be undertaken. The narrator does not tell, but instead, shows the reader what kinds of motives stir a king's activities. Calmness in peril, courage, strength, wit, a certain calculating manipulation of circumstance and emotion—these are the factors that explain the king's behavior. They appear more salient by their contrast with the motives of the other, lesser, characters. They make more impression by their illustration than by their exposition. It is only after the disgruntled would-be assassin has left the court in fright that the King's motives are explained to his servitors and (since we are listening in) to the readers.

Social Motivation

A second kind of motivation is social motivation, which includes reasons stemming from class, social, or occupational types, mores, and norms. It is this type of motivation that most often appears in the discussions; similarly, it is this type that is most readily identified in the stories. In this social framework, discourse is rarely clear. Communication must be short-circuited in order to prevent tragedy and the dissolution of the social fabric. The appropriate mode of intercourse is ambiguity, even duplicity.

The contrast between two stories which treat a similar situation reveals Marguerite's preference for ambiguity when communicating motive. In each story an honest wife unknowingly sleeps with someone other than her husband. In each case the facts become known to the husband first and in each case both deliberate and unwitting miscommunication takes place. However, in one tale the ending is happy and even edifying. In the other deepest tragedy prevails. Although there are several structural differences between these tales, the fundamental difference lies in Marguerite's attitudes towards comprehension and misapprehension of motive. These attitudes may be seen in the types of communication—appropriate or inappropriate—which take place.

The eighth tale deals with a husband who takes a fancy to his wife's maid. The maid, trying to flee his advances, confides in the wife who suggests that she agree to meet the husband secretly that very night. The wife's intention is to change places with her maid, catch the husband at his infidelity, and give him the scolding he deserves. She understands enough of his character to realize that what he needs is, as Marguerite put it, the pleasure that comes from changing diet from time to time. She knows that he is really not interested in a serious liaison. Thus, she hopes that she can shame him into changing his ways.

So far, the wife has shown an understanding of human motivation that should have kept her out of difficulty. However, what she does not understand about her husband is another sort of motivation, a male egotism that requires someone to boast to about his little conquests. The husband confides in his good friend and neighbor. Unknown to the wife, these two old friends decide to share and share alike, including their night with the "maid." They proceed to do just this, each spending part of the night in bed with the woman they think is the maid.

Of course, there's a hitch. The friend steals a ring from the wife's finger and then brags about this exploit to the husband the next day. When the husband realizes what has happened, he learns his lesson, although at far greater expense to both husband and wife than could have been foreseen. Fortunately, the husband wisely says nothing to the wife of his friend's part in the affair. The unclear messages are only partly deciphered; social harmony remains untroubled. The story, a very funny one told from a decidedly femininist point of view, owes much of its charm to the author's understanding of human nature. Underlying the details of the plot is an acute sense of the human capacity for self-deception, manifested in a witty and compassionate treatment of man's unerring ability to misinterpret motivation.

Tale 23 is as dark and unsubtle as Tale 8 is witty and satirical. In this story Marguerite's style is at its heavy-handed worst; the narrator details the lechery of a priest who connives to sleep with his host's unsuspecting wife in place of her husband and then to sneak away before the deception is discovered. Motivation is clearly interpreted by the middle of this story, and both husband and wife, disabused, react violently and tragically, to their own destruction. The wife, unable to bear the shame and repugnance, hangs herself, unwittingly killing their infant at the same time. Her brother, finding her dead and assuming she had died by the husband's hand, rushes off to avenge her. Although the husband meets his fate at the brother's hand, he does not die until the whole sordid story is brought to light.

In this tale there is no subtlety, no ambiguity of communication to preserve social fabric, only deliberate distortion on the part of the friar in order to dupe his hosts. Marguerite often distinguishes between the tragic, negative sort of misinterpretation when a victim is purposely fed false information or led to a wrong conclusion and the comic, healthy, sort when the dupe is the source of the misinterpretation and does not find out the truth. She also (quite predictably) forgives more readily the muddying of messages in the secular realm as opposed to the sacred one.

In the case of Tale 23, one wonders if the treatment of the story could have been more effective, indeed more damning to the monk and more positive in its impact had the wife remained ignorant as did her counterpart in Tale 8. Certainly the unraveling of the communication, the discovery of what the friar had actually purposed (the "why" behind his fair-seeming actions) contributed to a dissolution of order and the destruction of the whole family. Out of this enlightenment came darkness and chaos. Out of the obscurity of Tale 8 came at least a partial enlightenment.

Whether the tale is light or serious, short-circuited communication serves a constructive purpose. If nothing else, this deliberate ambiguity prevents quibbling. On a more didactic level, we may see the obscuring of motives as a positive social value. For instance, in Tale 30 a woman thinks so highly of her special immunity to temptation that she traps herself into sleeping with her own son. Later, she gives birth to his child. Seeking to hide her sin by silence, she rears the child away from her son and hopes for the best. However, ignorant of the relationship, the son later meets this young lady (who is his sister and his daughter) and marries her. Finally driven to confession by the turn of events, the woman tells all to church officials. Their advice to her is blunt: she must never tell the two of their real relationship. Although the woman's life with these two is a living punishment for her pride, there is a clear implication that the two children were blameless. Certainly, in their ignorance they remained safer, happier, and more innocent than they could ever have been had the truth been known by them.[4]

Personal Motivation

A final type of motivation in the *Heptaméron* is personal motivation, the revelation of personal characteristics and individual reactions to various situations (frequently crises). Like public and social motivation, this type includes nonverbal as well as verbal communication. However, in the case of personal communication, we can often find examples where the nonverbal messages are directly at odds with the verbal ones. In many cases, spoken communication remains short-circuited, messages stay scrambled, and ambiguity is cherished. Nevertheless, the nonverbal discourse is unambiguous.

For instance, the actions of the maid in Tale 8 should be easy to interpret. She literally fled her employer's advances. Although her actions said "no," he was more than willing to accept her deceptive but spoken "yes." The misinformation exchanged is, of course, the pivot on which turns the comedy of the story. Can we not find a deeper purpose here as well? It is on the level of personal motivation that Marguerite's style almost strains to remain contradictory. Nonverbal gestures, unspoken messages, are the most easily overlooked in the tales; word almost always takes precedence over behavior as the first item we scrutinize for meaning. Yet the actions, the motions, the betraying gestures, remain embedded in the text, teasing at our subconscious as we seek an appropriate explanation for the behavior of the characters.

Personal motivation, then, generates a mixed reaction. Messages are not readily decoded even though they should be clear. What short-circuits communication is frequently the contradictory nature of the human psyche. It says "yes" when it means "no." It promises eternal love when it knows it cannot deliver.[5] It invokes God's presence on the way home from a sinful rendez vous.

Even when the nonverbal message is not in conflict with the spoken signals, the question of motivation remains tantalizingly obscured. Not only do the characters in the tales seek to interpret each other's actions but the discussants often take on a similar task after the story is completed. What's more, Marguerite's skill at raising and probing questions of motive—and at leaving them at least partially unanswered—draws the reader into the same process. At some point in the *Heptaméron* the reader, like the discussant, will begin to ask some vital questions: "Why does he / she act that way?" "How would I act in the same situation? Why?" Answers to these questions stay unfocused. It would be more accurate to say that our choice of answers remains undifferentiated. In the realm of personal motivation especially, the protective aspect of ambiguity commands attention. Undeciphered messages cannot threaten delicate personal security.

A final example helps illustrate the finesse of Marguerite's ability to paint motivation. Story 31 recounts the kidnapping of a young wife by a lascivious Franciscan who, after killing all the woman's household servants, threatens her with the same fate unless she quickly changes her gown for the monk's habit he had brought with him. Cutting her hair off and disguising her as a monk, he leads her with him back toward his monastery.

When she is discovered and rescued en route by her husband, a scuffle ensues, and the husband is able to overpower the monk. The husband, needing further help, sends her to the house to get aid. Here is the way Marguerite tells this part of the story:

> Le gentilhomme ne le voulut point tuer, mais pria sa femme d'aller en sa maison quérir ses gens et quelque charette pour le mener. Ce qu'elle fit: dépouillant son habit, courut tout en chemise, la tête rase, jusqu'en sa maison. (293)

> (The man didn't want to kill him [the monk] but asked his wife to run to the house to seek his servants and a cart to transport him. This she did: tearing off the habit, she ran in just her underclothes, her head shaved, all the way to her house.)

As this story is relatively short and its prose style concise, one could wonder why Marguerite added an apparently gratuitous detail like this one. It may indeed be nothing more than an embellish-

141

ment, a superfluous detail in the richly crowded tapestry of the *Heptaméron*. But this detail is a useful one, extremely important if the reader is to understand the young wife's state of mind. We have already seen that Marguerite's style encourages the reader to ask why characters behave as they do. If we pose that question in this particular context, we will discover more about the inner workings of the woman's mind than we would if this detail were suppressed.

Why should the woman take off the habit and run to the house in her undergarments, her shaved head exposed for all to see when she could have covered herself from top to toe with the habit? This question teases at the reader subliminally, a question that now must be answered and yet would not even have been posed without the existence of that brief sentence. There are several possible answers. Perhaps the woman, frightened for her husband and still shaken by the events, felt encumbered in running by the uncustomary habit. But no, women of her day wore clothes no less restricting.

Another answer suggests itself. Perhaps the woman, released from her ordeal, had to free herself of all that reminded her of the monk and of the stifling, threatening violence that had oppressed her. Her prior helplessness relieved, she violently relieved herself of the most evident symbol of her captivity. And she was ready to do so at all costs. Whether or not this is the appropriate answer, whether or not this detail was consciously given to evoke our question, the effect of the sentence is clear. It focuses the reader's attention fixedly on the question of motive. The reader becomes a discussant, endlessly debating what he/she would have done in the same situation, what the wife should have done, and why she did what she did. Marguerite reveals just enough of her character's motives to intrigue us, to begin the debate; but not enough to resolve our uncertainties. The interpretations are many because the ambiguity resists closure.

Motivation—why people say and do what they do—dominates the discussions and more subtly the tales themselves. At each level of discourse, motivation understood or misunderstood, obscured or deciphered, ignored or obsessively regarded, is the force that advances or rearranges the figures on the chessboard of human activity painted by Marguerite. Except for the highest, (the most public) functions, clear communication of motivation incurs great risk and, curiously, muddies human comprehension. To maintain carefree, productive, harmonious social interaction is to resolve to short-circuit communication, to refuse to decipher the code, to allow ambiguity to reign.

Marguerite, discerning painter of her world, seems to have grasped this lesson without difficulty. Human motivation, which she understood well, is portrayed for her readers in all its aspects; but the safety net is always present. Ambiguity protects the social order, enhances the esthetics of the tales, assures the reader's participation, and prevents a communicative overload. There is, after all, a great advantage to preserving the atmosphere of a "bal masqué" in which all that is said and done rests in the shadow, the responsibility of a persona rather than a person. The game must be continued by all means, for as one of the *Heptaméron* discussants so astutely remarked: "au jeu nous sommes tous égaux" (49). "In games we are all equals."

Notes

A shorter version of this essay was presented at the Sixteenth-Century Studies Conference in October, 1982. I would like to thank those conference participants who shared their comments and suggestions with me at that time.

1. Notable among the discussions of ambiguity in Marguerite's work is Marcel Tetel's *Marguerite de Navarre's Heptaméron: Themes, Language, and Structure* (Durham, N.C.: Duke University Press, 1973). For a broader context in which to situate the question of the uses of ambiguity, see also Barbara Bowen's discussion of Renaissance stylistic conventions in *The Age of Bluff: Paradox and Ambiguity in Rabelais and Montaigne* (Urbana: University of Illinois Press, 1972) and Rosalie Colie's treatment of the literary paradox in *Paradoxia Epidemica: The Renaissance Tradition of Paradox* (Princeton, N.J.: Princeton University Press, 1966). And for a different viewpoint on the uses of ambiguity, see Stanley Fish's "Literature in the Reader: Affective Stylistics," in *Reader Response Criticism: From Formalism to Post-Structuralism,* edited by Jane P. Tompkins (Baltimore, Md.: The Johns Hopkins University Press, 1980).

2. The Prologue to the *Heptaméron* spells out this constraint and its reasons: "Et à l'heure, j'ouïs les deux dames dessus nommées, avec plusieurs autres de la Cour, qui se delibérèrent d'en faire autant, sinon en une chose différente de Boccace: c'est de n'écrire nulle nouvelle qui ne soit veritable histoire" (47–48). "And just recently I heard the two ladies mentioned above [Marguerite herself and Francis I's wife], with several others of the Court, who plan to do the same thing [as Boccaccio did in writing the *Decameron*], but with this one difference from Boccaccio: that is that they will write no story that isn't true." All citations from the *Heptaméron* are taken from the Flammarion edition. Page numbers are indicated in the text within parentheses. The translations are my own.

3. ". . . il passait par un monastère de religieux. Et avait si bien fait envers le prieur que toujours environ minuit le portier lui ouvrait la porte, et pareillement quand il s'en retournait. Et pource que la maison où il allait était près de là, ne menait personne avec lui. Et combien qu'il menât la vie que je vous dis, si était-il prince craignant et aimant Dieu. Et ne fallait jamais, combien qu'à l'aller il ne s'arrêtât point, de demeurer au retour longtemps en oraison en l'église" (255). ". . . he went by way of a monastery. And he had been so good to the prior that the porter always opened the door to him around midnight and also when he came back that way. And since the house where he went was near there, he took nobody with him. And even though he led the life I am describing to you, he was always a prince who feared and loved God. And he never failed, even though he didn't stop on his way, to stay there on his return trip, praying in the church for a long time."

4. An interesting twist to this story is provided by the fact that had the woman's motives been known to the children before they married, their sin could have been prevented. And had the woman herself had the needed insight to understand her own prideful motives early in her life, she could have avoided her sin. In this respect, Tale 30 is the exception that illustrates the general rule. Once the events had taken shape, however, social harmony depended on the woman's ability to hide from her children the true reasons for her actions and attitudes.

5. See Tale 16: "Et, comme si la volonté de l'homme était immuable, se jurèrent et promirent ce qui n'était en leur puissance: c'est une amitié perpétuelle, qui ne peut nâitre ni demeurer au coeur de l'homme. Et celles seules le savent qui ont expérimenté combien durent telles opinions" (176). "And as if human will were unchangeable, they promised and swore to each other what wasn't in their power to promise: that is, an enduring love, which cannot originate or last in man's heart. And those alone know this who have experienced how long such ideas last."

Works Cited

Navarre, Marguerite de. *Heptaméron*. Paris: Flammarion, 1982.

Reading Spenser's *Faerie Queene*— In a Different Voice

Shirley F. Staton

> The question asks itself how Spenser, himself imprisoned in so many impediments of circumstance, remote from us in time, in speech, in convention, yet seems to be talking about things that are important to us too?
> —Virginia Woolf, *"The Faery Queen,"* 1948

ender presuppositions shape our responses to narrative. For example, in the late 1960s Spenserian critics changed their minds about *The Faerie Queene*'s Book III (The Legend of Britomartis, or Of Chastitie) and Book IV (The Legend of Cambel and Telamond, or Of Friendship). Formerly, critics had described the structure of these middle books which recount the crisscrossing stories of several females-in-love as fragmented and disunified. They had contrasted them unfavorably with Book I (The Legend of the Knight of the Red Crosse, or Of Holinesse) and Book II (The Legend of Sir Guyon, or Of Temperance), whose accounts of the heroic adventures of a single knight possess "clearly outlined narrative structure[s]" (Williams, 102). Then, much as the 1580s critics had argued the merits of Italianate romances versus Aristotelian epics, the 1960s Spenserian critics began to reappraise Books III and IV, commending their particular kind of textual unity, their "entrelacement," or interweaving, of multiple feminine voices (Tuve, 359). As a result, scholars today laud the "narrative complexity that is shut out by the individualistic ethical codes of his [Spenser's] earlier heroes" (Kane, 461).

This changed critical opinion about Books III and IV has resulted, in large part, from the dissemination of feminist insights. New awareness of what it is like to be Other, to be a woman, has helped generate a paradigm shift. Critics have recognized that in these central books Spenser "sets himself the task of realizing the Otherness and complex reality of women by seeing life from the feminine point of view" (Berger, 398). Like the decentering perspectives of Marxism, the new historicism, and reader theory, feminism challenges the monological assumption that a literary work reflects a single historical vision "usually identical to that said to be held by the entire literate class or indeed the entire population" (Greenblatt, *Power of Forms,* 5). Indeed, today's critics can empathize more closely with the readers Spenser originally had intended for Book III, his Ladies Book. (We recall that in his correspondence with Spenser, Gabriel Harvey had depicted these sections as Spenser's attempt to "overgo" Ariosto, author of *Orlando Furioso,* the extremely popular Italian romance quite frankly designed to amuse the independent ladies of the Court of Este.)

This new understanding of women's reality enables scholars to relate gender and narrative: "As we move in *The Faerie Queene* from Book II to Book III, it is significant that we move from a man's to a woman's world" (Bean, "Cosmic Order," 72). Contemporary readers of *The Faerie Queen* no longer are constrained to value only the heroic narratives of the first two books. Now they can appreciate also the ambiguous, relational realities structuring the romance genre of Books III and IV.

While it is no doubt healthy that the literary community is more attuned to the feminine register, it is equally important to realize that this is only a first step to understanding just how thoroughly gender assumptions have shaped, and continue to shape, our ideas of narrative unity and textual meaning. For our next step—the concern of this essay—I find useful Carol Gilligan's study of male and female developmental patterns, *In a Different Voice: Psychological Theory and Women's Development* (1982). Gilligan researched gender differences by asking people how they defined moral con-

146

flicts in their own lives. Her studies indicate that men and women think very differently about ethics, themselves, and "reality." That is, each gender has its own ways for making sense of things. One way we construct ourselves and our universe is through narratives. In Catherine Belsey's words, "Fiction, as a location of meanings and contests for meaning, . . . defines and redefines the subject [i.e., our sense of self]" (6). Thus Gilligan's gender studies can provide a grid for analyzing how concepts of value, power, and identity inform our readings of certain narrative genres. Moreover, though some commentators have faulted her psychological, a-historical method for generalizing from a basis of white, middle-class subjects (Auerbach et al., 151–156), this group aptly describes most of us who read and comment on *The Faerie Queene.*

By contrasting the narrative structures, imagery, and ethical systems of Books I, II, and V with those of the two central books, we gain insight into how fiction shapes us as "masculine" or "feminine." Thus we not only can begin to move beyond the traditional male-is-human paradigm but also can explore a disguised form of that paradigm—the model that splits the human subject into binary oppositions of masculine/feminine. We can begin to analyze self-reflexively the Mars/Venus oppositions, the "Fierce warres and faithfull loues" (*The Faerie Queene* 1.1. Proem) that structure Spenser's poem.

Gilligan begins her study by showing that what has been accepted traditionally as the universal, human pattern of personal development is actually not a human, but a male, pattern. That is, the standard developmental theories of Freud, Erikson, Jay, Kohlberg, and others describe how the individual progresses through maturational stages first by separating himself from mother and home and then by learning to be independent. His idea of himself and of reality is bound up with concepts of what it is to be masculine, to be manly. His sense of standing alone, of self-sufficiency, allows him to feel integrated and centered in his world (8–18).

Extrapolating a little, we can easily see how such a masculine gender model emphasizing individuation informs the heroic quest narratives of *The Faerie Queene*'s Red Cross Knight (Book I) and of

she is his strength
—as a cornerstone

Sir Guyon (Book II). Red Cross, separated from his faithful Una throughout most of his adventures, continually struggles to become worthy by fighting off threatening monsters and seductive females. His quest culminates in a ritualized three-day battle when he kills the dragon terrorizing Princess Una's city, marries Una, and soon sets out alone on more knightly adventures. In Book II, whose structure parallels that of the first book, Sir Guyon's violent adventures supposedly teach him—the Knight of Temperance—to control his temper and play by the rules of chivalry. Guyon's quest climaxes in his destruction of the enchantress Acrasia's sensuous Bower of Bliss.

Scholars have praised these first two books for their "centralized biographical method" (Jones, 231) and for "their intellectual systems, theological and moral . . . [which support] a clearly outlined narrative structure: temptations are encountered and a quest achieved" (Williams, 102). Gilligan's studies, however, suggest that critics have valued such heroic quest narratives because these stories encode the culturally approved paradigm of male—generally assumed to be universally human—development. The formula for masculine maturation inscribes the narrative structures of the heroic epic: the young man achieves self-identity by separating himself from others.

—women as temptress

In contrast, the once condemned but more recently praised narrative strategies of Book III, Of Chastitie, and Book IV, Of Friendship, do not "fit" this masculine pattern. Instead of centering on a single hero like Red Cross or Guyon, these books interlace the voices of "pairs or groups" (Dasenbrock, 25), especially those of four females: Florimell, Amoret, Belphoebe, and Britomart. Moreover, each female protagonist is characterized not by independent acts and successful completion of a "heroic" quest in which she subdues an opponent but rather within a context of relationships to others. For example, beautiful Florimell seeks reluctant Marinell even while simultaneously fleeing would-be rapists; "womanly" Amoret, snatched from her courtly wedding ceremony seven months ago, has ever since been facing a fate worse than death at the hands of the evil sorcerer, Busyrane; virginal Belphoebe's identity depends on her remaining a desirable virgin and keeping suitors, but keeping them at a safe distance; the female knight Britomart for whom Book III is titled, adventures forth to find her pre-ordained husband yet spends her time en route succoring other knights and ladies. We might even add, as antiphonies, the voices of Book III's sexy Hellenore, characterized by her busy life-style with her satyr-consorts, and Book IV's false Florimell, surrounded by her gaggle of adoring knights.

Obviously, the central books' narrative strategies of multiple voices and interconnectedness do not conform to the masculine developmental pattern structuring Books I and II. Reed Way Dasenbrock sums up the differences: "The world of Books I and II, in which an isolated character needed to resist social entanglement in order to be virtuous and to accomplish his quest, is replaced by a more complicated world in which entanglement is inevitable and essential in order to achieve one's quest" (32). These narrational complexities, however, do suit Gilligan's description of the typical feminine developmental pattern, which emphasizes attachment to others. Gilligan's research establishes that the young woman understands herself by relating with others—be it as daughter, friend, lover, wife, or mother. Her identity takes shape by networking (8–17).

Along with foregrounding the relation between human developmental patterns and narrative plots, *In a Different Voice* helps explain why the violent imagery of epics differs from that of romance. Gilligan's research with male and female subjects establishes that while both men and women use destructive images to express fears of identity loss, the nature of these images differs along gender lines. Because entangling intimacy threatens masculine independence, the young man projects these fears in violent images of "entrapment or betrayal, of being caught in a smothering relationship or humiliated by rejection and deceit" (42).

Keeping this in mind, recall the first violent episode in *The Faerie Queene*--Red Cross's battle with the she-monster Error in Book I, canto 1. We remember that Red Cross routs this "most lothsome, filthie, foule" half-serpent, half-woman from her dark den where a thousand misshapen baby monsters are sucking on her "poisonous dugs." After battling furiously, Error enwraps her scor-

pion-like tail around Red Cross and begins to strangle him. He
manages to strangle her instead, causing her to spew

> out of her filthy maw
> A floud of poyson horrible and blacke,
> Full of great lumpes of flesh and gobbets raw,
> Which stunck so vildly, that it forst him slacke
> His grasping hold.

(1.1.20)

Red Cross's courage fails as Error pours forth out of "her hellish
sinke" (1.1.22; glossed by Hamilton as "her womb, or organs of
excretion") her cursed swarm of baby monsters which climb about
Red Cross's legs. Finally losing his temper, Red Cross strikes "at her
with more then manly force" (1.1.24; Hamilton notes that "manly"
here means "human") and at last manages to behead her. But the
goriness is not quite over, for her scattered brood, unable to climb
back into her mouth, flock about her bloody wound to suck up their
dying mother's black blood. "Having all satisfide their bloody
thurst," their swollen bellies burst and their bowels gush forth
(1.1.26).

I have detailed Red Cross's first battle to call attention to its
physical grotesqueness. As Hamilton notes, "The monster Error is
made repulsive to each of man's senses" (gloss on 1.20.9). Page Ann
DuBois suggests that these concretely repulsive images will be echoed in the eighth canto when Red Cross bares seductive Duessa's
"neather parts, the shame of all her kind" (1.8.48). A. Bartlett
Giamatti relates such imagery to the epic genre when he points out
that "in many ways, great epics illuminate man's need and man's
incapacity to control the demonic and destructive forces within him
and around him" (19). A feminist perspective complements these
readings. It suggests why heroic narratives are studded with female
bodies, why evil in such narratives takes the physical shape of the
dangerous female Other—or perhaps we should say, the devouring
Mother. According to Gilligan, intimacy poses the greatest threat to
manly independence. In order to achieve a masculine identity, the
young man must not only separate himself from others but also

continually ward off threats of (female) entrapment. Seen within this developmental context, the repulsive imagery of Red Cross's battle with the she-monster Error makes palpable the masculine dread of intimate sexual entanglement.

Such a gendered reading also helps explain Sir Guyon's violent destruction of the Bower of Bliss and enchaining of Acrasia at the end of Book II. Guyon's act, a "literary crux" that tests readers' "attitudes toward pleasure, sexuality, and the body" (Greenblatt, *Renaissance Self-Fashioning,* 170), has drawn both strong yeas and strong nays from critics. We recall that Guyon finds the lovely enchantress Acrasia dallying with the knight Verdant, his armor doffed for lovemaking, his sleeping head in her lap. In a replay of Vulcan's entrapment of Mars and Venus, Guyon catches the lovers in a net; he then releases Verdant while binding Acrasia in chains of adamant. In the standard critical reading, the capture signifies the masculine triumph of reason over the emotions, which are traditionally feminine (Hamilton, *Structure of Allegory,* 132). Guyon next razes everything on the island:

> all those pleasant bowres and Pallace brave,
> *Guyon* broke downe, with rigour pittilesse;
> Ne ought their goodly workmanship might saue
> Them from the tempest of his wrathfulnesse,
> But that their blisse he turn'd to balefulnesse.
>
> (2.12.83)

Since the garden is a time-honored metaphor for women's bodies, we may infer "the Bower of Bliss is itself a particular seductive, beautiful body" (DuBois, 55).

The key issue here, as Stephen Greenblatt comments, is "Why the particular erotic appeal of the Bower—more intense and sustained than any comparable passage in the poem—excites the hero's destructive violence?" (*Renaissance Self-Fashioning,* 171). He answers that Guyon's act is a violent attempt to secure the principle of difference necessary to fashion himself. Self-abandonment, here represented by Acrasia's Bower, endangers the progress of civilization, which must channel sexuality into reproduction. Indeed, this threat of sexual self-abandonment enables institutional power to exercise a "protective" control over sex and self (170–177). Guyon only binds but does not destroy Acrasia, moreover, because she and what she represents must remain "forever the object of the destructive quest. For were she not to exist as a constant threat, the power Guyon embodies would also cease to exist" (177). Athough such ideological readings reinforce feminist perspectives in many ways, they would benefit from gender analysis. Greenblatt's formula (sexuality equals difference equals self) needs to be modified as female sexuality equals difference equals male self.

Now contrast these violent images of masculine fears with comparable feminine ones from Britomart's and Amoret's confrontations with the evil sorcerer, Busyrane, at the end of Book III. While readers have remarked the violence of these concluding episodes, they have also remarked their strangeness. Unlike Red Cross's battle with the she-monster or Guyon's destruction of the Bower of Bliss, which critics generally have interpreted as ethical and meaningful, Britomart's climactic rescue of the imprisoned Amoret has mystified critical opinion. Readers seem unsure as to what the curiously static, silent, isolated images of empty rooms, the perverted midnight masque, the pinioned Amoret should mean (Lewis, 39; Bean, "Making," 245). Their "reality" perplexes scholars.

Gilligan's field studies, however, show that stasis and separation inscribe the violent images a young woman uses when she feels her identity threatened (39–48). Dreading separation from others because it threatens the human interconnectedness her identity depends upon, the young woman projects her fears in images of destructive isolation—the very terms often used to describe Britomart's silent and solitary forty-eight-hour vigil in Busyrane's house: "You go through room after empty room, all in silence, and the whole place ignores you" (Lewis, 30).

Isolation also characterizes Amoret's seven-month imprisonment by the vile enchanter Busyrane. We first see the dying Amoret, with "deathes owne image figured in her face," as she is led by the "two grysie villeins," Despight and Cruelty, in the "rigid and stylized" midnight masque (3.12.19; Kane, 478). Her chest has been slashed open, and her heart, "transfixed with a deadly dart" (3.12.21), is drawn from her bleeding body to be carried in a silver basin. When her weak steps flag, the two villains enforce "Her forward still with torture" (ibid.). From one perspective, the displacing of Amoret's heart—the symbol of human love and sympathy—from her body surely represents the feminine dread of separation, of being cut off from Others. On the following night, we see the wounded Amoret bound fast to a brazen pillar as the magician Busyrane sits before her, writing strange charms with Amoret's dripping "liuing bloud" (3.12.31).

Critics disagree as to how these odd images should be interpreted. Most tie them in one way or another to what they have assumed to be a female fear of sex. This assumption, however, was neatly undercut some time ago for one male critic, Thomas P. Roche, Jr., when Rosamund Tuve responded to his early draft of this position with "Hon, women do not fear sex." Roche admits that "to this day Tuve's comments are the most striking insights into my observations on this episode, because they bring up the possibility of a gulf separating readers of Spenser as great as that separating Scudamour and Amoret" ("Britomart," 129).

The first step in spanning this gender gap, or gulf, in readers is to describe it. Perhaps this final canto of Spenser's Ladies Book so perplexes yet intrigues readers not just because romance readers take delight in the unsolved and obscure—what some theoreticians see as the essence of the romance genre (Robert Guiette; cited in Jauss, 184). Perhaps the canto also perplexes because its imagery offers insights into the ambiguities of both feminine and masculine fears. Surely the cutting out of Amoret's heart with a knife (represented today by the sado-masochistic heart-with-a-dart valentine) seems to encode masculine fears of entrapment as well as feminine fears of separation. Then, too, remember that we watch all these horrors through the martial maid Britomart's eyes: from the shadows "the noble Mayd, still standing all this [the midnight masque] vewd" (3.12.5). Again on the following night we watch Britomart who watches Amoret who watches Busyrane as he writes magic characters with Amoret's dripping "liuing bloud." (3.12.31). The reader, reading letters on the page, reads Britomart watching Amoret (her heart in the basin) who watches Busyrane who writes magical letters—an unstable, circular dynamic that lets us experience a series of Others simultaneously. In an uneasy exchange of masculine fears of entanglement and feminine fears of isolation, we experience an oscillating anxiety. The palimpsest of contradictory imagery climaxing *The Faerie Queene*'s central book lets readers communicate with alterity. To genderize Jauss's term, each reader, male and female, simultaneously perceives the Other from the Other's position.

In addition to showing us how gender differences encode narrational strategies, gender studies can tell us something about how the male-equals-human paradigm affects a text's value systems. Of especial interest here is Gilligan's revisioning of Kohlberg's six stages of moral development. This authoritative scale depicts the individual moving from an egocentric understanding of fairness based on his own needs, through a concept of fairness based on a shared consensus, and finally to a principled understanding of fairness grounded in the logic of reciprocal equality. Kohlberg observes that females tend to halt midway, while males tend to ascend to the top stage.

Gilligan argues, however, that this influential model, which is widely used as a standard for all humans, describes only male, not female, moral development (24–38). Part of her proof lies in her reassessement of Kohlberg's own field data, most particularly those interviews with the two paired eleven-year-olds, Jake and Amy, in which each was asked to solve Heinze's dilemma: Heinze's dying wife needs a drug Heinze can't pay for. Should Heinze steal the drug? Jake answers Yes, because life is more important than money; furthermore, the law will understand this is the right thing to do. He points out that logically "there can only be right and wrong in judgment" (quoted in Gilligan, 27). Jake's responses are adjudged positively by the interviewers. On Kohlberg's moral scale, Jake's responses exemplify a self-confident view of reality which allows the individual to achieve the highest stages of moral maturation (25–27). In contrast, Amy's answer is deemed less satisfactory. She seems to hedge when asked if Heinze should steal the drug. "Well, I don't think so. I think there might be other ways besides stealing it" (quoted in Gilligan, 28). She wonders if the druggist might be made to understand Heinze's need, or, failing that, if Heinze could borrow the money. She points out that Heinze might go to jail for stealing; then if his wife got sick again, he'd be unable to help her (27–29).

Reinterpreting Kohlberg's data, Gilligan reasons that while both Jake and Amy understand the need for a solution, each approaches it in a different way. Because the young man sees the world as one in which he must stand on his own two feet, he would solve Heinze's dilemma "through the [impersonal] systems of logic and law," what Gilligan calls the ethics of rights. Because the young woman sees the world as a network of human connections, or what Gilligan terms the ethics of care, she would solve the problem "personally through communication in relationship" (29).

I have spent some time summarizing these differences in average female and male ethical development because I think they provide a model for explaining the readings of certain episodes in *The Faerie Queene*. Consider, for example, the incident at the outset of Book II when Sir Guyon promises to avenge the bruised and battered damsel who claims she has been raped by Red Cross. Guyon pledges,

> But now, faire Ladie, comfort to you make,
> And read, who hath ye wrought this shamefull plight;
> That short reuenge the man may ouertake,
> Where so he be, and soone vpon him light.
>
> (2.1.18)

Guyon charges furiously when he sees the accused knight approaching. But in mid-charge he suddenly veers aside, stops his attack, and humbly apologizes to Red Cross for his "offence and deedless hardiment / That had almost committed crime abhord" (2.1.27). That is, Guyon apologizes both because he charged Red Cross without issuing the usual formal challenge as decreed by the Chivalric Code and because he had almost attacked the "sacred badge," the symbolic red cross on that knight's shield, a shameful act, he says, that would have dishonored Guyon's status as a Christian knight (2.1.27, 29). This playing by the rules takes precedence over the issue of rape. Guyon's promise to avenge the Lady evaporates, as indeed does the Lady herself (whom the reader, but not Guyon, knows to be the false Duessa). The two knights forthwith declare friendship, bonded by the Chivalric Code and the masculine ethics of rights that prescribes who and what is right, and in what order. Keep in mind here Jake's solution to Heinze's dilemma. Jake felt confident that his choice to steal was the right one because he felt at home within the ethical system of hierarchized rights. The masculine logic of justice guarantees fairness—be it of the soccer game, of the corporation, or of Chivalry: each of us must play by the rules; you stay on your turf, and I'll stay on mine. Thus while a feminist critic might describe this episode as Guyon's lesson in How to Play by Old Boys' Rules, critics usually have interpreted it as Guyon's first lesson in learning temperance.

Contrast this positive response with that accorded Britomart's dinner table dalliance with the wanton Malecasta at the outset of Book III. We remember how, during the feasting, the enamoured Malecasta propositions Britomart; Malecasta mistakes the martial maid for a man because Britomart "would not disarmed be" (3.1.42). Moreover, according to the Chivalric Code, Britomart has "won" Malecasta's love by defeating that lady's six knights. Now, instead of revealing herself to be a woman, Britomart seemingly encourages Malecasta's attentions because "She would not in discourteise wise, / Scorne the faire offer of good will profest" (3.1.55). Yet while critics have had no trouble in interpreting Guyon's broken promise to the battered lady as an example of a noble soul's misplaced pity (Morgan, 32–33), they have been perplexed and disconcerted about Britomart's seemingly immoral behavior in misleading Malecasta. They ask, Why doesn't Britomart take off her helmet and let her hair down? (Lanham, 432).

Gilligan's research suggests an answer. We recall that Amy saw the world and Heinze's problem as a network of human connectedness. Instead of viewing ethical situations in terms of competing rights as Jake did, Amy perceived them as conflicting responsibilities. He asks, What is the right thing to do? She asks, Who will be hurt the least? Gilligan's account of the feminine ethics of care calls attention to the poem's own cues, which tell us that "by self-feeling of her feeble sexe" Britomart sympathizes with Malecasta's "strong extremitie" (3.1.54, 53); "For great rebuke it is loue to despise; Or rudely sdeigne a gentle harts request" (3.1.55). As Paul Alpers points out (379), Britomart's identification with Malecasta's need enables her, in Spenser's words, to "judge what pains do loving harts perplexe" (3.1.54). Along with the Ariostan undertone of homoeroticism, we also hear the voice of the sisterly woman who does not want to hurt another's feelings. Britomart asks not Who has the right? but Who will be harmed the least?

Of course, no figure in the poem so sparks the ethical implications of the gender gap than the ambiguous figure of the female knight Britomart—woman in man's armor. While she is probably the most popular figure in the poem, critics have a field day arguing whether to read her as a successful union of masculine and feminine qualities, a kind of perfect androgyne, or as an inconsistent character who becomes a man only when she's got her armor on. In either case, this martial maid constantly foregrounds the issue of gender. She demands that the reader fill in the gaps between her masculine aggressiveness and feminine nurturance; she makes us question "the simple antithetical labels of male and female" and search for a new definition (Shepherd, 8).

These sexual ambiguities are resolved in the original 1590 conclusion of Book III. Here Britomart breaks Busyrane's (and our) spell, rescues Amoret, and restores her to both health and husband. In what is probably one of the most famous embraces in literary discourse, and surely an emblem of Britomart's success in overcoming gender differences, the lovers—Amoret and Scudamore—fuse as one:

No word they spake, nor earthly thing they felt,
But like two senseles stocks in long embracement dwelt.
Had ye them seene, ye would haue surely thought,
That they had beene that faire *Hermaphrodite.*
(3.12.46; 1590 ed.)

Again Gilligan offers us a model that explains in psychological terms what Spenser says in poetic ones. In Chapter 6, "Visions of Maturity," she depicts the apex of both male and female psychological development as a coming together, like two halves of an arch, of the feminine and masculine developmental routes. These "divergent constructions of identity" merge as each sex discovers the other's perspective and understands their interrelationship: male independence with its morality of rights and female interconnectedness with its morality of responsibility become complementary and intersecting routes to maturity (157–167). In these terms, the lovers' embrace signifies that the feminine fear of separation has been withstood and overcome (Amoret's imprisonment and Britomart's vigil) and the masculine dread of attachment has vanished—albeit magically, like Busyrane himself. Sir Scudamore and Amoret become one. The hermaphrodite emblematizes the mature human being created by the intersecting arcs of the hitherto separated masculine and feminine patterns of growth (Paglia, 62–63). The androgynous emblem caps "the gradual restoration of sanity experienced by the reader in Book III" (Bernard, 20).

But as we all know, Spenser discarded this happy hermaphroditic ending and deferred the lovers' reunion, ostensibly to continue Amoret's adventures throughout the next book on Friendship. For me, however, the change in endings signals the poem's resumption in Book V (The Legend of Artegall, or Of Justice) of the masculine epic structures of Books I and II. Like the first two books, the fifth book narrates the heroic adventures of a central knight—here Artegall, Britomart's husband-to-be (Stump, 88). More importantly, Book V's theme of justice codifies a masculine-equals-human paradigm in which the ethics of rights, ensconced in the Chivalric Code, lords it over the ethics of care. For "the essence of chivalry," as Huizinga has claimed, "is the imitation of the ideal hero" (quoted by Leslie, 133). As a result, Britomart and the other female voices of the central books are framed by the patriarchal value system of Books I, II, and V.

Take, for example, Artegall's first dispensation of "true iustice." He is to decide which of two men—Sir Sanglier or a squire—will get to keep a lady whom each man claims as his own (5.1.14–30).

Another lady who has just been beheaded by Sir Sanglier bloodies the nearby ground. But Artegall never asks the living lady which man she prefers: Hamilton suggests that this is because Artegall "knows that the lady might not tell the truth" (*Structure of Allegory*, 172). Nor is Artegall interested in finding out "to whom the living lady rightfully belongs. Rather he wants to assert the lore of justice by discovering which knight is worthy to have the living lady, and which the dead" (ibid., 17). Using Solomon's ploy, Artegall gives the Squire his living lady back and saddles Sir Sanglier with the dead lady's head, not because Sanglier is a murderer, but because he "loue so light esteeme[s]" (5.1.28). Critics have generally seen Artegall's solution as a restoration of "harmony between the sexes" (Lewis; quoted in Paglia, 54). But a feminist reading would point out that the woman here becomes what Gayle Rubin, building on Levi-Strauss, has described as a medium of sexual exchange, a piece of property (Greene and Kahn, 8). Even if Artegall's judgment may express the prevailing sixteenth-century view of what was just and "natural," a feminine ethics would fault Artegall, the model of "true justice," for being more concerned with (male) property than with human needs.

In Book V no feminine voices counter Artegall's ideal of true justice. Even Britomart, whose main task is to rescue the enthralled Artegall from the the beautiful Amazonian Queen Radigund, is co-opted by the masculine ethics of rights. Recall, if you will, how Britomart prepares for her confrontation with the Amazon by staying overnight in the Temple of Isis, Goddess of Equity and sister-wife of Osiris, God of Justice. (Equity represents a personal justice ancillary to or outside of the Law.) Of importance here is that during the night Britomart experiences a violently sexual dream-vision "which did close implie / The course of all her fortune and posteritie" (5.7.12). Her fortune, of course, is to reproduce the royal progeny; in addition, as Equity, she is to restrain her husband Artegall's "cruell doomes" (5.7.22). Critics take this dream-vision to be an omen of Britomart's and Artegall's ideal union as man and wife (Hieatt, 135–145). But as the phrase "man and wife" (not "husband and wife") so aptly reveals, it is only "ideal" from a masculine point of view. From this hierarchal perspective, the term "man" includes woman, Justice encompasses Equity, and Chivalry commands Chastity. The ethics of rights has subsumed the ethics of care.

Britomart's dream in the Temple of Isis thus prepares her to serve "true justice," the masculine ethics of rights. So after hacking and hewing each other's "dainty parts . . . as if such vse they hated" (5.7.29), Britomart lops off Radigund's head, doles out equity by restraining Talus from murdering all the city's inhabitants, and restores patriarchal rule to the Amazonians:

> And changing all that forme of common weale
> The liberty of women did repeale,
> Which they had long vsurpt; and them restoring
> To mens subiection, did true Iustice deale.
>
> (5.7.42)

We last glimpse Britomart as she mopes for the now-absent knight of "true Iustice": Artegall's honor has compelled him to set forth alone on more heroic adventures. The narrative structures are once again monolingual.

In a Different Voice foregrounds these relations between gender and narrative. As a kind of meta-narrative, Gilligan's book underscores the differences between "masculine" epic and "feminine" romance and so frames our readings of *The Faerie Queene* within a sexual politics. Gender analysis makes us, as readers, more alert to how textual values fuse with systems of power—in fiction and in the "real" world.

Works Cited

Alpers, Paul. *The Poetry of "The Faerie Queene."* Princeton, N.J.: Princeton University Press, 1967.

Auerbach, Linda Blum, Vicki Smith, and Christine Williams. "On Gilligan's *In a Different Voice.*" *Feminist Studies* 11 (1985): 149–161.

Bean, John C. "Cosmic Order in *The Faerie Queene:* From Temperance to Chastity." *Studies in English Literature, 1500–1900* 17 (1977): 67–79.

————. "Making the Daimonic Personal: Britomart and Love's Assault in *The Faerie Queene.*" *Modern Language Quarterly* 40 (1979): 237–255.

Belsey, Catherine. *The Subject of Tragedy: Identity and Difference in Renaissance Drama.* London: Methuen, 1985.

Bennett, Josephine Waters. *The Evolution of "The Faerie Queene."* Chicago: University of Chicago Press, 1942.

Berger, Harry, Jr. *"The Faerie Queene,* Book III: A General Description." In *Essential Articles for the Study of Edmund Spenser,* edited by A. C. Hamilton. Hamden, Conn.: Archon Books, 1972.

Bernard, John D. "Pastoral and Comedy in Book III of *The Faerie Queene." Studies in English Literature* 23 (1983): 5–20.

Dasenbrock, Reed Way. "Escaping the Squires' Double Bind in Books III and IV of *The Faerie Queene." Studies in English Literature* 26 (1986): 25–45.

DuBois, Page Ann. " 'The Devil's Gateway': Women's Bodies and the Earthly Paradise." *Women's Studies* 7 (1980): 43–58.

Dunseath, T. K. *Spenser's Allegory of Justice in Book Five of "The Faerie Queene."* Princeton, N.J.: Princeton University Press, 1968.

Giamatti, A. Bartlett. *Play of the Double Senses: Spenser's "Faerie Queene."* Englewood Cliffs, N.J.: Prentice Hall, 1975.

Gilligan, Carol. *In a Different Voice: Psychological Theory and Women's Development.* Cambridge, Mass.: Harvard University Press, 1982.

Gohlke, Madelon S. "Embattled Allegory: Book II of *The Faerie Queene." English Literary Renaisance* 8 (1978): 123–140.

Greenblatt, Stephen. *Renaissance Self-Fashioning: From More to Shakespeare.* Chicago: University of Chicago Press, 1980.

————, ed. *The Power of Forms in the English Renaissance.* Norman, Okla.: Pilgrim Books, 1982.

Greene, Gayle, and Coppélia Kahn. "Feminist Scholarship and the Social Construction of Woman." In *Making a Difference: Feminist Literary Criticism,* edited by Gayle Greene and Coppélia Kahn. London: Methuen, 1985.

Hamilton, A. C. *The Structure of Allegory in the "Faerie Queene."* Oxford: Oxford University Press, 1961.

————, ed. *The Faerie Queene.* By Edmund Spenser. London: Longman, 1977.

Hieatt, A. Kent. *Chaucer, Spenser, Milton: Mythopoeic Continuities and Transformations.* Montreal: McGill-Queene's University Press, 1975.

Jauss, Hans Robert. "The Alterity and Modernity of Medieval Literature." *New Literary History* 6 (1979): 181–229.

Jones, H. S. V. *A Spenser Handbook.* New York: Appleton-Century-Crofts, 1930, 1958.

Kane, Sean. "Spenserian Ecology." *English Literary History* 50 (1983): 461–483.

Lanham, Richard A. "The Literal Britomart." *Modern Language Quarterly* 28 (1967): 426–445.

Leslie, Michael. *Spenser's "Fierce Warres and Faithful Loves": Martial and Chivalric Symbolism in "The Faerie Queene."* Cambridge: D. S. Brewer, 1983.

Lewis, C. S. *Spenser's Images of Life.* Edited by Alastair Fowler. Cambridge: Cambridge University Press, 1967.

Morgan, Gerald. "The Idea of Temperance in the Second Book of *The Faerie Queene" The Review of English Studies* 37 (1986): 11–39.

Paglia, Camille A. "The Apollonian Androgyne and the *Faerie Queene." English Literary Renaissance* 9 (1979): 42–63.

Roche, Thomas P., Jr. "Britomart at Busyrane's Again, or, Brideshead Revisited." In *Spenser at Kalamazoo: 1983,* edited by Francis G. Greco. Clarion, Pa.: Clarion University of Pennsylvania, 1983.

————. *The Kindly Flame: A Study of the Third and Fourth Books of Spenser's Faerie Queene.* Princeton, N.J.: Princeton University Press, 1964.

Shepherd, Simon. *Amazons and Warrior Women: Varieties of Feminism in Seventeenth-Century Drama.* New York: St. Martin's Press, 1981.

Silberman, Lauren. *"The Faerie Queene,* Book II: A Surfeit of Temperance." In *Spenser at Kalamazoo: 1984,* edited by Francis G. Greco. Clarion, Pa.: Clarion University of Pennsylvania, 1983.

Stump, Donald V. "Isis versus Mercilla: The Allegorical Shrines in Spenser's Legend of Justice." In *A Renaissance Poetry Annual III,* edited by Patrick Cullen and Thomas P. Roche, Jr. Pittsburgh, Pa.: University of Pittsburgh Press, 1982.

Tuve, Rosamund. *Essays: Spenser, Herbert, Milton.* Edited by Thomas P. Roche, Jr. Princeton, N.J.: Princeton University Press, 1970.

Williams, Kathleen. "Venus and Diana: Some Uses of Myth in *The Faerie Queene." English Literary History* 28 (1961): 101–120.

Woolf, Virginia. "The Faery Queen." In *The Moment and Other Essays.* New York: Harcourt Brace Jovanovich, 1948.

THREE

ole and Representation
in English
Renaissance Texts

Presentations of Women in the English Popular Press

Sara J. Eaton

> Now is there not one end, and one only, in philosophical exposition, in
> oratory, and in the drama? . . . All have one and the same end—persuasion.
> —Scaliger, the *Poetics* (Lyons, 1561)

caliger was one of the first translators and interpreters
of Aristotle in the Renaissance, and he argues a point
often forgotten by subsequent literary critics and historians. Not only could generic considerations be subsumed by rhetorical goals, but for Renaissance writers,
philosophical expositions, oratory, and the drama were used as
examples of Rhetorica. In their works, Renaissance writers followed
these literary and rhetorical conventions for depicting women—
conventions established early in Western culture and modified
some under the influence of neo-Platonism and Courtly Love
rhetoric.

Women were described in Petrarchan terms and in the familiar
metaphors of Courtly Love. Perceived as either queenly virgins or
dissipated whores, they inspired virtuous male behavior. From the
male writer's viewpoint, women were perfectable. Women's failure
to be so—or seem so—elicited condemnations that resonated with
religious convictions because the psychology of Courtly Love combined sexuality and love with religiosity. Idealized women enabled
the writer "to discover a whole new reality, *another* reality, the
eternal ideas in which one's own nature participated and for which

it ought to renounce every other value," as Frederick Goldin has put it (50). Anti-Petrarchan rhetoric described women as "monsters" who failed masculine ideals of feminine perfection. The language surrounding these dispraised women had its sources in Petrarchan conventions and in the Roman satires of, for example, Martial and Juvenal: animalistic and sensual images support a sententious authorial tone, and minor faults threaten the stability of society.[1] But Scaliger asserts that the purpose of rhetoric is persuasion, even in the demonstrative mode, which praises and dispraises. The question this essay attempts to answer, then, is what we are persuaded of by these conventional (dis)praises of women, particularly those printed by the English popular press between 1554 and 1645.

The courtesy books, pamphlets, and ballads published during this period are well-known for their misogynist viewpoints. These tracts are evidence of a cultural concern about women's behavior or, more precisely, about errant female behavior.[2] Certainly, the steady stream of publications during the period indicates substantial interest from readers on this topic, but modern readers should be leery of taking these tracts as a priori evidence of how the English actually viewed women. It is just as likely that these works are examples of persuasive demonstrative rhetorical practice in the period, so persuasive that readers still succumb to the rhetoric as its practioners intended.

These portrayals are literary constructions, the results of ascribed feminine "qualities" sanctioned over centuries, and they catalogue how men "see" women. For the Renaissance writer, written/spoken language which focused on discernible qualities produced a more persuasive rhetoric.[3] And the speaker was more persuasive when he demonstrated that he had been personally affected by the passions he spoke or wrote of. As Thomas Wright, the protégé of Henry Wriothesley, 3d Earl of Southampton, put it in his philosophical exposition *The Passions of the Minde in Generall* (London, 1604), "for *Cicero* expresly teacheth that it is almost impossible for a oratour to stirre vp a passion in his auditors, except he be first affected with the same passiō himself":

Wise men are most moued with sound reasons, and lesse with passions: contraiwise the common people or men not of deepe iudgement, are more persuaded with passions in the speakers; the reason is, because as we haue two senses of discipline especially, the eyes & the ears: reason entreth the eares; the passion wherewith the oratour is affected passeth by the eyes, for in his face we discover it, and in other gestures: the eyes are more certain messengers and lesse to be doubted . . . but those passions we see, nature imprinteth them deeper in our hearts. (174–175)

A persuasive rhetoric creates images of "passion" meant to be "seen" by the heart. Wright argues that, of sensory impressions, what can be seen is "lesse to be doubted." His explanation, however, because it suggests that rhetoric can be supplemented by a physicality manipulated to increase the words' affect, addresses "doubts" about the speaker's sincerity of purpose when the "passions" are thus enacted to be "seen."

How does the audience trust what it sees? As Wright suggests in his allusion to Cicero, the question of the speaker's sincerity plagues theoretical discussions of rhetoric's efficacy from its beginnings in Plato and Aristotle. Doubt is resolved by accepting that certain kinds of rhetoric, particularly the demonstrative, reflect on the virtue of the speaker—that is, efficacious rhetoric is produced by virtuous speakers. Since this is obviously a more hopeful than realistic resolution to the problem, rhetoricians tend to take both the producers and the recipients of the rhetorical experience into account as judges of effective rhetorical practice. If the orator's job is to convince the audience that he has indeed experienced the passion he so vividly describes and abstracts from, it is the audience's job to determine how *convincingly* that passion has been portrayed.

The skilled use of rhetorical figures and tropes supplements and enforces both ends of this rhetorical transmission; they "paint" the image of experienced passion *and* reveal its veracity. Rhetorical emphasis shifts, however, from the orator as a purveyor of truth to one whose performance of linguistic acts may convey truth to an audience prepared by rhetoric itself to "see" it. For the Renaissance theoretician, practitioner, and audience, truth values lay hidden in the performance of a rhetorical form of art. Even in the tracts printed by the popular press, the emphasis is on the writer's theatrical abilities to portray passionate feeling visually. The object of the discourse—woman—is displaced as a referent for the rhetoric by this emphatic shift; instead, women become examples of *ut pictura poesis* or textual representations of how women are perceived by men.

The consistent publication of these works and the reissue of popular ones like *The Scholehouse of Women* (London, 1557) or *The Praise and Dispraise of Women* (London, 1558), as they are listed in *A Transcript of the Registers of the Company of Stationers of London* for the years 1554 through 1645, indicates a flourishing market. This was a transitional period for the popular press; it became an industry, supplying relatively inexpensive reading to an increasingly literate public, began to regulate itself as an industry through the *Stationer's Register,* and established a working relationship with the government censors to determine what the public could read. Just as plays were owned by the companies that performed them, printed works were owned by the stationers and inherited or sold to each other. Modern copyright laws were nonexistent; prior to Ben Jonson, who is credited with being among the first to be concerned with how his work appeared in print, an author relinquished control of his work once he sold it to a stationer, if he sold it at all. Consequently, authorial attribution and accurate dating—for a signature may consist of only initials, or earlier editions of a text may be undated or lost—are a significant bibliographic problem, especially for scholars wanting to trace the evolution, if any, of specific contemporary concerns in this press.

A rigorous statistical study of the *Stationer's Register* would confirm my impression that the textual forms for writing about women shifted during this period. Around 1565, most titles dealing with women's behavior were printed as ballads or broadsides. In the 1580s a more permanent form of text, the book, was frequently given over to this material. By 1615, published sermons also addressed issues surrounding female behavior, but by 1631, the ballad was again the topic's predominate form. Clearly, the public's taste for reading in some form about women was dulled only by periodic censorship (for example, during the last years of Elizabeth's reign). The authors writing on this topic, ranging from hack writers to rhetoricians and dramatists to, most likely, Puritan clergy, knew their market; as Sandra Clark notes in *The English Pamphleteers,* women were a "stock subject," as were "social upstarts, foreigners, atheists, and puritans . . . despite an increasing awareness of women as social beings and the growth of the ideal of monogamy" (177).

Too often, these tracts seem oblivious to contemporary attitudes towards real women's lives in Renaissance England, and allusions to political or social events create merely a background for conventional rhetorical treatments of women. Their structural and imagistic similarities suggest that many were written as rhetorical exercises and followed traditional conventions for praise and dispraise in demonstrative rhetoric established by Aristotle and more fully articulated by Quintilian. The sheer numbers of texts published are evidence of a preoccupation with women's roles in society, but the ways in which these writings present women argue as well that rhetorical conventions mediated between social concerns and the intended effects of the rhetoric on readers. As George Puttenham (d.1590) explains it when he defines hyperbolic praise in *The Arte of English Poesie:*

> Now when I speake that which neither I my selfe think to be true, nor would haue any other body beleeve, it must needs be a great dissimulation, because I meane nothing lesse then that I speke, and this manner of speach is used, when either we would greatly aduance or greatly abase the reputation of any thing or person, and must be used very discreetly, or els it will seeme odious, for although a prayse or other report may be allowed beyōd credit, it may not be beyōd all measure. . . . Nevertheless as I said before if we fall a praysing, especially of our mistresses vertue, bewtie, or other good parts, we be allowed now and then to over-reach a little by way of comparison. (192)

Puttenham repeats his authorities' advice on "praysing." For the Renaissance rhetorician and writer, praise and dispraise were equivalent rhetorical modes. Generalized heuristic *loci* or places—the person's moment in history, personal background and heritage, what others said or had been prophesied—were amplified or portrayed through the same rhetorical figures.[4] Aristotle's instructions on praise in the *Rhetoric* insist that the writer focus on praiseworthy actions and assume that "for the purpose of praise or blame, that qualities which closely resemble the real are identical with them" (1.9.24–29; p. 97). Aristotle's point, with its emphasis on identical praised and real qualities, heavily influences Renaissance authors' points-of-view when they "fall a praysing." Note Puttenham's assertion that he means "nothing lesse then that I speke" as he dissimulates. The writer must appear sincere to be persuasive.

But it is Quintilian's formulation of how praise dissimulates that informs Puttenham's explanation and, more generally, results in a rhetorical pattern common to both praises and dispraises in this period. Quintilian generally agrees with Aristotle; praise, he suggests, is "reserved solely for the delectation of audiences, which indeed is shown to be its peculiar function by its name [epideixis], which implies display" (3.7.1–2; p. 465). However, Quintilian focuses more closely on the rhetorical difficulties of praising: "Aristotle also urges a point, which at a later date Cornelius Celsus emphasized almost to excess, to the effect that, since the boundary between vice and virtue is often ill-defined, it is desirable to use words that swerve a little from the actual truth" (3.7.25–26; p. 477). In order to appear sincere and be persuasive, the writer must "swerve a little from the actual truth." The words lie. Methods of amplification particularize the portrayal by focusing on personal details and actions, but they also *generalize* because they are less than truthful. This rhetoric requires the writer and the reader to measure excess and employ it in the pursuit of what the author means. Thus, the tendency of the epideictic to emphasize outward appearances focuses attention on the "garments of style," the aspect of praise where lies can be apprehended.

Both Aristotle and Quintilian, in their definitions of the *loci* and in their explanations of amplification, stress the role of appearances in determining how the person praised should be perceived by the rest of society. The speaker's goal is to persuade his hearers to agree with his exposition on discernible qualities which affect the entire society. This particular rhetorical strategy explains why the portrayals of women in the popular press emphasize physical details in relation to their effect on observers. For example, Barnaby Rich (1540?–1617), the self-educated soldier-pamphleteer whose works were popular with the bourgeoisie, claims in his dispraise, *Faultes, Faults and Nothing Else But Faultes:*

> Men you see are full of Faults, but amongst women (some will say) there are but two Faults, and those are, they can neither doe or say well. . . . There hath bin good and bad women from the beginning; but for those that haue beene accounted ill, they were neuer halfe so detestable in times past, as they be at this houre: nay, those women that now be accounted good, and would be angrie if there should be any exceptions taken to their honesty, are more Courtezan-like (to the show of the world) that euer was *Lais* of *Corinth,* or *Trine* the famous Curtezan of *Thebes.*
>
> What newfangled attires for the heades, what flaring fashions in their garments, what alteration in their ruffes, what painting of shamelesse faces, what audacious boldnes in company, what impudencie, and what immodestie is vsed by those that will needes be reputed honest, when their open breasts, their naked stomachs, their frizled haire, their wanton eie, their shameless countenance, are all the vaunt errours of adulterie. . . .
>
> What is become of that age, when simple beutie was best beseeming an honest woman, when bashfull modestie inclosed in a vertuous breast was their best lewre, whereby to induce an honorable reputation. (G3r–G4v)

But what Rich dispraises, William Bercher, a personal retainer of Norfolk's instrumental in his fall from royal favor, praises in his *Nobylytye of Women,* presented to Elizabeth in the first year of her reign:

> Who doe not see that the bodye of wymen / doth ftir passe and excell all thynges / , the bewtye of hyr face / wth a certyne dyvyne brightnes / shynyge in hyr countenauce / wythe all other partes so

well proporcõned, as all the world dothe confesse hyr, to be / the
moste notable creature, in the whiche nature thaught to prove hyr
connynge / insomuch as the goddes and their chyldren have byn
caught wythe their love / as doth well appere by awntient lear-
enge / and one pryveledge they have geven in the hed / that is the
pryncypall part / wch in a woman is never devoide of heare / as it
is in a mã / and whear the fface of man is for the most parte
deformed by the growthe of his berde / the woman's remaynethe
ever smooth and pure / , and is of Suche vertue, as yf yt be once
ffayre wasshed / the water never receaveth the spott thear bye /
whear as contrary in man / lett hym washe never so ofte, the water
remaynethe trowbled and ffowle. (97–98)

The image that inspires Rich's longing for a Golden Age of female
modesty, influenced by the opening lines of Juvenal's Sixth Satire,
can also inspire flights of logic in Bercher. The amplified details,
drawn from close observation of the body, move the reader to a
contemplation of an ideal. For John Ford (1586–1639), the poet and
dramatist, that ideal becomes specifically religious:

Being overcome with the affection of some excellently deserving
beauty, with admiration of the singular perfection thereof, with
what curious workmanship it is framed, with what glorye of majesty it is endowed, it is an immediate occasion, to bring [male
observers] in serious conceit of weighing the wonders of the
heavens in compacting such admirable quintessence in so precious a form, by which they will deeply resolve the dignitye of
God in that mould, and truly acknowledge the weaknesse of their
owne nature in comparison of beauty. (29)

In the majority of these writings, the depiction of a woman's
faults or virtues moves the readers toward thoughts of something
else. This movement of thought is accomplished by comparing what
is described in concrete hyperbolic detail to an idealized abstraction. These details are chosen for their potential affective impact on
the reader. As Thomas Wright explains in *The Passions of the Minde:*
"Passions are not onely, not wholy to be extinguished (as the Stoiks
seemed to affirme) but sometimes to be moued, and stirred vp for

the service of virtue" (17).[5] He is clear about the method: "Passions then must be moued with vrgent reasons, reasons vrging proceed from solid amplification, amplifications are gathered from commonplaces, commonplaces fit for oratoricall persuasion concern a part of Rhetoric called Invention" (185). In this context, hyperbolic portrayals of women are part of a didactic rhetoric; amplified to move the reader's mind, they stir the passions "for the service of virtue." Wright's point is reiterated by others: Richard Brathwait (1588?–1626), the Oxford-educated poet and would-be dramatist, thought women were "mouing objects of imitatio, both in life and death" (159); Nicholas Breton (1545?–1626?), one of the most highly praised and popular poets and writers of his day, whose patron was Mary Sidney, the Countess of Pembroke, agreed, saying "for, indeed, it ought to be written wooman, and not woman: For that she doth woo man with her virtues, who weds her with vanity. For man being of wit sufficient to consider of the virtues of woman, is (as it were) ravished with the delights of those dainties, which do (after a sort) draw the senses of man to serve them" (18–19). Sensitive to how women appear as a text, these writers use rhetorical terms to describe their subjects. Women are "mouing objects of imitatio" and inspire considerations of virtue. Breton's suggestion that woman should be written "wooman" reflects a general consensus in the period that women serve to help the reader visualize the message of the text.

Particularized hyperbolic female images of women moved readers by their example to serve virtue or contemplate abstractions. The structural pattern of these tracts as a whole likewise mimed that process of movement from the particular to the abstract. The first of these praises to appear in English, *The Defence of Good Women,* by Thomas Elyot (d.1546), the famous diplomat and Christian humanist, is also credited with being its first neo-Platonic dialogue because it moves readers in this way. The dialogue between Candidus, women's defender, and Caninius, the woman-hater, initially dwells on details. Candidus asks, "Wherein do you note her to be imperfitte? Is it in the soule or bodie?" Caninius retorts: "In both of them trewly, for they be weaker than men, and haue their fleshe softer, less hearc on their visages, and their voice sharper, and as I have redde, they haue in some parts of their bodies, their boones fewer. And as concernyng the soule, they lacke hardinesse, and in perilles are timerous, more delicate then men, unapt to peinefulnesse, except thei be thereto constrained or stered by wilfulnesse" (Bbr).

Midway through the dialogue, Caninius asserts that "for the word man, which I named, included as well woman as man, when it is written or spoken so generally" (C3v). Caninius is being slowly persuaded by the force of Candidus's "urgent reasons" to a consideration of the similarities between men and women at this point, but Candidus responds by pointing out women's exemplary qualities. In particular, he portrays Queen Zenobia as the image of a good woman and good ruler. Caninius, converted, says "I wolde neuer haue loked for suche a conclusion. I see well enoughe, that women beying wel and vertuously brought up, do not onely with men participate in reason, but some also in fidilitie and constancie be equall unto them" (Db3r). The overall rhetorical structure of *The Defence of Good Women* moves the reader from depictions of soft flesh and sharp voices to the contemplation of fidelity and constancy. The passions are carefully mitigated by reasoning. But the consolatory conclusions are qualified ones: Caninius's assertion that the word man includes woman is moderated by Candidus's praise of extraordinary female qualities. Only certain women are, finally, "equall" to men.

Even a commentary on a topical event, *The Just Downfall of Ambition, Adultery, and Murder,* attributed to Thomas Overbury (1581–1613), the popular poet and pamphleteer allegedly murdered for interfering in the love affair between Robert Carr, Viscount of Rochester, a favorite of James I, and Frances Howard, Countess of Essex, follows this pattern of abstraction and exclusion:

> All you that haue your hearts pierced with sad consideration, take this for a remembrance of greefe, that is, that when a woman of noble Parentage, placed on the mountaine of smiling chance, hauing the dignity of greatnesse shining on her forehead, should humble herselfe to base condition, giving her whole mind to malicious hatred, secret consents of iniquity, selfe-will and wicked proceedings, never pacified till the end of damned performances.

Oh: was not this woman created for a deepe furrow to her Aliance, a great greefe vnto her Country, and foule staine vnto her
owne reputation? (C2r–C2v)

This woman's fall from the "mountaine of smiling chance," where
she is by virtue of her position potentially equal to men, to the
"deepe furrow" of iniquity shames herself, her family, and her
country. She moves from society into a "damned performance,"
artificiality, and exile. The abstractions—"Aliance," "Country," and
"her owne reputation"—become equivalent terms through their
placement in the sentence structure. All are endangered because of
the woman's actions; the consequences of her "performance,"
"great greefe" and "a foule staine," place her in juxtaposition to the
abstractions reified by her actions.

In all these examples, the descriptions of frequently trivial attributes have momentous effects. Rich's women's hair and eyes
become the "vaunt errours of adulterie." Bercher's woman's facial
beauty leads to a contemplation of men's less virtuous counte-
nances, while Ford sees the face of God. Elyot's depictions of sexual
differences are negated and transformed into social differences,
much like Overbury's, which threaten or maintain social stability.
The result is that the woman being described "falls" from her ele-
vated position or transcends her human one and endangers or
inspires her society.

But it is rhetoric that creates the sense of movement. One exaggerated feature is linked to a hyperbolic effect, and that linkage
creates the cause-and-effect "logic," the urgent reasons, portrayed
in the text. The extended phrases and long periods augment the
hyperbolic figures so the rhetoric seems to gather weight and mo-
mentum as it is read. The style is Ciceronian, and the stylistic exag-
geration of feminine appearances and behavior is responsible for,
in a sense produces, the results of feminine transgression or tran-
scendence within the text for the reader.[6]

"The real trouble with hyperbole," Keir Elam argues in his
work on Shakespeare's rhetoric, "is that it surpasses (or 'throws
beyond') the limits of *sense* and invades the territory of *reference*"
(300). Rudolf Agricola, one of the most influential rhetoricians for

Renaissance writers, notes in *De inventione dialectica libri tres* that this shift from the praised person to effects, to what the praise refers to, is exactly what interests the audience: "For virtue, vice, and the like are things indeed which, when seen, move the mind: and the person is a sort of pathway to the things, in that we be moved by the things even without the person, whereas we think the person of no concern to us apart from the things" (416). The flamboyant prose style which characterizes the pamphlets accents the "things" because these visual representations arouse the readers' passions to a point where they could "take heede," in P. Thomas Wilson's words, of the distinctions between words, things, and meanings. Wilson (1525?–1581), the ambassador and secretary of state for Elizabeth, a man accused of heresy by Queen Mary and perhaps tortured by the Inquisition at her instigation for having written his rhetorics, urges readers to see that "when such speeches are used, that we take them not as they bee spoken, but as they are ment" (75). The historical ironies of Wilson's life suggest the seriousness with which such assertions were taken and used in the Renaissance. In a neo-Platonic world, portrayals of women were "pathways," figures augmenting readers' perceptions of authorial intent because, presumably, the author is dissembling stylistically so that the truth could be revealed in the act of reading.

Readers and authors are involved in a complex hermeneutic in these secular allegories. Discernment of the work's rhetorical truth depends on a set of shared perceptions of the less than ideal or idealized woman for revelation to occur. Consequently, these tracts indulge in stereotypes; women who deviate from expectations of how women should behave are "monsters," while women deemed praiseworthy are "stars." Neither are human. In an anonymous work, *Hic Mulier: or, The Man-Woman,* the woman becomes a metaphorical horse and deceives others in her disguises:

> But whan they thrust vertue out of doores, and giue a tham lesse libertie to euery loose passion, that either their weake thoughts ingenders, or the discourse of wicked tongues can charme into their yeelding bosomes (much apt to bee opened with any pick locke of flattering and deceitfull insinuation) then they turn mask-

ers, mummers, nay monsters in their disguises, and so they may catch the bridle in their teeth, and runne away with their Rulers, they care not into what dangers they plunge either Fortunes or Reputations, the disgrace of the Whole Sexe, or the blot and obloquy of their priuate families. (B2r)

Thomas Overbury said similarly in *The Just Downfall* that "an Ambitious woman shewes her selfe to bee a troublesome disturber of the world, powerfull to make smale things great, and great monstrous" (B3r). Their intentions disguised, women who show themselves to be other than how they are perceived are potentially "monstrous," as is their impact on society. Or this is what their rhetorical rendering demonstrates.

Virtuous women, on the other hand, are "especiall Objects," as Richard Brathwait proclaims them: "Here, Gentlewomen, haue yee heard in what especiall Objects you are to be *Honorable Presidents.* You shine brighter in your Orbe than lesser Starres. The Beames of your reflecting virtues must submit of no Eclipse. A Thousand eyes will gaze on you, should they observe this in you" (205). Virtuous women induce observation from others. Moreover, seeing encourages observers to imitate those virtues. Bercher argues: "Thear is such a nature in wymen / as maketh men devyse / how they maye be excelent in vertues / and ffeates to be able to appere in their presens" (134). Elizabeth, of course, used attitudes like this to her advantage during her rule, but Hic Mulier both expresses and questions this rhetorical usage when she asks her attacker in *Haec Vir or the Womanish Man,* an anonymous companion piece to *Hic Mulier,* "And will you haue poore woman such a fixed starre, that shee shall no so much as moue or twinkle in her owne Sphere?" (B1r). Women in these depictions have no "sphere" of their own. As images constructed of "monstrous" or "especiall" metaphors, their depictions serve the pursuit of authorial intentions. They do not contain them.

Whether praised or dispraised, these women are depicted as alterior to society; they twinkle above it or are disguised monsters relegated to its boundaries. The emphasis is on how these women appear to observers, that is, on how they seem. The monsters gull observers by being "mummers," while a praised woman seems to be how she looks. As Thomas Tuke, the royalist divine, puts it in *A Discourse Against Painting and Tincturing* (London, 1616): "It is not enough to bee good, but she that is good, must seem good: she that is chast, must seem chast" (quoted in Clark, 178). For the Ideal woman there is no difference between being and seeming. What is perceived should correspond to feminine intentions. The result of this rhetorical treatment is that the writers dramatize the *effects* of a woman's behavior, what Agricola calls the "things," not the rationale. Psychological explanations do not obtain.

Brathwait claims that the reward for a virtuous woman's portrayal of a correspondence between her physicality and her moral inclination is to be written about: "Many have purchas'd praise in Oylie lines, that neuer merited applause all their liues. [The praiseworthy woman's] desire is to *be,* rather than seeme, lest *seeming* to *be* what she *is not,* she gull the world, but her selfe most, by playing the counterfeit. Resolute is she in this her Impreze; My prize is her owne prayse" (Epilogue, Gg3). Brathwait also explains how the observer can see this feminine state of being: "the *Habit* of the mind is discerned by the state or posture of the body; the condition or quality of the body by the *Habit,* which either adds or detracts from her beauty" (91). This tautological correspondence between inside and outside, so to speak, assumes that what is true about women can be seen and therefore expressed rhetorically.

Brathwait is particularly concerned about the connections between female virtue and the language used to describe it: "*Words,*" he says, "corrupt the disposition; they set an edge or glosse on depraved liberty: making that member offend most, when it should be imployed in profiting most" (139). For Brathwait and for other authors, a woman who is as she appears results in a correspondence between word and thing. If Brathwait seems to overstate his case, it is because the rhetoric of praise requires him to. A hyperbolic description draws attention to the rhetoric, away from the person praised, and makes the connection between the ideal and the words used to signify it clear.

Incidentally, men's capacity to manipulate how they are perceived is not viewed as "monstrous" by authors during this period.

With the obvious exception of the Machiavell, the masculine ability to act, to seem other than what one is, is analysed, encouraged, and admired as exemplary behavior. This point-of-view is echoed in the drama and in influential books like Castiglione's *The Courtier*. Readers of Giovanni della Casa's *Galateo of Manners and Behaviors* (London, 1576) were told: "It is no enoughe for a man, to doe things that bee good: but hee must also haue a care, hee doe them with good grace" (quoted in Barish, 177). Thomas Wright tells his readers:

> Besides, it were good to dispraise in words before others, that passion thou art most addicted vnto; for by so doing thou shalt make men beleeve in deed, that thou abhorrest much that vice; & question lesse, if the passion be not pregnantly known. . . . I say not this, because I would have a man doe one thing, and speake another, but that if he cannot but sometime of fragilities slide, it may bee a good way to recall him again, and not to fall so often, if he speak in dispraise of his own fault. . . . and besides, it repaireth anew his credit. (93–94)

Aristotle's idea that "for the purpose of praise or blame . . . qualities which closely resemble the real are identical with them" is taken as literal truth for women but as a rhetoric of politic social behavior for men.

But Aristotle's claims for "real qualities" are never fully addressed in the praises of women. The writers identify apparent qualities as evidence of seemly or disruptive behavior to demonstrate how closely rhetorical depictions can approximate the "real" or, more precisely, how they can *only* approximate the real. This results in an odd dislocation between the praised woman and her qualities because rhetoric serves to paint them. Brathwait's extravagantly strained portrayal of *ut pictura poesis,* for example, calls the sincerity of "shamefastnesse" into question precisely because it is "painted" vitality:

> Painters are curious in their choise of their colors, lest their Art become blemished, through those decaied colours, wherewith their Pictures are portrayed. Some are of the opinion, that the

receit of Painting or Colouring the substance of glasse through, is utterly lost; neither that these late succeeding times can regain, as yet, that mysterious perfection. Farre more is it to be doubted, lest vertue, which we haue proued by infallible arguments to be the best *Coat,* want her true colour, and consequently become deprived of her chief lustre. Some Pictures, I know will doe well in white; yet it is colour that gives them life, Beauty neuer darts more loue to the eye, nor with quicker conuoy directs it to the heart, then when it displays her guiltlesse shame on a crimson blush. There is *one flower* to be loued by women, which is the chiefest flower in all their garden; and this is a *good* red, which is shamefastnesse. (167)

This figure of a woman modestly painted with virtue is similar to the one of Dame Rhetoric described by Sidney and Puttenham, to name two familar sources. For Brathwait, and we must assume, for other writers in this period, the "colours" of rhetoric reproduce feminine appearances; rhetoric and looks are treated as though they are analogous. Written language reveals itself as a visual experience. But as a sensory experience in a neo-Platonic world, the writing approximates the real and represents the Ideal only as far as a visual illusion can.

The "stars" and "monsters," the preoccupation with appearances, the comparisons between men and women, contemporary women and their predecessors, and between their appearance and their thoughts, all reveal themselves as rhetorical fabrications—as "lies," in the service of virtue. The depictions motivate a "correct" reading of the text, a didactic one in which female images move representation towards persuasion, towards imitation. In their alterior rhetorical function, above or outside the culture that observes them, these women reflect on the masculine norms of an androcentric world. Overbury expresses this in the *Characters* in much the same terms as Caninius, the woman-hater: "A Good Woman is a comfort, like a man" (63) and conversely, "A very Whore . . . is a woman" (114). And Nicholas Breton expands on the point: "For let a man not quite forget himself and but a little look into himself; he shall see so great a part of a woman in himself, as that except he will run from himself, he can not but with as great honour account of them as of himself" (2). Breton then comments on the rhetorical representations of women: "Some have a delight to term women by nick-names; as in the door she is an image. But how wise is the man that hath his wits so cozened, to take one thing for another. They be lunatic, or in love, that worship such idols. And this I will say further, if she be an image she is like nothing than a man" (19).

What Breton identifies as a function of the image—to mirror its maker—is seconded by Overbury in his long poem, *A Wife,* as it ends:

As *Good,* and *wife;* so be she *Fit* for mee,
That is, To *will* and *Not to will,* the same
My wife is my *Adopted-selfe,* and shee
As mee, so what I loue, to Loue must frame.
    For when by Marriage, both to one concurre,
    Woman conuerts to Man, not Man to her.

                                           (*Newes,* 61)

The praised woman is like a man; and as a "star," she leads readers to a contemplation of virtues desired in men. The dispraised woman, a "monster," a "whore," implicates the reliance on appearances that ordered Renaissance life. She, likewise, leads readers to a consideration of the physical, psychological, and finally linguistic corruption of ideals in men's lives. Explicitly didactic, the (dis)praises function to reveal truths about masculine lives in the Renaissance through the false depictions of feminine ones.

Notes

Fellowships from the University of Minnesota Graduate School and the Newberry Library enabled me to complete the research for this essay. I am grateful for their support.
1. The best description of this prose style is still Erich Auerbach's *Mimesis: The Representations of Reality in Western Literature* (49).
2. For studies of these tracts, see Utley; Camden; Clark; Woodbridge; and Whigham. Lawrence Stone's *The Family, Sex, and Marriage* is a good example of how these writings are used in historical studies; in literary criticism, Simon Shepherd's *Amazons and Warrior Women: Varieties of Feminism in Seventeenth-Century Drama* correlates "feminist attitudes" in the popular press with those dramatized.

3. For a discussion of the cultural effects of ascription in the Renaissance, see Frank Whigham's *Ambition and Privilege;* for a similar discussion of its effects on our own culture, see Kenneth Burke's *A Rhetoric of Motives.*

4. Quintilian defines the *loci* most clearly in the *Institutes;* Renaissance rhetoricians usually follow his definitions.

5. Modern critics, notably Rosamund Tuve in *Elizabethan and Metaphysical Imagery* and O. B. Hardison in *The Enduring Monument: A Study of the Idea of Praise in Renaissance Literary Theory and Practice,* have shown how much Wright's point here governs use of the demonstrative in seventeenth-century lyric poetry.

6. Sandra Clark argues that this literary style focuses on women's appearances because how they look is evidence of manifest pride (212 ff.).

Works Cited

Agricola, Rudolf. De inventione dialectica libri tres. Translated by J. R. McNally. *Speech Monographs* 34 (1967): 393–422.

Aristotle. *The "Art" of the Rhetoric.* Edited by John Henry Freese. New York: G. P. Putnam & Sons, 1926.

Auerbach, Erich. *Mimesis: The Representations of Reality in Western Literature.* Translated by Willard Trask. Princeton, N.J.: Princeton University Press, 1953.

Barish, Jonas. *The Antitheatrical Prejudice.* Berkeley: University of California Press, 1981.

Bercher, William. *The Nobylytye of Women.* London, 1559.

Brathwait, Richard. *The English Gentlewoman, drawne out to the full Body: Expressing, What Habillments doe best attire her, What Ornaments doe best adorne her, What Compliments do best accomplish her.* London, 1631.

Breton, Nicholas. *Praise of Virtuous Ladies and Gentlewomen.* London, 1606. Edited by Sir Egerton Brydges. Kent: Press of Lee Priory by Johnson and Warwick, 1815.

Burke, Kenneth. *A Rhetoric of Motives.* Berkeley: University of California Press, 1962.

Camden, Carroll. *The Elizabethan Woman.* Houston: Elsevier Press, 1952.

Clark, Sandra. *The English Pamphleteers.* East Brunswick, N.J.: Farleigh Dickinson Press, 1983.

Elam, Keir. *Shakespeare's Universe of Discourse: Language Games in the Comedies.* Cambridge: Cambridge University Press, 1984.

Elyot, Thomas. *The Defence of Good Women.* 2d ed. London, 1534.

Ford, John. *Honor Triumphant: or the Peeres Challenge.* London, 1606. Shakespeare Society of London Publications 10, no. 19. Nendeln, Liechtenstein: Kraus Reprint, 1966.

Goldin, Frederick. *The Mirror of Narcissus in the Courtly Love Lyric.* Ithaca, N.Y.: Cornell University Press, 1967.

Hardison, O. B. *The Enduring Monument: A Study of the Idea of Praise in Renaissance Literary Theory and Practice.* Chapel Hill: University of North Carolina Press, 1962.

Overbury, Thomas. *Characters or Witty descriptions of the properties of sundry Person, The "Conceited Newes" of Sir Thomas Overbury and His Friends.* London, 1604. Edited by James E. Savage. Gainesville: Scholars' Facsimiles and Reprints, 1968.

————. *The Just Downfall of Ambition, Adultery, and Murder.* London, 1615.

Puttenham, George. *The Arte of English Poesie.* London, 1589. Edited by Gladys Doidge Willcock and Alice Walker. Cambridge: Cambridge University Press, 1936; 1970.

Quintilian. *De Institutio Oratorio, I.* Edited and translated by H. E. Butler. New York: G. P. Putnam & Sons, 1920.

Rich, Barnaby. *Faultes, Faults and Nothing Else But Faultes*. London, 1606. Reprint. Edited by Melvin H. Wolf. Gainesville: Scholars' Facsimiles and Reprints, 1965.

Scaliger, Julius Caesar. *Select Translations from Scaliger's Poetics*. Translated by Frederick M. Padelford. Yale Studies in English, no. 26. Edited by Albert S. Cook. New York: Henry Holt, 1905.

Shepherd, Simon. *Amazons and Warrior Women: Varieties of Feminism in Seventeenth-Century Drama*. New York: St. Martin's Press, 1981.

Stone, Lawrence. *The Family, Sex, and Marriage*. New York: Harper and Row, 1977.

Trundle, J. *Haec Vir or the Womanish Man*. London, 1620.

_____. *Hic Mulier: or, The Man-Woman*. London, 1620.

Tuve, Rosamund. *Elizabethan and Metaphysical Imagery*. Chicago: University of Chicago Press, 1947.

Utley, Francis Lee. *The Crooked Rib: An Analytical Index to the Argument about Women in English and Scots Literature to the End of the Year 1568*. Columbus: Ohio State University Press, 1944.

Whigham, Frank. *Ambition and Privilege: The Social Tropes of Elizabethan Courtesy Theory*. Berkeley: University of California Press, 1984.

Wilson, P. Thomas. *The Rule of Reason, Conteining the Arte of Logique*. London, 1567.

Woodbridge, Linda. *Women and the English Renaissance: Literature and the Nature of Womankind*. Urbana: University of Illinois Press, 1984.

Wright, Thomas. *The Passions of the Minde in Generall*. London, 1604.

The *Feme Covert* in
Elizabeth Cary's *Mariam*

Betty S. Travitsky

ecognized in her own time as a linguist, religious writer, and dramatist, Elizabeth Tanfield Cary (1589–1639) was, despite herself, an unconventional Renaissance Englishwoman. A precocious only child, she persisted, in her early years, in the face of sometimes formidable obstacles, in mastering esoteric subjects that *she* considered important, but refused to learn anything that she did not want to know. In adulthood, Cary struggled bitterly to live by those ideals which she professed and occasionally to propagate her views through publication, but she obediently withdrew her works from public view when her family insisted that she do so (Henderson, Murdoch). Those works, and her life itself, demonstrate the ambiguous reality that characterized the Renaissance woman's position.

An heiress, Cary was married in 1602, when she was fifteen, to the opportunistic Henry Cary, later 1st Viscount Falkland. Accounts, including those by her children, suggest that the unhappy course of the marriage notwithstanding, Cary valued the usual caveats of wifely chastity, silence, and obedience (R. S.). This claim is supported by the motto, "Be and Seem," which Cary had inscribed on her oldest daughter's wedding ring, advice that is echoed in one of the speeches of the chorus in her *Tragedie of Mariam:*

Tis not enough for one that is a wife
To keepe her spotles from an act of ill:
But from suspition she should free her life.

(3.3.1219–1221)

Despite such firm espousals of the convention of wifely submission, however, Cary was herself unable to repress her independent idealism. In 1625, after twenty-three years of marriage and during the particularly inopportune period when her husband served as Lord Deputy of religiously torn Ireland, she publicly professed Catholicism. Such an independent stance by a married woman was remarkable in this period, and Cary suffered bitterly as a result of her profession: she was disinherited by her father, separated from her husband and children, and reduced to a relatively beggarly standard of living as a direct consequence of her public conversion.

The extent of Elizabeth Cary's strength in maintaining a secretly independent position while living with her husband and in maintaining her independent ideas despite her difficult estrangement from him is impressive. It is true that alternative and convincing claims have been made for the greater religious independence within the Renaissance family of committed Catholic or committed Protestant wives in the wake of the Elizabethan Settlement of 1559 (Bossy, esp. 149–160; Warnicke, esp. 170–179; Haller and Haller, 252; Roelker).[1] Despite these small, though important advances, however, the family continued to be viewed as a kingdom during the Renaissance, with the husband its ruler, and the wife, his subject. One male writer on law in the early seventeenth century noted sympathetically that the *feme covert* (married woman) had no public rights, no separate legal personality, and no redress under law for physical, economic, or social brutalization by her husband.[2]

Because the Carys were prominent, Elizabeth Cary's plight (during the years of her separation) was considered scandalous. Nonetheless, despite the anomaly of intervention on her behalf by the king, queen, and privy council, the vindictiveness of her husband could not be totally overcome. Lady Falkland never fully recovered her rightful position, although something of a reconciliation between the Carys was effected before the Viscount's death in 1633. Remarkably, none of Cary's severe trials ended her intellectual, creative, or religious activities. That her experiences were nevertheless harrowing to her is suggested by her writings.

Even a cursory examination of these materials demonstrates Cary's interest in the mentality and position of women. While her verse lives of women saints are apparently nonextant, the fact that she composed them attests to her interest in the religious experiences of women, a subject of obvious importance in her own life. In her preface to her translation of Cardinal Perron's *Reply,* she gave voice to a consciousness of the precariousness of the woman writer's position, when, among other reasons for dedicating the work to Queen Henrietta-Maria, Cary described that queen as "a woeman, though farr above other woemen, therefore fittest to protect a woman's worke" (A2). Most intriguingly, both her complete and her embryonic dramas deal with the difficulties of assertion of independent-minded women like herself: unhappy Isabel in the two versions of the downfall of Edward II, and Salome, Doris, Alexandra, and Mariam in the play which she based on the tragedy of Herod and Mariam. Her interest in the dilemma of the *feme covert* is indeed marked in these plays.

Suggestively, the preface to what I believe to be her later version of the history of Queen Isabel and Edward II alludes rather cryptically to the "deep and sad passion" (*Life, Reign, and Death,* A2) that led Cary to compose that "wedding," as Donald Stauffer has described it, "of biography and the drama."[3] And her treatment of the adulterous Isabel, in both versions of this prototypical drama, is unusually, if not totally, sympathetic to the queen, who is described early in the play as "a jewel, which, not being rightly valued, occasioned his [Edward's] ensuing ruin" (*Most Unfortunate Prince,* 93).[4]

In the charming but mistreated Queen Isabel, we surely have a wife whose position is ambiguous. And we never completely lose sight of the wrongs done Isabella by Edward: "Had he not indeed been a Traytor to himself, they could not all have wronged him"

(*Life, Reign, and Death,* 160).[5] It would be less than straightforward, however, not to mention Cary's many double-edged carpings at the nature of women—"poor wretched woman." Nor should we ignore her negative judgments about "womans Wit [which] sometimes can cozen Statesmen," or her devastating statement that "we may not properly expect Reason in Womens actions" (*Life, Reign, and Death,* 149, 105, 130).[6] We take heed when, late in the chronicle, Isabella describes herself as "a Woman fitter to hear and take advice than give it" (153).[7] I will return to Cary's negative comments on womankind before concluding, merely noting, for now, the ambivalence of her judgments about Isabel, another married woman, in these histories.

For the clearest and most sustained expression of Cary's interest in the experience of women, and particularly of married women, we must turn to her *Mariam,* a highly regular, Senecan closet drama of the type written by the followers of Mary Herbert. *Mariam* is one of the subgenre of dramas termed "Mariamne tragedies" by Maurice Valency, but it differs from other Renaissance dramas in this group, such as Massinger's *Duke of Millaine* and Markham and Sampson's *Herod and Antipater,* in assessing the tragedy primarily from the point of view of Mariam, rather than primarily from that of her partner. In his study, Valency defined "Mariamne tragedies" as dramas which "involve three elements—a man loves a woman excessively; he does or has done something which causes her to turn cold toward him; this coldness he is incapable of separating in his mind from the suspicion of infidelity, . . . and he is driven to kill the woman he loves" (15). Valency had few good words to spare for Lady Falkland's play; indeed, in my opinion, he misread it in several important ways. Despite his judgment, however, the work has significance: it is the earliest original drama written in English by an Englishwoman, and it provides fascinating and explicit instances of both wifely rebellion and irresolute wifely smoldering, demonstrating the importance to Lady Falkland of the ambiguous position of the adult but dependent *feme covert.*

Furthermore, it is significant for the light that it sheds on the experience of marriage of Renaissance women. For it is the marriage relationship which is at the hub of Cary's play, in contrast to the other Renaissance dramas of the group that concentrate on the jealousy of the husband-ruler rather than analyzing equally the related stirrings of personhood in the subordinated wife. The world of *Mariam* is a kingdom ruled by a male despot, and in it the position of even noble women is most insecure. Substantive decisions are the monarch's and are executed by his officers, who are male; women are effective in this world only if they can influence male decision-makers, a tenuous and insecure type of dependence, which is found both in society at large and within marriage. Patriarchal marriage systems, we note, are remarkably alike in ancient Judea and in seventeenth-century England, and married women in both societies are energized or inactivated by the surges and shutdowns of male power.

Doris, a once cherished wife, was cast aside by Herod nine years before the opening of the drama, when he decided to satisfy his love for Mariam and to strengthen his claim to the Hasmonean throne. She is "haples" (2.3.785), having "nothing but the sence of wrong" (2.3.779). And she bemoans her impotence piteously: *"Mariams* purer cheeke / Did rob from mine the glory" (2.3.776–777). Over time, Doris has learned that her "weakenesse must to greater power give place" (2.3.835), but she has unceasingly implored Mariam's fall in revenge for her own fallen state. Using "petticoat power,"[8] Doris seeks the downfall of Mariam's children so that her own son, Antipater, may be reinstated as Herod's heir. When Mariam is imprisoned, Doris turns the full force of her only weapon, her loud but impotent tongue, on her rival. Cursing Mariam and her children, she exclaims:

Had I ten thousand tongues, and ev'ry tongue
Inflam'd with poisons power, and steept in gall:
My curses would not answere for my wrong,
Though I in cursing thee imployed them all.

(4.8.1883–1886)

Interestingly, the chorus that follows immediately on Doris's exit denounces revenge but ignores Doris's ineffectual, though vengeful, curses. Instead, it indicts Mariam for her much less aggressive efforts to avenge Herod's wrongs to herself: Mariam should not have been so disloyal to Herod as to "have bene by sullen passion swaide" (4.8.1936).

Like Doris, Mariam's mother, Alexandra, is developed quite suggestively beyond Cary's source (Josephus).[9] Single-mindedly joying in the reported downfall of Herod at the beginning of the play, she attempts to strengthen Mariam's resentment of her once beloved husband. Her comments reek of family pride, and her simultaneous ridicule of Salome and praise of Mariam indicate *her* use of the means of "petticoat" government to undermine the patriarchal conditions that stifle her. The real and pitiful limits to Alexandra's power are underlined by her denunciation of her daughter when Mariam passes her on her way to execution. While Josephus gives Alexandra's speech in full, however, Cary softens the act with merely a brief report of this desperate effort at self-preservation (15.12.5).[10] She also underlines Mariam's nobility by reporting that "she scarce did notice take" of her mother's denial of her (5.1.1993–1994). The mistreated relict, it seems, had Cary's sympathy.

Interestingly, however, Cary hardens Josephus's account of Cleopatra (see especially book 15:2.5,6; 3.2,5,8; 4.1–4; and 5.1): she omits his illustrations of the Egyptian's sympathy for the plight of the Hasmonean women and their kin and of her intercessions on their behalf, and she refers repeatedly to Cleopatra's immorality and beauty—in contrast to Mariam's immutable, if still insufficient, physical chastity. Unlike her predecessor, Mary Herbert, who chose to translate a play portraying Cleopatra as maternal, Cary depicts the Egyptian only as a siren (1.2.195–207 and 4.8.1819–1826). Cary, apparently, had internalized the contemporary male conflation of female rule and out-of-bounds sexuality.[11]

The machinations of these dependent women provide an important backdrop to the crux of Cary's play—the sacrifice of Mariam to Herod's jealousy despite his doting love for her. And Mariam's death, despite her undoubted physical chastity, underlines Cary's thesis that physical chastity alone is inadequate in the wife:

When to their Husbands they themselves doe bind,
. . . .

> . . . give they but their body not their mind,
> Reserving that though best for others pray?
> No sure, their thoughts no more can be their owne,
> And therefore should to none but one be knowne.
>
>   (3.3.1237–1242)[12]

In one sense, it is true that Mariam's destruction is largely the result of the schemings of her aggressive sister-in-law, Salome, who deliberately misinterprets Mariam's dissatisfaction with Herod's murders of her kin as unfaithfulness to Herod. But to an even greater degree, it is a result of Mariam's own independence. For Mariam learns too late that, "had I but with humilitie been grac'te, / As well as faire I might have prov'd me wise" (4.8.1833–1834). Had she, she states, ignored Herod's murders of her grandfather and brother and his orders, on the two occasions when he left Judea, to have her put to death if he failed to return, and had she not made her displeasure clear by denying him his conjugal rights, she would neither have aroused his suspicions nor have been marked for execution. The propriety of such meek behavior is hammered home repeatedly by the choruses which follow each act.[13]

Mariam's fatal lesson, however, is not visited universally on the women of the play. For Salome, unlike Mariam, indeed is guilty of extreme disloyalty to two husbands in succession, disloyalty that leads to their deaths through her plotting. Predictably, her disloyalty is associated with lust, "a shamefull life, besides a husbands death," in Mariam's words (1.3.254). Salome admits to this lasciviousness and changeableness when alone. Married for the second time she is in the same position she had been in before when she had plotted to rid herself of her first husband. Chafing at the bit because her now despised husband stands in the way of her marriage to another man, she muses:

> Had I upon my reputation stood,
> Had I affected an unspotted life,
> *Josephus* vaines had still bene stuft with blood
> And I to him had liv'd a sober wife.
> Then had I never cast an eye of love

On *Constabarus* now detested face,
Then had I kept my thoughts without remove:
And blusht at motion of the least disgrace.

(1.4.295–302)

At first, Salome resolves upon a revolutionary, but nonviolent, method of ridding herself of Constabarus: divorce. Though law and precedent bar this method to her, since, under Jewish law, only men can divorce a marriage partner, this is but a frail impediment to a strong-willed woman who insists that she has the right to shed unwanted husbands and remarry:

Why should such priviledge to man be given?
Or given to them, why bard from women then?
Are men then we in greater grace with Heaven?
Or cannot women hate as well as men?
Ile be the custome-breaker: and beginne
To shewe my Sexe the way to freedomes doore,
And with an offring will I purge my sinne,
The lawe was made for none but who are poore.

(1.4.315–322)

Salome closes her arguments with the statement: "My will shall be to me in stead of Law" (1.6.468).

Not surprisingly, Constabarus greets her resolution with comments that would have gratified any Elizabethan. And we recognize his questions as demonstrations of the patriarchal bias of the double standard (Thomas):

Are Hebrew women now transform'd to men?
Why do you not as well our battels fight,
And wear our armour? suffer this, and then
Let all the world be topsie turved quite.

(1.6.435–438)

However, when Salome learns that Herod is still alive, she is able to pursue an easier, if even more sinister, path to her freedom:

the execution of Constabarus by Herod on the grounds of his disobedience to various of the king's orders. Thus, although we may
admire Salome's pluck, we may not altogether disagree with Constabarus's characterization of her. She is a "painted sepulcher"
(2.4.880), "ever readie . . . / To aime destruction at a husbands
throat" (2.4.884–885). And she is beastly, "like a Serpent, [which]
poysons where it kisses" (2.4.889–890). Bitterly confronting her
betrayal and his impending death, Constabarus offers "no farewell
to any female wight," to "creatures made to be the humane curse,"
"giddy creatures, sowers of debate," "the wreake of order, breach
of lawes" (4.6.1578–1600).

Descriptions such as these, common in other Renaissance dramas that portray "female villainesses" (Taylor, 3 and passim), evoke
Jung's comments on the "negative, evil meaning" of the archetype,
which is "made visible . . . in [such] products of . . . creative
. . . fantasy" as these dramas (especially, 75–84).[14] And the internalization of negative imagery and of patriarchal constructs of wom-
en by a woman writer—particularly by a woman writer as learned
and pious as Elizabeth Cary—is surely chilling evidence of the
pervasiveness of the patriarchal attitudes that underlay and determined women's place in Renaissance English society.[15]

Still, Cary's attitudes towards this insubordination seem to be
ambivalent. We may, indeed, wonder whether the Elizabeth Cary
who lived out her own beliefs so unequivocally did not, perhaps
unconsciously, approve on occasion of other women's defiance.
While Mariam's guilt vis-à-vis Herod, or her lack of adequate "chastity" (or loyalty to him) seems to be upheld by the important commentators of the play, the message sent by Salome's lighter fate
belies this thesis and perhaps attests to Cary's own doubts.[16]

Although one would not want to interpret a literary work solely
as the product of an author's own life experience, one surely adds a
dimension of interest and meaning to the reading of Cary's play by
remembering that it was written when her own efforts to subordinate herself wholly to her husband were presumably at their height
and by recognizing that the play provides a mirror for the somber
facts of woman's subordination in marriage in seventeenth-century
England.[17] In Mariam and Salome, Cary provides us with two well-

developed, eloquent spokespersons for the woman's point of view about patriarchal marriage customs. Indeed, these two characters are better-rounded than their counterparts in the "Mariamne tragedies" by Renaissance English men. In conjunction with Doris, the rejected, scheming wife, Alexandra, the futilely embittered mother, and Cleopatra, the siren who fails to charm Herod and whose shadow lies over the play, they provide a broad range of portrayals of the *feme covert* within this unique drama. Perhaps even more significantly, they portray a woman's ambiguous view of the reality which governed women's lives in Renaissance England.

Notes

1. For balanced evaluations of woman's position in marriage during the Renaissance, see Davis, especially 65–95; "City Women and Religious Change"; and Slater. For a more polemical evaluation, see Fitz.

2. In his standard text Baker gives this careful description of the "unity of person" that governed the relationship of husband and wife (*baron et feme*) in English law (in some cases until 1970):

> In the eyes of the law husband and wife . . . were but one person. . . . This one person was the husband, since the very being or legal existence of a woman is suspended during the marriage, or at least is incorporated and consolidated into that of the husband. . . . The married woman was said to be . . . a *feme covert* and her husband was both her sovereign and her guardian. . . . He looked after her and her property during 'coverture,' while she was incapable of owning property or making contracts. She could not sue or be sued at common law without her *baron* and this prevented her from suing him for any wrong done to her. Like feudal wardship, therefore, the guardianship of a wife by her husband was more beneficial to the guardian than the ward. (258)

A contemporary description of the Renaissance matrimonial norm is given in *Certayne Sermons*. The sympathetic contemporary discussion of the position of English women under Renaissance law is T. E.'s *The Lawes Resolutions*.

3. Stauffer (314). Stauffer states: "There is, of course, no positive proof that the short edition is not the original text, of which the longer account is a poetic elaboration. This, however, seems unlikely" (295n). On the contrary, and for that very reason, I would reverse the order he suggests.

4. The line is echoed in *Life, Reign, and Death:* ". . . he [was] seised of a Jewel, which not being rightly valued, wrought his ruine" (19).

5. The *Most Unfortunate Prince* notes: "Kings, that once falsify their faiths, . . . grow . . . fearful to their own peculiar subjects" (96).

6. The *Most Unfortunate Prince* mentions "a woman's passion" (112) and speaks of "the vanity of female passion" (111).

7. The *Most Unfortunate Prince* states: "We may not properly expect reason in women's actions, whose passions are their principal guide and mover" (119).

8. By this term, I mean the manipulative sort of behavior that Joan Kelly has much more elegantly termed "the social formation of 'femininity' . . . [and defined as] an internalization of ascribed inferiority which serves, at the same time, to manipulate those who have the authority women lack" (6).

9. Indeed, Doris is merely mentioned in passing (14.12.1 and 17.1.3). And Alexandra (treated in book 15: 2.5,6,7; 3.2,4,5,9; 7.4,8) is not fleshed out except in the denunciation of her daughter, an act that Cary treats lightly, as already noted.

10. Cary refers to this act in 5.1.1975–1990.

11. Knox's badly timed attack on the "horrible monster Jesabel of England" is a well-known instance of this disapproval.

12. Cary also states: "That mind for glory of our sexe might stand, / Wherein humilitie and chastitie / Doth march with equall paces hand in hand" (4.8.1837–1839).

13. Josephus makes a penetrating comment that Cary does not quite incorporate into her drama:

> She [Mariam] did not also consider seasonably with herself that she lived under a monarchy, and that she was at another's disposal, and accordingly would behave herself after a saucy manner to him [Herod] because she saw he was so fond of her as to be enslaved to her. . . . she took too unbounded a liberty . . . and at last greatly provoked both the king's mother and sister, till they became enemies of her; and even he himself also did the same, on whom alone she depended for escaping the last of punishments. (15.7.4,6)

14. I endorse the efforts of such scholars as Pratt, Lauter, and Rupprecht to build on Jungian insights rather than to reject them totally.

15. Pratt notes:

> For thousands of years women have been forced to disguise and deny the heady mixture of intellectual, sexual, inventive, political, and procreative powers embodied in the ancient goddesses, . . . a single author may take different attitudes toward such a figure within a single text, creating an ambivalence in tone and ambiguity in attitude that literary critics need to scrutinize. (101)

16. In an interesting article brought to my attention by Elizabeth Hageman, who was kind enough to read an earlier draft of this paper, Beilin states that "Cary chose at the end of the play to view politics and morality from a transcendent religious perspective, one more suited to her own knowledge and personality" (62). Sandra K. Fischer takes a similar view. I think it more consistent with Cary's vivid and realistic portrayals of her female characters, and her remarkable fidelity to her sources, to interpret the play along lines suggested by Pratt's approach (see note 14, above).

17. For the legal position, see T. E. and/or Baker (note 2, above). A most striking individual case is discussed by Harris.

Works Cited

Baker, John Hamilton. *Introduction to English Legal History*. London: Butterworths, 1971.

Beilin, Elaine. "Elizabeth Cary and *The Tragedie of Mariam*." *Papers on Language and Literature* 16 (1980); 45–64.

Bossy, John. *The English Catholic Community, 1570–1850.* New York: Oxford University Press, 1976.

Cary, Elizabeth. *The History of the Life, Reign, and Death of Edward II, King of England, and Lord of Ireland. With the Rise and Fall of his great favourites, Gaveston and the Spencers. Written by E. F. in the year 1627. And Printed verbatim from the Original.* London: J. C. for Charles Harper, Samuel Crouch, and Thomas Fox, 1680.

_____. *The History of the most unfortunate Prince, King Edward the second: with choice Political Observations on him and his unhappy Favourites, Gaveston and Spencer: Containing several rare Passages of those Times, not found in other Historians; found among the Papers of and (supposed to be) writ by the Right honourable Henry Viscount Faulkland, some time Lord Deputy of Ireland.* In *Harleian Miscellany.* Vol. 1. London: John White, John Murray, John Harding, 1808.

_____. *The Tragedie of Mariam, Faire Queene of Jewry. Written by that learned, vertuous, and truly noble Ladie, E. C.* London: Thomas Creede for Richard Hawkins, 1613. Reprint. Malone Society. London: Charles Wittingham and Co. at the Cheswick Press, 1914.

_____. trans. *Reply of the Cardinall of Perron to the Answeare of the King of Great Britaine.* Douay: M. Bogart, 1630.

Certayne Sermons appoynted by the Queenes Majestie, to be declared and read, by al Persones, Vycars, & Curates, every Sundaye and holyday in their Churches: where they have curre. London, 1562.

Davis, Natalie Z. *Society and Culture in Early Modern France.* Stanford, Calif.: Stanford University Press, 1975.

E., T. *The Lawes Resolutions of Womens Rights: Or, The Lawes Provision for Woemen.* London: John More for John Grove, 1632.

Fischer, Sandra K. "Elizabeth Cary and Tyranny, Domestic and Religious." In *Silent but for the Word, Tudor Women as Patrons, Translators, and Writers of Religious Works,* edited by Margaret P. Hannay. Kent, Ohio: Kent State University Press, 1985.

Fitz, Linda T. [Woodbridge]. "'What Says the Married Woman'?" *Mosaic* 13 (1979): 1–22.

Haller, William, and Malleville Haller. "The Puritan Art of Love," *Huntington Library Quarterly* 5 (1941–1942): 235–272.

Harris, Barbara. "Marriage Sixteenth-Century Style: Elizabeth Stafford and the Third Duke of Norfolk." *Journal of Social History* 15 (1980): 371–382.

Henderson, Thomas F. "Elizabeth Cary, Lady Falkland (1589–1639)." *Dictionary of National Biography* 3:1150–1151.

Herbert, Mary, trans. *The Tragedie of Antonie Doone into English by the Countesse of Pembroke.* London: For William Ponsonby, 1595. Reprinted as *The Countess of Pembroke's Antonie.* Edited by Alice Luce. In *Litterarhistorische Forschungen.* Vol. 3. Weimar: Verlag von Emil Felber, 1897.

Josephus. *Antiquities of the Jews.* In *Complete Works,* translated by William Whiston. Grand Rapids, Mich.: Kregel Publications, 1960.

Jung, C. G. *The Archetype and the Collective Unconsciousness.* In *Collected Works,* edited by Sir Herbert Read et al. and translated by R. F. C. Hull, vol. 9, pt. 1, Bollingen Series, no. 20. Princeton, N.J.: Princeton University Press, 1959.

Kelly, Joan. "The Social Relations of the Sexes." In *Women, History and Theory: The Essays of Joan Kelly,* edited by Catharine R. Stimpson. Chicago: University of Chicago Press, 1984.

Knox, John. *The First Blast of the Trumpet against the monstruous regiment of Women.* Geneva: J. Crespin, 1558.

Lauter, Estella, and Carol Schreier Rupprecht, eds. *Feminist Archetypal Theory: Interdisciplinary Re-visions of Jungian Thought.* Knoxville: University of Tennessee Press, 1985.

Markham, Gervase, and William Sampson. *The true Tragedy of Herod and Antipater: With the Death of faire Marriam.* London: G. Eld for Mathew Rhodes, 1622.

Massinger, Philip. *The Duke of Millaine. A Tragaedie.* London: B. A. for Edward Blackmore, 1623.

Murdoch, Kenneth B. *The Sun at Noon: Three Biographical Sketches.* New York: Macmillan, 1939.

Pratt, Annis. "Spinning among Fields: Jung, Levi-Strauss, and Feminist Archetypal Theory." In Lauter and Rupprecht, pp. 93–136.

Roelker, Nancy L. "The Appeal of Calvinism to French Noblewomen in the Sixteenth Century." *Journal of Interdisciplinary History* 2 (1972): 391–418.

S., R., ed. *The Lady Falkland, her Life From a ms. in the Imperial Archives at Lisle.* London: Catholic Publishing and Bookselling Co., 1861.

Slater, Miriam. "The Weightiest Business: Marriage in an Upper Gentry Family in Seventeenth-Century England." *Past and Present* 72 (1976): 25–54.

Stauffer, Donald A. "A Deep and Sad Passion." In *The Parrott Presentation Volume,* edited by Hardin Craig. Princeton, N.J.: Princeton University Press, 1935.

Taylor, William E. "The Villainess in Elizabethan Drama." Ph.D. dissertation, Vanderbilt University, 1957.

Thomas, Keith. "The Double Standard." *Journal of the History of Ideas* 20 (1959): 195–216.

Valency, Maurice. *Tragedies of Herod and Mariamne.* New York: Columbia University Press, 1940.

Warnicke, Retha M. *Women of the English Renaissance and Reformation.* Westport, Conn.: Greenwood Press, 1983.

The Myth of a Feminist Humanism: Thomas Salter's *The Mirrhor of Modestie*

Janis Butler Holm

ntil recently, discussions of Tudor attitudes toward women's education focused mainly on the accomplishments of female figures of the English aristocracy and on the works of well-known male humanists who were associated with them. As proof that the humanist movement opened up new educational possibilities for women, historians pointed to such learned ladies as Catharine of Aragon, the daughters of Sir Thomas More, the daughters of Sir Anthony Cooke, Lady Jane Grey, and Elizabeth I—to those women whose achievements were idealized in their own time and celebrated by succeeding generations. As evidence for the humanist hope that women be educated in the liberal arts, they adduced passages from the treatises, dedications, prefaces, and personal letters of an elite group of educators: for example, Erasmus, Juan Luis Vives, Sir Thomas More, Richard Hyrde, Sir Thomas Elyot, Roger Ascham, and Richard Mulcaster. From this tiny sample of learned women and their prestigious champions, scholars developed the myth of a feminist humanism, a literary movement that encouraged women to enter the exclusively masculine sphere of arts and letters and to share the joys of classical erudition.[1]

possibly, use in note - Cavy's learning perh
not entirely unusual due to her high
birth - encouraged (at least initially) by prev
→ see Fischer 228

Recent scholarship has begun to examine more critically the evidence used in support of this notion; the newer studies present a much less cheerful picture of attitudes toward women's education in the sixteenth century. They point to the exceptionally privileged positions of the few women who were renowned for their learning and to the relative lack of evidence for learning among women in lower social positions. One study, based on document signatures, estimates that ninety-five percent of English women were illiterate at the time of Elizabeth's accession and that ninety percent could neither read nor write at the time of the civil war (Cressy, 176). (The same study calculates male illiteracy as having been as high as eighty percent at the accession and seventy percent at the time of the war.)[2] Furthermore, as scholars begin to examine humanist writings in their totality, they are finding considerable ambivalence in the attitudes of many of the authors traditionally presented as the defenders of women's intellectual rights. For example, a recent analysis of works by Juan Luis Vives, an educator long regarded as one of the most influential proponents of humanist feminism, suggests that his "feminist remarks are easily matched by his anti-feminist dicta" (Kaufman, 891). And increasingly, as readers of humanist pedagogy scrutinize the proposed ends to which female learning was to be turned, they are finding that, for the most part, these purposes were quite different from those of male learning and remarkably consistent with traditional expectations of women's lives (Jardine, 37–67; Kelly-Gadol).

As scholars grow more reluctant to characterize a historical period by its most illustrious members and less inclined to limit textual evidence to such works or passages as may sustain an idealistic view of the past, research on Tudor attitudes toward women's education will undoubtedly become more inclusive—not only incorporating new readings of the traditional canon but also expanding that canon to include materials previously considered minor or insignificant. As the collection of evidence grows larger, we are less likely to base a discussion of English pedagogical trends on the contents of a few "master" works, less likely to let the extremely small part stand for the prodigious historical whole. As we begin to consider, for example, the notions of women's instruction that are embedded in numerous religious and moral tracts and domestic conduct books published in the sixteenth century, we may come to see these as more representative of contemporary English attitudes than are the classical curricula devised for a handful of noble-women. From our reading of pedagogical works from less priv-ileged classes of Tudor society, we can begin to understand the extent to which specific social contexts shaped the expression of attitudes toward female learning, if not the attitudes themselves. And as we examine such evidence in detail, not only on its own terms but also in relation to the courtly works we already "know," we may discover commonalities and differences where we least expected them—and so find all of our materials newly illuminated. In the process of recovering and reintegrating the less renowned works addressing women's education, we lose the fixity of ster-eotypes and gain a clearer sense of the complexity of historical ideas.[3]

Thomas Salter's *The Mirrhor of Modestie* (London, 1579) is among those works that promise further to confound the comfort-able myth of feminist humanism and to complicate the terms with which we have traditionally characterized sixteenth-century theo-ries of female instruction. Addressed to "all Mothers, Matrones, and Maidens of Englande," *The Mirrhor* articulates one of the most con-servative of Early Modern positions on women's education. Ostensi-bly the work of an obscure schoolmaster, the text has been largely neglected by scholars who have investigated sixteenth-century En-glish pedagogy. No modern edition of *The Mirrhor* is available,[4] and, to date, the only serious review of its contents is that by Ruth Kelso in her *Doctrine for the Lady of the Renaissance*. Kelso appears to have been the first to discover that Salter's work was not an original composition but an early translation of Gian Michele Bru-to's *La Institutione di una Fanciulla Nata Nobilmente* (Antwerp, 1555), a work that was to appear in English translation nineteen years later under Bruto's own name.[5] Authors of subsequent studies addressing Tudor attitudes toward women's education, even those who mention Kelso in their notes and sources, have overlooked *The Mirrhor* and its implications for the reconstruction of English ped-agogical ideas; one study points to the 1598 translation of Bruto as evidence of a new pedagogical conservatism, a late sixteenth-century movement in opposition to liberal education for women in the last years of Elizabeth's reign (Hogrefe, *Tudor Women,* 115–116). By examining *The Mirrhor of Modestie* we risk upsetting this, and other, tidy theoretical schemes, but the disturbance promises to be salutary.

The paraphrase of *The Mirrhor* that follows this prefatory essay is intended as an introduction to the treatise—not, in any way, as a substitute for the treatise itself. My hope is that its appearance here, with the speculative questions raised below, will help to complicate not only our notions of humanism and feminism but our sense of history in general.

What is it that distinguishes *The Mirrhor* as particularly reactionary, as contrary in spirit to some other Tudor writings on women's training? In answering this question, we need first to consider what the work clearly shares with other educational treatises of its time. The textual analyst, even the reader only casually acquainted with Early Modern attitudes toward female instruction, will find that many of the teachings in *The Mirrhor* are familiar, commonplace. Following his source, Salter advises that, from the time a maiden is able to learn, she should be encouraged to acquire the virtues of chastity, piety, and humility. In demeanor she is to be modest and temperate, and given to truthfulness, courtesy, and discretion in speech. A thorough education in the domestic arts is essential to her dower; cooking, cleaning, spinning, and stitching will prepare her for her appointed future. To preserve the young woman from worldly wickedness, her guardian must warn against the mundane temptations to vice, alert her to the dangers inherent in ornament, gossip, and evil company.

Though the particulars of the model may vary according to the class and prospects of the girl to be trained, sixteenth-century educators are generally agreed as to what constitutes ideal Christian womanhood. Whether liberal arts training might have any role in developing a virtuous womanly character, however, is a question that seems to divide the writers into distinct camps. Thomas Salter, in rendering Bruto's position, takes his place among the conservatives: "It is not mete nor convenient for a Maiden to be taught or trayned up in learnyng of humaine artes, in whome a vertuous demeanour & honest behavior, would be a more sightlier ornament, then the light or vaine glorie of learnyng" (Clr–Clv). Philosophy, poetry, and rhetoric are inappropriate studies for a woman who would be thought chaste and modest, as these studies may lure one away from simple Christian truths and promote a dangerous, even wanton, self-expression. Because it may lead to public performance, the study of music offers similar hazards. Ethical inquiry is generally to be avoided, since its lessons affirm our natural proclivity for evil, "whiche knowledge is not requisite to be in young women" (B6r). Even reading per se, as a process of interpretation, may put the feminine soul at risk—if the maiden must read, her books should be restricted to those works whose moral message is without ambiguity: the Bible, the teachings of Church fathers, narratives of virtuous women.

What relation, precisely, do the conservative contents of *The Mirrhor* bear to the humanist movement of the sixteenth century? The author of the original text, Gian Michele Bruto, was a prolific historiographer and translator of the classics, an Italian humanist who enjoyed an international reputation on the Continent and was guest to courts of both Eastern and Western Europe. The prototype for *The Mirrhor* issued from a thoughtful, learned Catholic and— given that accusations of heresy forced Bruto to leave his country for a time—we may suppose from a man who could question received tradition. As rightfully as Erasmus, or Vives, or Sir Thomas More, Gian Michele Bruto may serve as a representative of sixteenth-century humanism. (Like More, he was to live in a household comprised mostly of women—Bruto married three times and fathered a large number of daughters—but he seems to have been disinclined to repeat More's educational experiment.) That he wrote a detailed curriculum for young women might indicate his "humanist" concern for feminine training; sadly, there is little that may be termed "feminist" in his belief that women should be excluded from all liberal arts study.[6]

As we contemplate the origins of Thomas Salter's program for English women, we begin to question still other labels that traditionally have functioned as terms of scholarly classification. Because Salter presents Bruto's position as his own—he invokes, in his epistle to his readers, several conventions of authorial humility—*The Mirrhor for Modestie* assumes a troubling multiple identity for the historian who wishes to define its place in sixteenth-century pedagogy. Salter's apparently easy assimilation of Bruto's ideas makes for a merging of what, conventionally, have been categories of difference for scholars of the Early Modern period. Whereas we tend to associate particular notions with this *or* that nationality, religious association, and/or social class, *The Mirrhor* offers us a set of convictions that speak for this *and* that—the Italian and the English, the Catholic and the Protestant, the aristocratic and the bourgeois. However much we might wish for a single label that differentiates by locating within a discrete tradition, the multiple descriptors of *The Mirrhor* deny us even the temptation of such comfortable generalizations as "native conservatism" or "middle-class values." (Insofar as Bruto's treatise was first published in Antwerp as a bilingual text in Italian and French, the descriptors are even more various—and so the cultural distinctions even more difficult to assign.) Confronted with the clearly overdetermined text, we perceive the inadequacy of cultural stereotypes and are reminded that the contexts that helped to determine attitudes toward women's learning in sixteenth-century England were complex and, in many ways, collaborative.[7]

If the identity of *The Mirrhor* is multiple in that many cultural contexts serve to produce a particular ideological position, it is multiple also in that an ideological position may serve many functions within a particular cultural context. Some of the functions for which *The Mirrhor* was intended are pronounced explicitly and consciously in the work itself. For example, the text is clear in its message that formal study for women is perilous and that women's reading should be, if not prohibited, severely restricted. Other functions, however, are implied by the text, rather than expressly articulated, and these are often more difficult to define. For example, when we begin to examine more closely one of Salter's apparently superficial alterations to Bruto's text, his decision to address his treatise not to the father of a motherless girl but to "all Mothers, Matrones, and Maidens of Englande" (A4r), we are on the trail of an

202

unarticulated function. At the same time that Salter presents an argument to discourage women from study, he directs that argument to a female audience for which he appears to assume a high level of intellectual sophistication—*The Mirrhor* is studded with classical allusions and learned references clearly beyond the comprehension of a textually innocent reader. Neither Salter nor his publisher, Edward White, seems to have been troubled by this incongruity; White dedicated the treatise, with elaborate compliments, to Lady Anne Lodge, for "perusying it at [her] beste leasure" (A3r). What do we make of the contradiction, the simultaneous presence of an explicit proposal to limit women's reading and of what seems to be an implicit assumption of women's literary breadth? Were Salter and White simply careless of their audience? Were the esoterica retained in order to impress upon the female reader (or listener) the scope of the "author's" knowledge and thereby to convince her of his authority? Do we see in *The Mirrhor* a combination of wishful thinking and economic opportunism: women ought not to be educated and reading—but if they *are* educated and reading, why not take advantage of the market? Did a work such as *The Mirrhor* provide its propagators a means of appropriating and so, in some sense, controlling a potentially threatening trend?

The questions that could be generated from a single such inconsistency are numerous, and, like most treatises on women from this period, Salter's text is rank with inconsistencies. But suppose that, for the moment, we elect not to trouble ourselves about the multiple and contradictory functions that *The Mirrhor* may have served. Suppose that we choose simply to grant arbitrary privilege to Salter's work—to induct it (as a somewhat philistine member) into the canon of treatises considered representative of Tudor intellectual trends. How does the inclusion of this conservative tractate alter our perception of sixteenth-century thinking about women's education? Does the publication of *The Mirrhor* in 1579 necessarily signal the beginning of a backlash movement, the inception of a clear and sustained offensive against progressive notions of female learning?

Although Salter's translation of Bruto presents a position on liberal arts training for women that looks extreme when compared to positions articulated by well-known Tudor educators, its 1579 appearance need not, in itself, indicate a new tide of pedagogical conservatism. Given the publication, two years later, of Richard Mulcaster's *Positions,* in which we find one of the most detailed, persuasive, and liberal of Tudor arguments for training women in the arts and letters,[8] and given the reprinting of Vives' *Instruction of a Christen Woman* in its eighth and ninth editions in 1585 and 1592, it would be difficult to argue for a dramatic and pervasive shift in educational theory.[9] Moreover, since the later translation of Bruto (printed in a trilingual edition containing the original Italian and French and a scrupulous English transcription) appears to have been intended primarily as a language textbook, we may doubt whether Bruto's 1598 revival could represent either the crest or the commencement of a late sixteenth-century reactionary wave.[10] Even when we limit our discussion of Tudor pedagogy to "the canon," the tidy schema eludes us. And as we contemplate the circumstances of these publications, we may begin to wonder what relation the printed treatise in fact may bear to dominant cultural attitudes toward women's education. Do publication dates provide a true chronology of fixed or changing perspectives? Do they help us to locate real trends—that is, real educational practices? Do we get an accurate picture of educational beliefs when we count "conservative" treatises against "liberal" ones and claim the greater number as more representative of the times? Why do we want to characterize a historical period as mostly one thing or the other, instead of as a messy mix of both?

   An investigation of a text such as *The Mirrhor of Modestie* calls into question any number of scholarly habits—not the least of these our penchant for creating an artificial order when tolerance for the motley might bring us closer to the understanding we seek. As we expand our sense of canon, look more carefully at social contexts, learn to read contradictions, and become more innovative in our concepts of chronological significance, our paradigms are less systematic, our generalizations less general, our labels less misleading. Perhaps most important of these methodological advances is that, as we rethink Tudor pedagogical trends, the use of "feminist" as a descriptor for attitudes toward women's learning is likely to disappear. Generous gestures toward women may arise from a variety of motives—affection, kindness, chivalry, ingratiation, concession, appeasement, condescension, tradition, and fashion among them— and such gestures by themselves cannot function as signs of progressive and liberating movements. However much we might wish to see the seeds of more enlightened times in sixteenth-century discussions of women's education, our task is to read closely and inclusively, and to resist imposing our own categories when they distort Early Modern works. As we are careful to define and locate feminism in ourselves as historical readers, we can better identify the diverse and conflicting uses of female training in a culture whose dominant institutions interpreted women's subordination as divinely ordained and natural.

A Paraphrase of *The Mirrhor of Modestie*

[The Need for Good Instruction]

As we are naturally inclined to imitate that which is harmful instead of that which is beneficial, in my judgment there is nothing more suitable for maidens than a mirror by which they may see and order their actions. I do not mean a crystal mirror for vain reflections but a more worthy mirror for learning how to dress the mind for virtue. Therefore, this *Mirrhor* is made for matrons who are charged with the bringing up of maidens and for maidens who would themselves learn proper and reputable behavior.

Just as the lack of care or training may cause plants and animals of even the best stock to lose their natural excellence, so the absence of proper instruction may make a maiden less virtuous than her parentage would promise. Those who are responsible for a maiden's education must be diligent in preserving her good qualities. Therefore, I would wish all mothers and other female guardians to avoid placing their children with such as are too lenient (and thus demoralizing) or too severe (and thus unduly intimidating). The woman to whom a maiden is entrusted should be grave, prudent, modest, and wise, so that children in her keeping may learn from her chaste and womanly demeanor. Above all, she ought to take care that their tender minds, filled with God's bounty, be shielded from improper behavior.

If the maiden, when before a crystal mirror, will not tolerate so much as a spot on her face, how much more ought the blemish of sin to be kept from her mind? Mothers and mistresses are so fastidious as to forbid so much as a speck to settle on their garments, but most are unmindful of the behavior of their daughters and maidens.

But why should I talk here of mothers, or even of fathers, since, however wise they may be, their judgment is commonly clouded by affection? It is best that children be sent out for instruction. And in seeking an instructor, parents ought to take much care, for by training children are forever made or marred. In order that you may recognize the mistress suitable for teaching children, I will describe for you her qualities and those that every maiden should be taught.

[Eradicating Evil, Implanting Virtue]

First, she who is to train a young maiden should have the ability to discern what is to be hoped and what is to be feared in the child. Thus she may from the beginning prevent the growth of bad qualities and nourish the good qualities toward perfection. Our matron should cut from the maiden's heart all that threatens to be evil, sowing there instead the seeds of goodness. Once virtue has taken root in the child, she must stay that virtue against the tempests of passion, lest it perish entirely for want of support.

In determining the maiden's essential character, our matron should have the shrewdness of Ulysses (who by a clever ruse identified the male Achilles, concealed among Lycomedes's daughters). When identifying vice for the maiden, she must take care to teach her the corresponding virtue, praising the good and condemning the bad. She also should give her to understand the beauty and honor of chastity in young women. If the maiden attends to such instruction and wishes truly to be virtuous, the signs will be in evidence. Should the matron perceive that the child is disposed other than wisely and prudently, she must take every opportunity to tell her stories of women who by their virtue achieved great renown.

[Forbidden and Commended Reading]

Here I must pause to denounce the practice of foolish fathers who encourage their daughters to read and to know by heart amorous books, ballads, songs, and sonnets. Since that which is first learned will take precedence in the memory, I would have our matron avoid this practice and instead provide biographies and exempla of virtuous ladies, chosen from the Holy Scripture and other histories. These will not only delight young women but also incite them to follow virtue and to abhor wickedness.

[Evil Company; Gossip]

Our maiden shall be kept not only from injurious books and verse but also from all those things that may in any way damage her reputation. Among these is familiarity with young gossips, who, beneath the aspect of nobility or (worse) of pious morality, hide corrupt and wicked manners. I do not think, as do some, that a matron need keep her maidens from the company of other children the same age. But to preserve them from harmful influences, she should forbid their acquaintance with kitchen servants or with such idle hussies as would insinuate themselves among those of good calling and proceed to do great mischief. There is nothing more disreputable for a maiden of good name than to be seen and heard among such women, gossiping and telling foolish tales.

[Proper Discourse]

Our matron shall induce her maidens to discuss instead, among themselves and commonly in her presence, ethical questions, moral proverbs, and stories of godly virgins. And she herself, who ought to be ready with prepared questions and skillful arguments, shall participate in the discussion in a dignified manner. To those who show merit she should offer commendation, by such means to encourage others to do well.

[Companionate Teaching; Gravity and Mirth]

And it would be fitting were she to make example of some modest and well-behaved maiden who not only shall incite the rest to virtue but also shall cause them to delight in serious matters. (There are some things that, although by nature delightful and in the proper context pleasurable, may sometimes appear disagreeable. And if this be so, how much ought our matron to beware lest things *not* naturally delightful should appear disagreeable?) As the understanding of children cannot continually support grave and weighty matters, the wise matron will temper gravity with honest mirth.

[Correction]

If at any time a maiden should require correction, let the matron be inclined to mildness rather than harshness, just as the good physician, to cure a corporal malady, will sweeten with honey a bitter remedy. Moreover, our matron shall show to her maidens a gentle, pleasant countenance. If they do wrong, she must rebuke them in such a way that, without bitter words or lashes, they will know they have greatly offended. She should reserve severity for the last resort, and then it is to be of short duration, lest through too much use it cease to avail.

Should the maiden be frightened by her mistress's sharp frowning, our matron shall quickly smile and coax her out of dread. I would never wish any to be oppressed by fear, for thereby some become simple, like fools.

[The Dangers of Philosophy]

Some parents, thinking it an honor for their daughters to be thought learned, are of a mind that maidens should become skillful in philosophy. But I am of the contrary opinion, for by philosophy they are made to understand the evils immanent in human life. Thereby do they learn of our natural inclination to vice, a knowledge that is not requisite in young women. Likewise do they discover a host of worldly evils, from which the wise and wary man (much less the tender virgin) may hardly defend himself with the armor of great learning.

If I should flatly declare that more often the evil use of learning has been harmful than the laudable use of it has been profitable, I should be taken for a detractor of learning. Yet I could cite infinite examples to prove my proposition—among these Rome, Athens, and Sparta, which flourished unconquered only while eloquence and philosophy were in exile. Because I have undertaken to instruct a Christian maiden, I might bring in the example of our Savior, who utterly condemned worldly wisdom as inimical to good life and religion. But my intent is not to impute all human evil to the sacred study of learning, to which I have given my life. My purpose is rather to prove that, in a virtuous and modest maiden, learning is more dangerous and harmful than necessary or praiseworthy.

Some may allege that a maiden trained in the reading of sundry authors may become chaste and godly by reading chaste and godly lives. But who can aver that, if she may by herself read and understand the Christian poets, she will not read also the lascivious works of classical poets? And (seeing that parents will be so ambitious as to have their daughters debate in philosophers' schools) who can warrant that she will not as well defend the opinions of Epicurus as those of the Stoic philosophers?

[Learned vs. Virtuous Women]

Some, choosing from among a few learned ladies, may allege the excellence of Cornelia, mother of the Gracchi. But it is known that she taught her sons to be no less ambitious and violent than eloquent and learned, and some have judged that she instructed her daughter to put her husband to death. Porcia, the wife of Brutus, was less commended for her knowledge of Stoic doctrine than for her patience and loyalty to her husband. As regards the others who were famous in the study of philosophy, some of whom forsook their womanly attire and entered manlike into the schools of Plato, there to debate among lascivious youths—they, I say, were never so famous for their learning as infamous for their unvirtuous living.

And I am sure there is no man of reason who would not love a chaste and unlearned maiden before one suspected of unchastity, however famous in philosophy. Wherefore I wish all parents to beware how they suffer their daughters, who are frail of nature, to be bold disputers.

I further maintain that, where these obstinate defenders of female learning may bring in one example, I can cite a number to the contrary. The histories, ancient and modern, are full of the worthy deeds of excellent ladies who had no learning. And these ladies, known as well for their courage and magnanimity as for their chastity, will be eternally renowned, having occasioned more writing about their own virtuous lives than Sappho, Erinna, or Corinna ever themselves wrote about famous and excellent men.

[Learning vs. Woman's Place]

I would therefore advise that training in the liberal arts is unsuitable for a maiden, in whom a virtuous demeanor and chaste behavior would be more seemly than the vanity of learning. In the study of the liberal arts there are two things intended: recreation and professional gain. But such gain is not to be expected of her who ought to be wholly devoted to the government of her household. And those studies that yield recreation will endanger the beauty and brightness of her mind. Therefore, inasmuch as women are to be neither magistrates nor professors of law and philosophy, and inasmuch as pleasurable studies may as easily make them artful lovers as clever writers of verse, women should be restricted to the care of their families.

They should be taught to emulate such ladies as have, with true virtue, put to shame those who would wish to appear learned. Those who compare the small rewards of learning with its great dangers will soon perceive that needlework with good repute is far preferable to erudition with dishonor. Moreover, who can doubt the accomplishment of a maiden who, by virtuous instruction and ample experience, has learned to govern a household wisely? I will never concede that any maiden, choosing to rise above her role as active wife, should venture to climb the ladder of philosophy to that level of contemplation which even the most learned of men rarely achieve.

Given the dangers of such aspiration, I think it necessary that the matron to whom maidens are committed be one who through long practice has become wise and prudent in her guidance. It ought to suffice that a maiden, having profited by the instruction of her prudent mistress, give promise of governing a family and household with discretion.

[Permissible Reading]

Yet, notwithstanding all this, I would not forbid reading altogether, as reading may benefit wise and virtuous women. But if she would read, I should permit our maiden only such books as are written by Christian teachers for our souls' health and instruction, and not such indecent books and ballads as most commonly are for sale. She who would dress her mind by this *Mirrhor* ought to read the Holy Scripture or the histories of virtuous ladies made by Plutarch, Boccaccio, and others nearer our time.

And let her, while reading, ponder what she reads, for in such books she shall find not only words but also godly deeds of ancient worthy women, whose lives may spur her to virtuous imitation. Let these be imprinted on her mind, for no doubt she will learn by them devotion to her country and true loyalty to her husband. Likewise, in books of Christian martyrs she shall find examples of virtue and piety in those who were tormented for profession of a godly faith.

[Piety and Humility]

Returning to our matron, I would advise her to frame in the minds of those she governs a true religion and piety, untainted by superstition. Also, I would wish her to teach our maiden humility, the pillar of all Christian and civil virtues, for through humility we gain knowledge of ourselves and of God's infinite sapience, bounty, and power. And humility will show our maiden that all human capacity for goodness and wisdom, in comparison to that of God, is but abominable wickedness.

To instruct the maiden in these things, our matron shall daily set before her Christian teachings on the virtue of humility. And no doubt our maiden may easily attain this virtue, if our matron would carefully instruct her to heed both those who are more noble and those who are more virtuous. For, knowing that there are many noblewomen superior to her, the maiden will be less inclined to arrogance, and, perceiving that there are some who are more virtuous, she shall strive to achieve their level of virtue.

[Bodily Adornment]

Likewise, our matron shall show our maiden how shameful and unseemly it is for any woman to learn of another how to adorn herself after the latest fashion, so to display her bodily beauty without respect for the comelier virtues of the mind.

[The Dangers of Music]

Nowadays most believe that it also becomes a maiden to show herself a fine singer or an expert player of musical instruments. But

211

I hold that such practice is dangerous and ought to be eschewed by all women. Music is not in itself evil, if used with laudable intention, but under the cover of virtue it may lead to vice. Therefore, I wish our maiden to refrain from the performance of music. And she should be all the more cautious of it as its dangers are less apparent.

I confess that music may be a sweet solace for those who, spent with grief or care, have need of comfort or refreshment. But in practice it becomes not a remedy but a poison, for it is only to banquets that musicians are called, and there the pleasant harmonies are joined with lascivious songs, to move the hearers' hearts to lewd affections. It is said that from the false sweetness of the Sirens' song the wise Ulysses could barely escape. Can we then suppose that a tender maid, not only hearing but also learning this immoral art, will not become wanton and luxurious?

Plato and others of ancient time disdained all music as would corrupt and weaken the hearts of men. And truly, the more we are acquainted with such dainty fare, the more, to our great peril, we may find it pleasing. But lest it seem that I have set out to malign music, I will grant it necessary to those who have no other means of passing their time. Yet when music is to be heard, it more behooves a maiden to listen than to perform.

[Domestic Training]

I would wish her to learn instead all manner of stitching and spinning. And so that she, when a wife, may understand the duties of household servants, let her observe their cleaning and cooking and other domestic business. Let her be present at all things pertaining to household affairs, for her early experience will persuade others of her promise as an expert housewife.

[Temperance]

Should our maiden be of noble estate or position, she must take especial care to order and maintain her life according to good judgment. For, having grown accustomed to moderation, she will cease to desire and indeed will shun that which might provoke her to gluttony. And it would be fitting were she to learn, by looking in this *Mirrhor,* to abhor gluttony and all other loathsome practices (just as Pallas Athena, upon observing in a mirror how the flute caused her cheeks to swell in an unseemly fashion, flung that instrument away, renouncing its use).

[Truthfulness]

Also, I would wish our maiden not to lie but always to confess truthfully when she has offended. The secret sin, concealed by a false virtue, may persist in the heart, but the confessed sin may be routed and forsworn.

[Avoiding the Multitude]

Moreover, our maiden ought to be kept from large gatherings, inasmuch as in the multitude evil is more contagious and speedily achieved. It would most befit a maid to live chiefly in the company of one other. Yet she is not to be taught to hold the multitude in horror.

[Courtesy]

I would wish her to learn to be friendly and gracious to all, deferring always to others, whether they be equals or inferiors. By her manner she may be a virtuous influence, for her commendable courtesy will persuade others to refrain from prideful behavior.

[Prudent Speech]

Further, she ought to bear in mind that too much talking, or babbling, is always the occasion of error. She should speak seldom and attend carefully to all, heeding especially the words of grave and wise women. I would wish her to note that which is told in praise or dispraise of others and to observe carefully the behavior of the listeners, as they will look with favor upon commendable speech and frown upon the unseemly. Thereby our maid may judge what is to be spoken and what is to be checked, and so may learn to use her tongue discreetly.

[Modest Apparel]

I would wish her always to be modestly attired, neither envying others nor giving others cause for envy.

[Deportment]

Because I have advised our maiden to shun the company of kitchen maids and gossips, I think it wise once again to counsel her to conduct herself in such a way that none may think her arrogant. Let her participate in their household affairs with a modest dignity. Yet she should remember that the conversation of such tattlers is seldom to be taken in earnest.

She should strive to obtain, through courtesy and reverence, the approval of those who are good. And she is not to incur, through disdain and repudiation, the hatred of those who are evil.

[Commensurate Shamefastness]

Also, I must caution her against an inordinate shamefastness. Just as too much boldness is more appropriate for actors than for modest maidens, so too much fearfulness is more suited to babes than to such a one as I would wish our maiden to be. Therefore, if she should err, let her confess her fault simply, without grovelling, for confession in itself will convey her desire for amendment. And surely no punishment can be more painful than her own conviction of sin.

Likewise, when she is called upon to display her virtue before others, let her be willing but not too bold. With modest blushes and downcast eyes she may do what is praiseworthy without seeming to desire praise.

[Avoiding Affectation]

Should she be asked to recite a psalm or some other godly work, let her at first demur, but in demurring she is not to affect a false and incongruous modesty. And so that our maiden may continually be wary of such affectation, her prudent matron shall question the sincerity of her protestation.

In history are numerous examples of men who have sought glory by pretending to despise it. But just as glory is not to be desired with prideful ambition, so it is not to be rejected with arrogant self-righteousness. If those who reject fame do not truly despise it, they act with affectation.

Therefore, let our maiden learn truly to disdain that which merits disdain, but let her learn to express her judgment prudently. Likewise, when it is fitting that she be pleased, let her show her pleasure politely and quietly, without needless display. And at such time as she is invited to do what is praiseworthy, it most behooves her to be disinterested. In disclaiming the praise that others would speak of her, she will be thought to merit all the more.

[Avoiding Feasts and Entertainments]

Our maiden ought not to attend feasts and corrupting entertainments, for the immediate perception of evil deeds may make a greater impression in the hearts of youth than may stories of laudable behavior. She should instead resolve to seek refreshment and pleasure in gardens and pleasant orchards, whenever such leisure may be appropriate.

[Benediction]

Bringing this work to an end, I pray that God may guide all mothers, matrons, and maidens so that their lives may even surpass the pattern I have proposed and thus bring them to heavenly felicity.

Notes

An earlier version of "The Myth of a Feminist Humanism: Thomas Salter's *The Mirrhor of Modestie*" was published in *Soundings* 67, no. 4 (1984): 443–452. Used with the permission of *Soundings*.

1. In part, this myth can be traced to Jacob Burckhardt's *Die Cultur der Renaissance in Italien* (1860), a work which directed historical thinking for several generations. Though Burckhardt wrote only of Italian culture, his notion of a new parity in education and in other social institutions influenced students both of the Renaissance in other countries and of women's history. Compare John Langdon-Davies in his popular *A Short History of Women* (1927): "A sixteenth-century Englishwoman was more of a companion to her menfolk than ever before, or, until very recently, ever since. She was indeed a co-partner in the revival of learning and of the art of living" (304). Later writers were less likely to claim an actual parity but saw in the works of prominent humanists a vision of parity. Francis L. Utley, in *The Crooked Rib* (1944), suggested that "when we speak of the feminism which begins in the Renaissance it is largely of such educators as Vives that we are thinking" (69). Pearl Hogrefe, in *The Sir Thomas More Circle* (1959), made a similar claim: "With their comprehensive view of life and its regeneration, More and his friends also seemed to think of all human life as

one—not fragmented into life for men and for women. . . . Hence, they did not have one kind of education for men and another for women" (249).

Ruth Kelso's study, *Doctrine for the Lady of the Renaissance* (1956), is exceptional in its recognition of restrictive attitudes toward women's learning in Early Modern Europe and England. Kelso was one of the few scholars in the century following Burckhardt's work to examine in detail the contents of Early Modern treatises on women's training. Her work was largely ignored until the emergence, in the last decade, of the new scholarship on women.

2. Cressy bases his estimates of the size and character of the literate public on the evidence provided by marks and autograph signatures on extant documents. Critics of his methods have noted that the absence of writing skills need not necessarily indicate the absence of reading skills.

3. Those who take on the tasks of recovery and reinterpretation will find their work made considerably less onerous by three bibliographies in particular. The earliest of these, Chilton Latham Powell's *English Domestic Relations,* offers a list of "Early Books of Domestic Relations, Etc." (243–252). Kelso's study includes a lengthy bibliography of English, French, Italian, and Spanish texts addressing what a lady should be (326–424). Suzanne W. Hull's recent publication, *Chaste, Silent & Obedient,* offers a finding list of books that appear to have been intended, wholly or in part, for a female audience (144–217). Also useful is Hull's supplemental list of "Books with Other Female Associations" (218–233).

It is not within the scope of this introduction to address the complexity of Early Modern attitudes toward humanistic learning for men. I should like to note, however, that not only the less glamourous pedagogical treatises of the period but also the well-known defenses of classical learning and poetry suggest that the goals of humanism were under attack by a number of thinkers who saw them as threatening to male morality and good conduct, and that those who believed in the value of humanistic learning did not necessarily advocate such learning for *all* men.

4. The sole attempt to bring *The Mirrhor* in its entirety to the attention of a post-Tudor public was that of the Victorian editor, John Payne Collier, who included Salter's work in his *Illustrations of Old English Literature.* Collier's remarks in his preface to the text, however, suggest that his interest in the treatise, which he believed to be an expression of Puritan fanaticism, stemmed primarily from his antiquarian's fascination for the quaint and curious artifact. (Collier's incunabular series, by modern standards a bibliographical embarrassment, is now itself considered quaint and curious.)

5. Kelso provides details of Bruto/Salter's educational theory (41, 43–45, 54, 59–60, 67–68) and bibliographical entries for *La institutione, The Mirrhor,* and *The Necessarie, Fit, and Convenient Education of a yong Gentlewoman* (London, 1598; 344).

I have discussed the provenance of *The Mirrhor* at greater length in "Thomas Salter's *The Mirrhor of Modestie:* A Translation of Bruto's *La Institutione di una Fanciulla Nata Nobilmente.*"

6. Mario Battistini has provided a useful biography of Bruto. A much briefer account can be found in the *Dizionario biografico degli italiani.*

7. The scholar's predilection for attributing particular ideological positions to "monolithic" cultural movements has generated some curious contradictions in historical studies of attitudes toward women. Consider the following observations:

> The Protestant ideology inaugurated new attitudes to women and coalesced with the practical concern of Humanists like More and Erasmus to reform women's education (Dusinberre, 1–2).

It had been Luther's view, repeated by countless Protestant moral theologians, that "Women should remain at home, sit still, keep house, and bear and bring up children." As a result, the rise of Protestantism in the late sixteenth and early seventeenth centuries coincided with the decline of the learned lady in England (Stone, 203–204).

8. In describing Mulcaster's attitude as more liberal, I do not intend to represent it as more feminist. Mulcaster viewed liberal arts training for women as chiefly ornamental: "The bringing up of young *maidens* in any kind of learning, is but an accessory by the waye" (133). The passage just quoted has been omitted from some modern abridged editions of Mulcaster's work.

9. Vives's *Instruction* first appeared in English translation in an undated edition that is now believed to have been published in 1529.

10. According to its title page, *The Necessarie . . . Education* was "printed with the three languages togither in one Volume for the better instruction of such as are desirous to studie those Tongues" (Alr).

Works Cited

Battistini, Mario. "Jean Michel Bruto, humaniste, historiographe, pédagogue au XVIème siècle." *De Gulden Passer* 32 (1954): 29–156.

"Bruto, Gian Michele." *Dizionario biografico degli italiani.* Rome: Istituto della Enciclopedia italiana, 1960.

Bruto, Gian Michele. *La institutione di una fanciulla nata nobilmente.* Antwerp, 1555.

———. *The Mirrhor of Modestie.* [Translated and revised by] Thomas Salter. London [1579.]

———. *The Necessarie, Fit, and Convenient Education of a yong Gentlewoman.* Translated by W. P. London, 1598.

Burckhardt, Jacob. *Die Cultur der Renaissance in Italien.* Basel, 1860.

Collier, John Payne. *Illustrations of Old English Literature.* London, 1866.

Cressy, David. *Literacy and the Social Order: Reading and Writing in Tudor and Stuart England.* New York: Cambridge University Press, 1980.

Dusinberre, Juliet. *Shakespeare and the Nature of Women.* New York: Barnes and Noble, 1975.

Hogrefe, Pearl. *The Sir Thomas More Circle.* Urbana: University of Illinois Press, 1959.

———. *Tudor Women: Commoners and Queens.* Ames: Iowa State University Press, 1975.

Holm, Janis Butler. "Thomas Salter's *The Mirrhor of Modestie*: A Translation of Bruto's *La Institutione di una Fanciulla Nata Nobilmente.*" *The Library* 5, no. 1, 6th ser. (1983): 53–57.

Hull, Suzanne W. *Chaste, Silent & Obedient: English Books for Women, 1475–1640.* San Marino, Calif.: Huntington Library, 1982.

Jardine, Lisa. *Still Harping on Daughters: Women and Drama in the Age of Shakespeare.* Totowa, N.J.: Barnes and Noble, 1983.

Kaufman, Gloria. "Juan Luis Vives on the Education of Women." *Signs* 3 (1978): 891–896.

Kelly-Gadol, Joan. "Did Women Have a Renaissance?" In *Becoming Visible: Women in European History,* edited by Renate Bridenthal and Claudia Koonz. Boston: Houghton Mifflin, 1977.

Kelso, Ruth. *Doctrine for the Lady of the Renaissance.* 1956. Reprint. Urbana: University of Illinois Press, 1978, 1981.

Langdon-Davies, John. *A Short History of Women*. New York: Viking, 1927.

Mulcaster, Richard. *Positions wherin those Primitive Circumstances Be Examined, Necessarie for the training up of Children*. London, 1581.

Powell, Chilton Latham. *English Domestic Relations, 1487–1653*. New York: Columbia University Press, 1917.

Stone, Lawrence. *The Family, Sex and Marriage in England, 1500–1800*. New York: Harper and Row, 1977.

Utley, Francis L. *The Crooked Rib; An Analytical Index to the Argument about Women in English and Scots Literature to the End of the Year 1568*. Columbus: Ohio State University, 1944.

Vives, Juan Luis. *The Instruction of a Christen Woman*. Translated by Richard Hyrde. London [1529].

"I Trust I May Not Trust Thee": Women's Visions of the World in Shakespeare's *King John*

Carole Levin

 trust I may not trust thee," Constance says to the messenger who informs her of the truce between Philip of France and John of England that ignores her son Arthur's claim.[1] Constance's awareness that she cannot trust the world in which she lives, a world that is a "moral swamp and has the 'smell of sin'" in the words of Herschel Baker (767), is one of the underlying themes of Shakespeare's play, *King John*. Critics have often applauded the character Faulconbridge, bastard son of Richard the Lionheart, for his clear vision of the corrupt world of *King John*,[2] and this assessment of Faulconbridge's character is certainly apt; he is, however, not the only character with this awareness. The women characters, Eleanor, mother of King John, Constance, widow of John's brother Geoffrey and mother of rival claimant Arthur, and Blanche, John's niece, are also far more insightful of the world in which they live. The women are also more honest, at least with themselves, than the male characters of the play.

Recently critics have begun to devote attention to the question of women's roles in Shakespeare's history plays, a genre in which traditional readings have more often emphasized male character and motivation in relation to questions of power. Such critics as Juliet Dusinberre, Margaret Loftus Ranald, Madonne Miner, Irene Dash, and Linda Bamber have noted the significant role of Margaret of Anjou in the *Henry VI* plays. In *Richard III* Shakespeare abandons historical accuracy to have the character Margaret return to England years after the actual Margaret's exile to curse the family of the House of York, and her curses more accurately foretell what will happen to these characters than they themselves believe at the time. So, too, in Shakespeare's *King John,* are the women characters more clearsighted about the world in which they live than their male counterparts. Eleanor, the most unscrupulous of the three, is also the only one able to exert power; Constance and Blanche attempt to use their insights to manipulate the world around them but are not successful at doing so. Eleanor's power is such that she is the guiding force behind her son, King John. She would, in fact, rule far more wisely than he does. She also acts as a parallel to Constance, mother of Arthur, who attempts unsuccessfully to protect her son's claim against John. Blanche, a pawn between the warring factions of France and England, is well aware how despairing her position really is.

In the early acts of the play, Eleanor demonstrates both the insight and the force of will that causes her to play such a decisive role in the action. While Eleanor is alive, King John is a far stronger character than he is after her death. Eleanor is cleverer than John, more forceful, and he is more successful when he listens to her advice than when he ignores it. Eleanor publicly supports John's claim to the throne of England, and objects to any question there might be about it. When Chatillon, the messenger from France, refers to John as "borrow'd majesty" (1.1.4), Eleanor interrupts, "A strange beginning: 'borrow'd majesty'!" (1.1.5) But while she will support her son's claim in public, this does not blind her to the reality of the situation. When she and John speak privately, John still boasts about his right to the throne, terming it "our strong possession and our right for us" (1.1.39). Eleanor, on the contrary, does not feel the need to lie to either her son or herself:

> Your strong possession much more than your right
> Or else it must go wrong with you and me:

So much my conscience whispers in your ear,
Which none but heaven, and you, and I, shall hear.

(1.1.40–43)

Eleanor knows John's claim is invalid, but she is willing to hide the fact and fight for him anyway.[3]

Eleanor is also far more insightful about Constance's role in raising support for her son than John is. The threatened war between France and England is due in part to Arthur's claim, which King John had refused to recognize or accommodate. Eleanor tells her son:

What now, my son! have I not ever said
How that ambitious Constance would not cease
Till she had kindled France, and all the world,
Upon the right and party of her son?
This might have been prevented and made whole
With very easy arguments of love,
Which now the manage of two kingdoms must
With fearful-bloody issue arbitrate.

(1.1.31–38)

It seems clear that had John listened to his mother's advice and made the effort of coming to a compromise with Constance over Arthur's claim, the war between England and France could well have been avoided. John, however, has no interest in negotiations at this point. It is not that Eleanor is afraid of fighting; she describes herself as a soldier: "I am a soldier and now bound to France," (1.1.150) she states when armed conflict is inevitable, and she goes to war with her son. She does realize, however, how chancy war is and the wisdom of attempting to avoid it.[4] In this regard, Eleanor reflects the values of the reigning queen, Elizabeth, who attempted for years to stave off war between England and Spain, though when it came she addressed her troops in most patriotic language, referring to herself as "king" and heaping scorn on any who might dare invade her shores. There are, however, some marked differences between Elizabeth and Eleanor and any comparison should not be taken too far.

221

Other characters also recognize Eleanor's position of influence over her son. Chatillon describes to King Philip, John and Eleanor's descent into France.

> With him along is come the mother-queen,
> An Ate, stirring him to blood and strife.
>
> (2.1.62)

Ate was the goddess of mischief in classical mythology. From the French perspective, Eleanor's support of her son makes him a more dangerous enemy.

Another example of Eleanor's astuteness is that she is also the first to recognize that Faulconbridge is really the Bastard son of Richard I.

> He hath a trick of Coeur-de-lion's face;
> . . . .
> Do you not read some tokens of my son
> In the large composition of this man?
>
> (1.1.85, 87–88)

Not only does Eleanor recognize Faulconbridge's identity, it is also Eleanor, rather than John, who first gives Faulconbridge the chance to join the royal family, which certainly suggests the power she wields with John.

> Whether hadst thou rather be a Faulconbridge,
> And like thy brother, to enjoy thy land,
> Or the reputed son of Coeur-de-lion,
> Lord of thy presence and no land beside?
> . . . .
> I like thee well: Wilt thou forsake thy fortune,
> Bequeath thy land to him and follow me?
>
> (1.1.134–137, 148–149)

This may well be the wisest decision the character Eleanor makes: Faulconbridge continues to grow in stature as a character throughout the play and by the end is the main prop of the monarchy. He states in the last act, for example: "Now hear our English king, for thus his royalty doth speak in me" (5.2.128–129). In choosing Faulconbridge, Eleanor demonstrates that her wisdom is sharply edged with wit, a quality she shares with her newly acknowledged grandson. Faulconbridge responds to Eleanor's offer by stating, "Madam, I'll follow you unto the death" (1.1.154), but Eleanor counters, "Nay, I would have you go before me thither" (1.1.155).

Another example of Eleanor's ability comes while they are in France. She is the first to agree with the solution of Hubert, a citizen of Angiers. He suggests ending France and England's enmity through a marriage of Prince Lewis to John's niece, Blanche. "Son, list to this conjunction, make this match" (2.1.468), admonishes Eleanor. John then agrees.

If Eleanor prefers negotiations to war, yet is willing to fully back her son's claim to the English throne, this is also true of her daughter-in-law and rival, Constance. Even though Constance is vehement in support of her son's claim, she does not want blood shed unnecessarily. When Philip orders the destruction of a resisting town, stating,

> We'll lay before this town our royal bones,
> Wade to the market-place in Frenchmen's blood
> But we'll make it subject to this boy.
>
> (2.1.41–43)

Constance instead urges Philip to wait:

> Stay for an answer to your embassy,
> Lest unadvis'd you stain your swords with blood:
> My Lord Chatillon may from England bring
> That right in peace which here we urge in war,
> And then we shall repent each drop of blood
> That hot rash haste so indirectly shed.
>
> (2.1.44–49)

Yet while Constance urges Philip to wait, her devotion to Arthur's cause is far stronger than that of Philip, who is as willing to make a truce as to shed blood, whatever seems most to his immediate advantage. In this, Philip is far more similar to his enemy, John, who also chops and changes, than to Constance, on whose side Philip is fighting.

If John and Philip share attitudes, so, too, do Eleanor and Constance, much fiercer enemies of each other than their male counterparts.[5] As soon as Eleanor and Constance see each other, they begin to wrangle and argue. The conflict begins between Philip and John when each accuse the other of usurping authority. Eleanor soon becomes involved, asking Philip, "Who is it thou dost call usurper, France?" (2.1.120) But it is Constance who insists on answering, "Let me make answer" (2.1.121), and soon the two women are trading insults. When Eleanor moves to the forefront, Constance cannot resist in doing likewise. Eleanor accuses Constance of wanting her son to be king so "that thou mayst be a queen, and check the world!" (2.1.123), a statement that could with even more truth be made about Eleanor herself. From questions of power, the two women move on to even stronger insults, showing a lack of control with each other that, while not politically astute, comes from their inner selves. Soon each woman is charging the other with adultery, a theme already introduced in the first act in regard to the claims of Faulconbridge and his younger brother. Not only is this, for a woman, the most dishonorable accusation that could be made,[6] but, if true, would negate the claim of each of their sons. Constance's defense of Eleanor's accusation is oddly worded.

> My bed was ever to thy son as true
> As thine was to thy husband.

(2.1.124–125)

Given the many rumors current in sixteenth-century history and literature about Eleanor's infidelities,[7] for Constance's bed to be as true as Eleanor's was to assume it to be hardly true at all.[8] The two women's enmity is so strong they goad one another into making statements that, even if they believe them to be true, are far from wise.

Constance and Eleanor continue to argue until the men refuse to listen anymore, and the Duke of Austria cries "Peace!"—however, Austria quiets the women only to immediately begin verbal sparring with Faulconbridge. The wrangling of all the characters ends with Prince Lewis commanding: "Women and fools, break off your conference" (2.1.150). Lewis's implication, accepted not only by the other characters but also by the dominant culture, is that women and fools are equivalent and, also, implicitly, without power. Yet though Eleanor, Constance, and Blanche lack power to influence events in the play, the male characters have little success at controlling them. King John tells Constance, after she has further insulted his mother, "Bedlam, have done" (2.1.183). Even Philip, though he is fighting on Constance's side, finds her a dubious ally:

> Peace, lady! pause, or be more temperate:
> It ill beseems this presence to cry aim
> to these ill-tuned repetitions.

> (2.1.195–197)

I would suggest that Constance continues to bewail the situation with such vehemence in part because that is all she can do. She cannot control events in any way, a fact which becomes tragically clear to her when France and England decide to make peace through the marriage of Blanche and Lewis and ignore Arthur's claim to the throne. While demonstrating how helpless the outraged Constance is, the alliance also demonstrates how much of a pawn Blanche is—an object to be used for political reasons, despite Lewis's initial assertions of affection.

When the idea of the marriage is bruited about, Lewis responds by claiming great passion for Blanche in the typical rhetoric of courtly love. However, even though Lewis is extravagant in his claims of affection, he actually states his feelings solely in terms of self-love.

> . . . and in her eye I find
> A wonder, or a wondrous miracle,
> . . . .

I do protest I never lov'd myself
Till now infixed I beheld myself
Drawn in the flattering table of her eye.

(2.1.496–497, 501–503)

Blanche, while positive in her assessment of Lewis, is also more tempered.

Further I will not flatter you, my lord,
That all I see in you is worthy love,
Than this: that nothing do I see in you,
Though churlish thoughts themselves should be your judge,
That I can find should merit any hate.

(2.1.516–520)

While Lewis claims to be making the marriage for love, Blanche admits her sense of duty is also a strong motivation. She describes herself to her uncle as one that

. . . is bound in honour still to do
What you in wisdom still vouchsafe to say.

(2.1.522–523)

This sense of duty will eventually tear Blanche apart, as her duty to her uncle comes into conflict with the duty she owes her new husband. Blanche soon will be caught up between the warring factions, just as Constance already is.

While at peace, King Philip and John are concerned with Constance.

PHILIP: Brother of England, how may we content
         This widow lady?
         . . . .
JOHN: We will heal up all.

(2.1.547–548, 550)

But while they intend to compensate Constance with lesser titles for Arthur, they do not consult with her, and she is not assuaged. Rather, she is all too aware of her own weak position:

> For I am sick and capable of fears
> . . . .
> A widow, husbandless, subject to fears.
>
> (2.2.12, 14)[9]

Constance is indeed powerless to stop this coalition, and all that she can do is to withdraw herself and refuse to participate. When Philip summons her, his messenger tells her:

> Pardon me, Madam,
> I may not go without you to the kings.

Constance replies, "Thou mayst, thou shalt, I will not go with thee" (2.2.65–67). But the refusal will not change the course of events. While Constance is in her way as insightful as Eleanor, she lacks the power the older queen has. In certain ways this lack of power protects her person because she is treated so contemptuously. When Constance finally does appear for Blanche and Lewis's wedding day, the Duke of Austria responds to her mockery—the only weapon she has—by dismissing her as a woman: "O, that a man should speak these words to me!" (3.1.156). Words are the only weapon Constance has, which is why she uses so many. They are not, however, an effective method of gaining what she wants (Ranald, 59–60).

Constance is dismissed even more pointedly by the papal legate Pandulph, who has come to curse John due to his treatment of the Church. She is delighted by Pandulph and wants to join him, but he argues that in contrast to her grievance, "There's law and warrant, lady, for my curse" (3.1.110). When Constance continues to speak for another six lines, Pandulph simply ignores her and turns to Philip, asking him if he will risk potential damnation by continuing his association with John.

Yet though the male characters clearly see this question of ex-communication as "men's business," the women characters again attempt to influence the events. Eleanor is furious that Philip may forswear his recent peace treaty. "Look'st thou pale, France? do not let go thy hand" (3.1.121). Constance also attempts to pressure Philip and his son.

> O Lewis, stand fast! the devil tempts thee here
> In the likeness of a new untrimmed bride.
>
> (3.1.134–135)

Blanche, stung by Constance's interference, responds,

> The Lady Constance speaks not from her faith,
> But from her need.
>
> (3.1.136–137)

Blanche is correct in this assessment. It would be overwhelmingly to the advantage of Constance and her son if a rift developed between France and England.

But Blanche's needs are also very evident and also ignored by the male characters. When Pandulph convinces Lewis to take up arms, Blanche, like Constance, realizes just how powerless she is. She responds to Lewis:

> Upon thy wedding day?
> . . . .
> Now shall I see thy love: what motive may
> Be stronger with thee than the name of wife?
>
> (3.1.226, 239–240)

Earlier in the play Lewis used the rhetoric of a lover far more than Blanche, but Blanche obviously takes the marriage and what it represents far more seriously than her new husband. As Dusinberre points out (296), Blanche "transgresses the gentleman's agreement" that her marriage is only a serious political negotiation rather than a significant private relationship. The powerlessness of Blanche's position is at this moment at its most poignant.

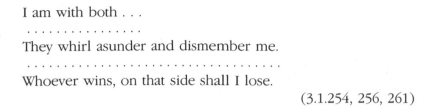

> I am with both . . .
> . . . .
> They whirl asunder and dismember me.
> . . . .
> Whoever wins, on that side shall I lose.
>
>   (3.1.254, 256, 261)

If Blanche really does not matter to Lewis, at least Eleanor does to John. During the battle he is most concerned about her welfare. He says to Faulconbridge:

> My mother is assailed in our tent,
> And ta'en I fear.
>
>   (3.2.6–7)

The Bastard, however, reassures him: "My lord, I rescued her" (3.2.7). It is significant as well that by Act III Faulconbridge is already beginning to take on kingly responsibilities. Eleanor chose well when she asked him to join the royal family. One can also see by Act III, however, that Eleanor's influence with her son is dwindling. Perhaps the most crucial, and in the long run disastrous, decision John makes in the play is to order the murder of his nephew Arthur. And Eleanor is neither consulted nor even informed about it.[10]

The capture and subsequent death of Arthur has great impact not only on John but also on Arthur's mother. Again powerless, Constance takes refuge in a highly rhetorical form of grief as her only possibility of comfort. Because of her excess, the male characters, Philip and Pandulph, are simply annoyed by her lamentations. Philip tells her, "O fair affliction, peace!" (3.2.36), adding later, "You are as fond of grief as of your child" (3.2.92). Pandulph concurs, "Lady, you utter madness and not sorrow" (3.3.43). Yet Philip had no interest in

Constance's grief or in aiding her, no matter *how* she framed it, and Pandulph cynically tells Lewis later that Arthur's death will simply help his own cause. It is obvious that the male characters do not take Constance seriously, and a number of critics assess her from this point of view. M. M. Reese doubts Shakespeare intended the audience to be sympathetic with Constance. "If [Shakespeare] uttered his own feelings at all, it is likelier to have been through those characters who blamed Constance for lamenting overmuch."[11] In *Macbeth,* Macduff's response, "He has no children," to Malcolm's "Be comforted" (4.3.216, 213) is an echo of Constance's reply when Pandulph states, "You hold too heinous respect of grief." She says of him, "He talks to me that never had a son" (3.3.90–91). Critics are far more generous about Macduff's response to his loss than about Constance. Yet Constance is right when she says,

> . . . never, never
> Must I behold my pretty Arthur more.
>
> (3.3.88–89)

And given that truth, it is difficult to see how there can be "overmuch lamenting."

The women characters of *King John* are the most clearsighted and honest; but as I mentioned before, they are also powerless to change the course of events. Even Eleanor, the most powerful of the three, is no longer being consulted in Act III as she was in Act I. Irene Dash has argued that "the ambiguous and uncertain limits" of the power Margaret of Anjou attempts to exert teaches about the condition of women (155). Certainly Eleanor's fading influence also works as an example of how, in Shakespeare's history plays, even the strongest women can exert power only indirectly. As the world of *King John* becomes ever more corrupt, even the possibility of their influence fades, and with it, so, too, do the women characters.[12]

As the situation for John worsens, he is also struck by the news that his mother is dead. He hears of an invasion and cannot understand why Eleanor did not warn him.

> . . . Where is my mother's care,
> That such an army could be drawn in France,
> And she not hear of it?
>
> (4.2.117–119)

The answer is the worst that John could imagine:

> My liege, her ear
> Is stopp'd with dust: the first of April died
> Your noble mother.
>
> (4.2.119–121)

For John this is indeed "dreadful occasion!" (4.2.125) Even many lines later, after he has recovered and begun to give orders, John keeps going back to this calamity. When finally left alone he cries out again, "My mother dead!" (4.2.181) And he is right to feel such desperation. It is after Eleanor's death that the character of King John begins to disintegrate, and the crises of his reign come hard and fast upon him. Immediately there are prophesies against his rule; Arthur, protected by Hubert, does really die in circumstances bound to lead to suspicions of John; John turns England over to the papacy and has to face a rebellion of his own subjects along with a French invasion. By the end of the play John is merely a cypher.[13]

Just as Eleanor and Constance balanced each other as opposing forces in life, so, too, do they in death. In the same speech that announces Eleanor's death, the messenger also provides the rumor that Constance "in a frenzy" (4.2.122) also died. And the character Blanche simply disappears from the action, her last words, "There where my fortune lies, there my life dies" (3.1.264) In fact, Constance died in 1201, three years before the death of Eleanor of Aquitaine. Blanche went on to a long and successful career as queen of France and regent for her young son, Louis IX (Gies and Gies, 97–119). Yet, for the point Shakespeare is making about women and powerlessness in an unjust world, these departures from historical accuracy are apt.

The world of *King John* is a corrupt political world in which characters lie to each other as well as to themselves—a "mad world" (2.1.561), as Faulconbridge, a bastard and thus also in some way out of the accepted action, proclaims. By the end of the play Faulconbridge has found his place in this world and, by assuming the kingly responsibilities of John, actually works to make it better. Neither Eleanor, Constance, nor Blanche had this opportunity. Despite their insight, what they have learned is that the only thing they could trust is that the world of *King John* is a world they cannot trust.

Notes

I would like to thank Professor Henry St. Onge for his useful suggestions about the similarities between *King John* and *Macbeth*. I also very much appreciate Sandy Uberbacher's help in checking references.

1. *The Arden Edition of King John,* 2.2.7. All subsequent citations are from this edition.

2. Useful discussions of Faulconbridge include Baker (767), Calderwood (34–53), Matchett (231–251), Reese (280), Smidt (78), and Tillyard (232).

3. In this Shakespeare is deviating from what is traditionally considered his source play, *The Troublesome Raigne of King John,* to specifically have King John *be* a usurper (Bullough 4:9). It is significant that it is Eleanor who is willing privately to admit it.

4. Dusinberre (303). While I would agree with Ranald that Eleanor is pragmatic, I disagree that she "courts battle" (58).

5. I would again disagree with Ranald (58), who sees Eleanor and Constance as complete contrasts. Dash points out that in the *Henry VI* plays, the women characters "have great difficulty liking or sympathizing with others of their sex" (156). The same could also be said of Eleanor, Constance, and Blanche, which demonstrates their ultimate powerlessness. They are all too aware that identifying with other women would not be of help to any of them.

6. As Lawrence Stone points out (503–504), honor was an important concept in early modern English society, but there were significant differences over what constituted male and female honor. While honor for men depended on the integrity of one's word and one's courage, for women, the sole determinant was chastity, not only of body but of reputation.

7. See, for example, Heltzel, and "Queen Eleanor's Confession" in Child, ed., *The English and Scottish Popular Ballads.* Eleanor is also the amorous villain of the Elizabethan play, *Look About You.*

8. As Smidt points out (95–97), the idea of unfaithfulness is one of the themes running throughout much of the play and, in Constance's case, a rather puzzling suggestion.

9. Shakespeare deviates from historical accuracy by making Constance a widow. In fact, she married twice more after her husband Geoffrey's death, and was survived by her third husband, Guy of Thonars (Norgate, 2: 369, 395, 404).

10. One can sense here some similarity to *Macbeth,* where Macbeth does not even consult with Lady Macbeth about the murder of Banquo.

11. Reese (262). E. A. Peers calls Constance "a sublime figure" but still refers to her as "half-crazy" (158). Tillyard, however, refers to Constance as one of the two most intelligent characters of the play and gives a sympathetic reading of her character (229–232). A number of critics, such as Baker (767), argue that by this point in the play Constance has lost her

individuality and is "hard to distinguish . . . from the wailing woman." Irving Ribner sees Constance as a means to sway the audience away from sympathy with John (20).

    12. As Smidt points out (83). I would disagree, however, that Shakespeare leads us to expect further participation from Eleanor. The disappearance of the women characters, I would argue, is an effective part of the developing theme of corruption in the play.

    13. See, for example, the works by Bonjour, Levin, and Simmons.

Works Cited

Baker, Herschel. "Introduction" to *King John* in *The Riverside Shakespeare*. Edited by G. Blakemore Evans. Boston: Houghton Mifflin, 1974.

Bamber, Linda. *Comic Women, Tragic Men: A Study of Gender and Genre in Shakespeare*. Stanford, Calif.: Stanford University Press, 1982.

Bonjour, Adrien. "The Road to Swinstead Abbey: A Study of the Sense of Structure of *King John.*" *Journal of English Literary History* 18 (1951): 253–274.

Bullough, Geoffrey. *Narrative and Dramatic Sources of Shakespeare*. 8 vols. New York: Columbia University Press, 1962.

Calderwood, James. "Commodity and Honor in *King John.*" *University of Toronto Quarterly* 29 (1960): 34–53.

Child, Francis James, ed. *The English and Scottish Popular Ballads*. 5 vols. Boston: Houghton, Mifflin, 1884–1898. Dover reprint edition, 1965.

Dash, Irene. *Wooing, Wedding, and Power: Women in Shakespeare's History Plays*. New York: Columbia University Press, 1981.

Dusinberre, Juliet. *Shakespeare and the Nature of Women*. London: Macmillan, 1975.

Gies, Frances, and Joseph Gies. *Women in the Middle Ages*. 1978. New York: Barnes and Noble, 1980.

Heltzel, Virgil B. *Fair Rosamond: A Study of a Literary Theme*. Evanston, Ill.: Northwestern University Studies, 1947.

Honigmann, E. A. J., ed. *The Arden Edition of King John*. 4th ed. Cambridge, Mass.: Harvard University Press, 1954.

Levin, Carole. "The Historical Evolution of the Death of King John in Three Renaissance Plays." *Journal of the Rocky Mountain Medieval Renaissance Association* 3 (1982): 85–106.

Matchett, William. "Richard's Divided Heritage in *King John.*" *Essays in Criticism* 12 (1962): 231–51.

Minor, Madonne. "Neither Mother, Wife, nor England's Queen: The Role of Women in *Richard III.*" In *The Woman's Part: Feminist Criticism of Shakespeare,* edited by Carolyn Lenz, Gayle Greene, and Carol Neely. Urbana: University of Illinois Press, 1980.

Norgate, Kate. *England Under the Angevins*. 2 vols. London, 1887. Reprint. New York: Burt Franklin, 1969.

Peers, E. A. *Elizabethan Drama and Its Mad Folk*. Cambridge: W. Heffer Sons, 1914.

Ranald, Margaret Loftus. "Women and Political Power in Shakespeare's English Histories." *Topic* 36 (1982): 54–65.

Reese, M. M. *The Cease of Majesty*. London: Edward Arnold, 1961.

Ribner, Irving, ed. *King John*. Baltimore: Penguin, 1962.

Simmons, J. L. "Shakespeare's *King John* and Its Source: Coherence, Pattern, and Vision." *Tulane Studies in English* 17 (1969): 53–72.

Carole Levin

Smidt, Kristian. _Unconformities in Shakespeare's History Plays._ London: Macmillan, 1982.
Stone, Lawrence. _The Family, Sex, and Marriage in England, 1500–1800._ New York: Harper and Row, 1977.
Tillyard, E. M. W. _Shakespeare's History Plays._ New York: Macmillan, 1947.

Recorder Fleetwood and the Tudor Queenship Controversy

Dennis Moore

ollack and Maitland's classic *History of English Law* (1895) contains a chapter on "The Sorts and Conditions of Men." The sort of men considered in section 11 of the chapter are women, discussed not only after earls and barons, knights, the unfree, the religious, and the clergy, but after aliens, Jews, outlaws and convicted felons, excommunicates, lepers, lunatics, and idiots. As if to explain why he gives women no precedence, Maitland observes that "no text-writer, no statute, ever makes any general statement as to the position of women," though a note does cite Bracton's observation "Et differunt feminae a masculis in multis, quia earum deterior est conditio quam masculorum."[1] Maitland then describes the legal status of women with a simple formula: "Private law with few exceptions [e.g., inheritance] puts women on a par with men; public law gives a woman no rights and extracts from her no duties, save that of paying taxes and performing such services as can be performed by deputy" (1:482). While he may be expounding medieval law, his evident approval shows that some things had not changed much by the end of the nineteenth century:

On the whole we may say that, though it has no formulated theory about the position of women, a sure instinct has already guided the law to a general rule which will endure until our own time. As regards private rights women are on the same level as men, though postponed in the canons of inheritance; but public functions they have none. In the camp, at the council board, on the bench, in the jury box there is no place for them. (1:485)

No public functions? No place? A sure instinct? Even if it be true that "in the thirteenth century the question whether a woman could inherit the crown of England must have been extremely doubtful" (1:483), it seems surprising that, six centuries later, a legal historian who could look back on a series of female monarchs from Mary I to Victoria would fail to mention queenship as the great exception to his general rule.

The History of English Law reminds us how remarkable it is that the daughters of Henry VIII occupied the throne for half of the sixteenth century. While humanist ideals had gained some ground, so that for instance the princesses enjoyed exemplary educations, women generally continued to suffer a *deterior conditio* in society.[2] Even so, fear of political instability proved greater than doubts about feminine frailty, and in the absence of a plausible male pretender, Mary and Elizabeth each came to rule in her turn. Yet both queens pursued controversial policies in troubled times, and the question of the legitimacy of their rule formed a rallying point for supporters and detractors alike. It is not surprising, then, to find a long, lively Tudor debate about whether a woman might rightfully rule at all. The most famous (or notorious) work in the resulting "gynecocratic literature," as it has been called, is undoubtedly John Knox's *First Blast of the Trumpet Against the Monstruous Regiment of Women* (1558), but Knox's tract by no means stands alone: it had its antecedents and successors, its reinforcements and counterblasts. We need not retrace the course of the whole dispute here, since it has been documented in detail by several historians whose accounts make for fascinating reading.[3] But those accounts completely ignore an important document.

Itinerarium ad Windsor, composed by William Fleetwood during the reign of Elizabeth, is a brief dialogue (in English, despite its title) concerning the regal authority of the queen of England. Although the issues raised fit *Itinerarium* neatly into the debate over female monarchy, the work was not published and seems to have played no role in the exchanges of public controversy, which may help explain why recent writers have overlooked Fleetwood. However, even though Fleetwood's dialogue was not as influential as better-known contributions, it has a different kind of significance. *Itinerarium ad Windsor* not only reinforces patterns established by the more familiar documents but also contains its share of surprises, providing some distinctive insights into Tudor ideas about queenship.

The Recorder

Itinerarium ad Windsor purports to relate a conversation conducted on horseback between London and Windsor in 1575. Two of the principal speakers are eminent Elizabethans: Robert Dudley, earl of Leicester, the queen's great favorite; and Thomas Sackville, lord Buckhurst (later lord treasurer and first earl of Dorset), known to students of English literature as a contributor to *Gorboduc* and *The Mirror for Magistrates.* The third main participant is the "reporter" of the conversation, William Fleetwood, who will be unfamiliar to many readers. While it is beyond the scope of the present study to present a full account of his life, one must know something of his public career to understand his writing.[4]

Leicester and Buckhurst consistently address Fleetwood as "master recorder," as do most contemporary references to him, for he spent twenty years as recorder of London after his first election to the post in 1571, perhaps under Leicester's patronage. Surveying the government of Elizabethan London, John Stow described the recorder as "a grave and learned lawyer, skillful in the customs of this city; also assistant to the lord mayor. He taketh place in counsels and in courts before any man that hath not been mayor, and learnedly delivereth the sentences of the whole court" (2:187). Recorder

Fleetwood was indeed a distinguished lawyer, a bencher of the Middle Temple who became serjeant at law in 1580 and queen's serjeant in 1592. A legal scholar, he published little yet left substantial evidence of his learning in twenty or so unpublished treatises on subjects ranging from admiral jurisdiction to the unlawfulness of marrying without proper consent. These studies show Fleetwood as more than just a diligent practitioner. He followed John Leland and other pioneering antiquaries in searching out the history of English laws, customs, and institutions. The subjects and method of the treatises show his further concern with the relevance of legal history to the political issues of his own day. *Itinerarium* belongs to this body of work.

Stow's description of the recorder's duties might lead a modern reader to underestimate the great importance of his office. As well as heading the legal bureaucracy and presiding in the lord mayor's court, the recorder (in those days long before Peelers) served as chief law enforcement officer: "He was largely responsible for the preservation of good order in London" (Harris, 108). Moreover, the recorder's wide-ranging responsibilities in the city made him useful to the crown in countless ways. Fleetwood's frequent letters to Lord Burghley show him busily engaged in Elizabeth's service, from presenting the new lord mayor to examining traitors and recusants.[5] The recorder was also a key intermediary between London and Westminster, carrying the city's concerns to the queen and her counsellors and conveying their views back to his fellows. For example, a 1571 pamphlet entitled *The Effect of the Declaration Made in the Guildhall by Master Recorder of London* reports an oration in which Fleetwood announced what the government wanted Londoners to know about the Ridolfi plot. He could pride himself on being among a handful of citizens so directly involved in royal affairs.

Recorder Fleetwood was clearly a man of authority in Elizabethan London, and that authority was enhanced by his prominence as a member of Parliament throughout a thirty-year career in Commons that began in Mary's reign, ending only after he had represented London in every session held during his long recordership. S. T. Bindoff describes him as "a leading figure in the Elizabethan Commons, active in debate and in committee" (2:148–149), and he cut so remarkable a figure in Parliament that J. E. Neale calls him "*sui generis* in his day," "one of the old incomparables" who "challenges a place among the significant 'characters' who have done so much to mould the traditions of the House of Commons." (1:243, 2:437).[6] Fleetwood was nothing if not a character, even appearing in a contemporary jestbook. His parliamentary performances were noted for their curious blend of what Anthony à Wood calls his "marvellous, merry, and pleasant conceit" (1:598) mixed with elaborate display of legal and antiquarian lore, a hobbyhorse he often indulged to the point of pedantry. His style and personality are recognizable in *Itinerarium.*

A pattern emerges from Fleetwood's career. He sought to advance his interests as politician, man of law, and antiquary by combining the three roles. The queenship question provided a subject ideally suited to this characteristic approach.

The Frame

At the opening of *Itinerarium,* Leicester is leading a large party to Windsor on the queen's business, and as they pass St. James Park, he notices two lone riders following along. Assuming the role of questioner that he will retain throughout the dialogue, the earl asks whether anyone knows them and expresses surprise when his kinsman John Dudley identifies them as Buckhurst and the recorder:

> "Nay," quoth the earl, "it cannot be they, for here be their men."
>
> "Yes," quoth Master John Dudley, "my lord, it is their condition to separate themselves from all company when they ride into the country, and then their manner is to use arguments of rare and very strange things, sometimes of parliament matters, sometimes of chronicles and histories, but chiefly of the antiquities of this realm of England, for they be both marvelously given to be antiquaries."

Then quoth the earl, "What mean you by that term 'antiquaries'?" (202v)[7]

Master John answers the question by listing some subjects the two can tell about: the antiquity of Leicester House, the Saxon history of the area between Temple Bar and Ivy Bridge, the origin of St. Clement Danes, and so on, with further historical references to St. Spirit's Chapel, the Savoy, Charing Cross, and St. James. This list is by no means the random assortment of topics it may appear, for Dudley's remarks pass systematically from one landmark to another along a path that begins at Leicester House, follows down Fleet Street and the Strand, then turns west to St. James. Thus his speech is a witty antiquarian itinerary of their trip so far.

Even so brief a summary of the first few pages indicates some ways *Itinerarium* stands out from other contributions to the queenship controversy. The dialogue is in part a tribute to antiquarianism, an illustration of its pleasures and its political utility. Indeed, Fleetwood differs from most other writers on female monarchy by emphasizing almost exclusively legal principles and political history rather than scriptural texts and moral philosophy. Furthermore, the narrative frame of the horseback ride, with its roundabout approach to the topic of queenship; the question-and-answer format, with Leicester as chief questioner; and the mingling of personal anecdote and scholarly research—all contribute to a tone relatively relaxed in comparison to the sobriety, relieved only by occasional vehemence, of other tracts in the debate.

Yet the contrast between *Itinerarium* and the other works should not be drawn too sharply in Fleetwood's favor, for like most sixteenth-century writers of didactic dialogues, he makes a minimal effort to portray the give and take of conversation. True, he takes some advantage of the imaginative possibilities of the dialogue form so beloved of the humanists, but Fleetwood is decidedly no More or Erasmus. The learning and craft of John Dudley's speech make it but the first of many highly improbable set speeches, some mere transcriptions from chronicle history and legal texts, their style and content undermining the fiction that the dialogue records an actual conversation. That it was inspired by one remains an interesting but undocumented possibility.

The Question

Intrigued by Master John's description of antiquaries, Leicester sends John's brother Thomas to fetch Buckhurst and the recorder. John then advises the earl "to move some questions of learning touching the state and policy of this realm." After Thomas returns with the antiquaries, Buckhurst explains that he and the recorder had been discussing "the excellency of the regal dignity of a king," particularly a king of England, and he invites Leicester to propose a related question. Having prepared one at John's advice, Leicester carefully stresses its hypothetical nature:

> My lord Buckhurst and you, master recorder, let me ride between you, and then I will move a question—the which, although I make no great doubt thereof, yet would I gladly hear what you think thereof. I do read that the most ancient statutes of this realm, being made by kings then reigning, do not only attribute and refer all prerogative, preeminence, power, and jurisdiction royal unto the name of king, but also do give, assign, and appoint the correction and punishment of all offenders against the regality and dignity of the crown and laws of the realm unto the king, by the name of a king, and not by the name of a queen. Hereupon would I gladly hear the reason why the queen our mistress should have and execute the like and the same prerogatives and other regal preeminences as have been given only by parliament unto her highness' most noble progenitors being kings, and by the special name of kings, and not unto them by the names of kings or queens. (204v–205)

The earl begins his question by saying "I do read that . . . " and continues in such legalistic language because his speech is a pastiche of quotation and paraphrase of "An act declaring that the regal power of this realm is in the queen's majesty as fully and absolutely as ever it was in any of her most noble progenitors, kings of this realm," the first statute passed in the third session of Mary's first parliament.[8] Although Fleetwood never identifies this act as the source of Leicester's question, he does say some extremely interesting things about it near the end of *Itinerarium.*

Since Leicester's question concerns the legitimacy of the queen's rule, Buckhurst immediately reaffirms the earl's disclaimer, assuring him that "your question is very honorably and wisely moved, for we do both perceive that your lordship doth not doubt thereof, but that for knowledge sake you desire to hear the very reason thereof" (205). Considering the strong and often harsh constraints on political discourse at the time, it seems worth noting that nothing in the dialogue hints at any insincerity in these disclaimers. No one in *Itinerarium* ever disagrees with the other participants or even tries to play devil's advocate. Once the earl has asked his question, his learned companions simply take turns offering support for queenship, Buckhurst beginning with legal arguments and the recorder with historical ones.

Buckhurst makes a long speech that surveys the entire English legal system with a truly Fleetwoodian pedantry and digressiveness, describing a dozen bodies of law from ecclesiastical canons to forest laws. Most appear to have little bearing on the question at hand, but the twelfth and final category is an exception:

> And yet there is another law, the which is *seorsum ab omnibus aliis regni legibus,* whereby certain especial and singular causes are absolutely deemed of, the which law is called *lex coronae,* and that law is the particular law of the crown. Mention is made of this law in the statute of 28 Henry 8, chapter 7. The words in effect are these: "By the law of the crown of England it hath been accustomed that the crown ought to succeed and go to the eldest daughter when the females are heritable," etc. (206v–207)

Although the printed version of this Henrician act of succession does not actually name the law of the crown per se, it does refer to the custom of succession to the female (*Anno XXVIII Henrici VIII,* fol. x verso). Buckhurst goes on to conclude his speech with its most intriguing passage, which reports the disappearance of the book of *lex coronae:*

There was a book wherein the especial laws of the crown were written, the which book did remain always in the custody of the lord chief justice of England, for it is his office to answer all doubts and questions that concern the law of the crown. This book, as I have heard Sir Richard Sackville my father say, that it was not permitted to come to the hands of Sir Richard Lyster, or of Sir Roger Cholmley, he thought that if the late earl of Southampton (who sometime was lord chancellor of England) were living, that he could make an account what is become of that book. (207)[9]

Buckhurst invites comments from the recorder, who responds with a variety of historical observations, from an Old English etymology of "king" and "queen," to a biblical example, and (finally) to English precedents. Unlike Maitland, he has no doubt that female monarchy has a long history in England, including Queen Cordelia, daughter of Lear ("who builded the ancient city of Leicester"). The precedent developed in greatest detail is Matilda's claim to the throne against King Stephen. Since both made title by the female, it would seem that female succession in the absence of male heirs had been admitted at least since the Conquest. (Apparently either the recorder sees no difference in principle between a queen ruling and a king succeeding through a female line, or he passes over the distinction in silence since it does his case no good.) In explaining the example of Matilda, the recorder presents an unusual interpretation of the treaty of Winchester and offers to show Leicester a twelfth-century copy, a manuscript borrowed from Fleetwood for Holinshed's *Chronicles*.[10] The recorder's historical reflections conclude with a review of the title of Edward IV, "who was son and heir unto Richard duke of York, who was son and heir unto lady Anne, who was daughter and heir unto Roger Mortimer earl of March, who was son and heir to the lady Phillip, who was daughter and heir to Lyonell duke of Clarence, who was the third son of king Edward the third," and so on (210v–211).

After this history lesson, Leicester expresses himself satisfied but asks Buckhurst if he has anything more to offer. Buckhurst then takes a remarkably swift glance at scripture and morality. Half his brief speech merely repeats the recorder's commonplace reference to the Old Testament; the rest quotes Augustine's disparagement of a Roman law against female inheritance (*City of God* 3.21). One could never guess from this speech, or from *Itinerarium* as a whole, how greatly other contributors to the queenship controversy were concerned with biblical and ethical arguments.

Law, history, and religion each having had some say, Leicester offers a brief benediction that would seem to wrap things up: "God be thanked that of his mercy hath now raised up unto us a woman for our queen, who is of such wisdom, learning, and clemency, gravity, judgment, government, and other noble and princely virtues, as have not been seen in many men. God increase her daily with his most holy spirit, and make her an old mother. Amen." (211v–212).[11] Yet this prayer is deceptive, for its "Amen" does not in fact mark the end of the dialogue. Two more sections follow, in certain respects the most interesting of the dialogue—the first for its historical testimony, the second for its theoretical implications.

The History of the Act

The recorder introduces the next section by restating the original question and then he makes a fresh assault on it in seven manuscript pages of monologue, tracing the issue back into the previous reign: "This question or doubt was first moved by Doctor Stephen Gardiner, late lord chancellor of England, rather to remove some scruple out of some simple heads . . . than for any doubt he had therein. And for that only cause did the same Stephen Gardiner with his own hand draw a bill and passed the same, first in the Lords' house, and then came the same into the Common house" (212). This bill, the Marian statute mentioned earlier as the source for the wording of Leicester's question, guarantees that the queen shall have all the powers of the kings who preceded her. The recorder goes on to present a unique behind-the-scenes account of the origin of this legal text central to the queenship controversy.

He first recounts at length the objections raised in Commons by "Raphe Skinner, late dean of Durham," who feared that the law was meant to usher in Roman Catholic tyranny. Skinner's speech concludes:

Ambassadors be come, and (as we hear) a marriage is intended between the infant or prince of Spain, son unto Charles the emperor, and the queen our mistress. If we by a law do allow unto Her Majesty all such preeminences and authorities in all things as any of her most noble progenitors kings of England ever had, enjoyed, or used, then do we give to Her Majesty the same power that her most noble progenitor William the Conqueror had, who seized the lands of the English people and did give the same unto strangers; and that King Edward I had, who was called the Conqueror because he conquered all Wales, who did likewise dispose of all men's lands in Wales at his own pleasure. If it be . . . that the said statute be intended for any such purpose, then is it not well. (213)

When the earl expresses amazement that Skinner dared speak so in those days, the recorder answers, "My lord, such as he and I at that time had little to lose and much less to care for. What we spake there we recked not, so our speeches tended to a troth and by any means might be a furtherance to God's glory, the honor and safety of the prince, and the public wealth of the realm" (213v). Yet despite this expression of solidarity, he explains that Skinner was wrong.

According to the recorder, Gardiner had only the best intentions, devising the statute to foil a truly tyrannous plot masterminded by a shadowy figure. Without actually naming the man, Fleetwood says enough to identify him as Sir Robert Rochester, chancellor of the duchy of Lancaster and a powerful privy councilor in Mary's reign. This man asked the queen to study a "platform" proposing that she "take upon her the title of a conqueror over all her dominions. Then might she at her pleasure reform the monasteries, advance her friends, suppress her enemies, establish religion, and do what she list. They alleged that by the law she was not bound. For (said they) there is not any statute extant, made either with or against the prince of this realm, wherein the name of a queen is once expressed" (214). Mary, who saw the proposal as a violation of her coronation oath and an open invitation to civil war, asked Gardiner to judge it, and Fleetwood describes a dramatic Maundy Thursday scene at Westminster Palace in which the bishop advises her to avoid the "pernicious devices of such lewd and subtle sycophants." The queen cast the book into the fire; the lord chancellor drafted the statute.

One historian uncritically hails this anecdote as "the history of the Act," while another observes somewhat more guardedly that "there is no reason to dismiss out of hand the essentials" of the tale (Dunham, 45; Graves, 192). Fleetwood's account is by no means easy to evaluate, and in the absence of further supporting evidence, one need not accept the story as more than an intriguing possibility. Moreover, the entire narrative is decidedly odd. One surprise involves the recorder's unexpected attitudes toward the participants. A protégé of Leicester and noted prosecutor of Roman Catholics, Fleetwood was a zealous Protestant. Such men generally blamed Gardiner for the deaths of the Marian martyrs and for the constant threat of Princess Elizabeth's execution: a look at Foxe or Holinshed will remove any doubts on that score.[12] By contrast, Rochester (the villain of Fleetwood's story) is a man whose influence with Mary was often thought to have helped preserve Elizabeth's life. Or consider Skinner, the late colleague whose arguments the recorder repeats at length, only to shove them aside in favor of the pro-Gardiner version of events. Still another puzzle involves the source of the anecdote. If the secret plot were known only to the queen, Gardiner, and the plotters, then who told Fleetwood? The anecdote is a well-told story of obvious historical interest. Is it "the history of the Act"?

The Queen's Two Bodies

After the recorder's story, Buckhurst requests a return to their original subject, "the nature, capacity, and dignity royal of the king or queen of England, in and by the laws of the realm; and the rather because the same doth so aptly depend upon our former argument" (215v). Note how Buckhurst here stresses the connection between the queenship question and the following speeches, for queens are never again mentioned in the last few pages of *Itinerarium.*

Buckhurst and the recorder expound the legal theory that the ruler has two bodies: first, the natural body that is born and dies, subject to the infirmities of infancy, sickness, old age; second, the political body, an abstract legal entity subject to no infirmity, not even death. When an individual becomes king, the natural body is subsumed by the body politic, the crown miraculously washing away any weakness. The *Itinerarium* speeches about the king's two bodies are largely copied verbatim from two famous law cases published in Plowden's *Reports,* the same passages Ernst Kantorowicz cited in his classic study *The King's Two Bodies.* Kantorowicz documented the development of the theory itself, but as Marie Axton observes, he "did not explore the Elizabethan setting in any depth" (*The Queen's Two Bodies,* 15). Examining how Elizabethan jurists actually applied this seemingly commonplace doctrine, Axton has revealed how politically charged it became. For instance, Plowden himself used it to justify the claim of Mary Queen of Scots to the English throne, and his arguments were repeated for decades by other defenders of a Stuart succession, as in the seditious *Leicester's Commonwealth* (1584).

The conclusion of *Itinerarium* suggests still another political application of the doctrine, one unique to Fleetwood. The dialogue merely *suggests* this new use of the idea because Fleetwood leaves the purpose of the final section implicit. Yet to expound the theory of the king's two bodies in the context of Leicester's question about queenship suggests an obvious application. Suppose womanhood a weakness: Could not gender too be wiped away like the minority of Edward III or the alienage of Mary Stuart, the limitations of the natural body transcended through a miracle of the crown? Even if one considered being female an infirmity, it need present no impairment to the monarch.

If Fleetwood had such an application in mind, why would he not have made that point explicit? Such a question can have no definite answer. Perhaps he feared that the queen would take amiss any emphasis on supposed feminine limitations, even in a defense of her authority that disposed of them miraculously. Or he may have felt that any use of "two bodies" arguments required the utmost caution, since they had been employed for questionable, even treasonous, ends (Axton, *The Queen's Two Bodies,* 22). However one might answer the question, the fact remains that Fleetwood does not explain the connection between the concluding section and the rest of the dialogue. He simply has Buckhurst assert their interdependence and leaves the rest to the reader.

Given the legal equation of kings and queens, as defined for instance in the Marian statute, there would be nothing surprising in applying the theory of the king's two bodies to a queen. However, it would be a bold innovation to use it to justify queenship itself as a miracle of the crown. Whether Fleetwood actually intended to do so must remain an open question, but the very possibility testifies to the anomalous nature of female rule in a society that restricted women's roles so severely that it afforded them no regular place of authority in church or state—with one most notable exception.

Notes

I would like to thank the Folger Shakespeare Library, Washington, and the Newberry Library, Chicago, for research opportunities. Special thanks to Marcia Culver, Carole Levin, and Mary Beth Rose for assistance and encouragement.

Tanner ms. 84 is quoted by permission of the Bodleian Library, Oxford. Quotations from this and other Renaissance texts have been modernized.

1. "And women differ from men in many things, for their condition is worse than that of men." Compare *Digests* 1.5.9.

2. Hogrefe provides a good introduction to the limits on women's roles in Tudor society, along with the extraordinary achievements of exceptional individuals.

3. In the primary survey of the queenship debate, Phillips noted that "the continued publication of gynecocratic literature . . . kept the issues alive until Spenser's day and into the next century" (5). Two notable recent studies are Levine, "Place of Women," and Scalingi. Henderson and McManus mention the *First Blast* and Aylmer's answer (12–13) but seem surprisingly unaware of the larger controversy.

4. The best recent biographical sketch is Hasler, 133–138. See also the fine study by Harris and, among older references, the *Dictionary of National Biography* and works cited, especially Woolrych 1:132–169. Concerning the recordership in general and Fleetwood in particular, see Foster, *Politics of Stability* and "Merchants and Bureaucrats," 152–153.

5. Over forty of the letters are preserved among Burghley papers in the British Library Lansdowne manuscripts. Strype drew upon them freely, particularly in *Annals of the Reformation;* many appear in Chambers and Greg, Ellis, Murdin, and Wright.

6. Additional references in Neale's index. Levine mentions Fleetwood's role in the *Tempestas Halesiana* of 1563 (*Early Elizabethan Succession*, 71, 75).

7. *Itinerarium ad Windsor* is preserved in three seventeenth-century collections of state papers. The text quoted here is Bodleian Tanner ms. 84, fols. 201–217v; the other

complete copy appears in British Library Harley ms. 6234. The only published text (Bruce, 354–362) presents the first half of the dialogue from an incomplete copy in British Library Harley ms. 168.

8. *Anno Mariae Primo,* fol. ii. John Leslie cites a long passage from this act (137); for his debt to Plowden, see Axton, "Influence."

9. When Lyster became chief justice of the king's bench in November 1546, Cholmley succeeded him as lord baron of the exchequer. When Lyster resigned in March 1552, Cholmley succeeded him in the higher post as well. The following year Lyster died and Cholmley found himself in the Tower for having witnessed the will in which Edward VI sought to alter the succession (*DNB*). For a reassessment of Southampton, removed from the chancellorship in 1547, see Slavin.

10. Fleetwood describes the treaty as a legal judgment of right rather than as a negotiated peace settlement. Tudor chronicles unanimously echo the latter view, found in such contemporary documents as *Gesta Stephani* and Henry of Huntingdon's *Historia Anglorum*. Holinshed, after repeating the standard explanation, then translates the treaty from "an authentic book containing the old laws of the Saxon and Danish kings, in the end whereof the same charter is exemplified, which book is remaining with the right worshipful William Fleetwood, esquire, now recorder of London" (389–390). This manuscript, which contains the earliest exemplar of the treaty, is now John Rylands Library Latin ms. 420 (see Taylor, 13–14).

11. The conclusion of Leicester's prayer may be less strange than it appears: the petition that Elizabeth live to be "an old mother in Israel" seems commonplace, appearing for instance in Jewel's letter to the queen in *Defence of an Apologie,* and in a later prayerbook (Compare the song of Deborah, Judges 5:7.) The phrase "in Israel" may have been omitted accidentally.

12. See the discussion of Lever in Moore (174–184). Graves also notes "Fleetwood's surprisingly favourable account of Gardiner's conduct" (192).

Works Cited

Anno Mariae Primo. Actes Made the Seconde Daye of Apryll. London, 1554.

Aylmer, John. *An Harborowe for Faithfull and Trewe Subjects.* Strasbourg, 1559.

Axton, Marie. "The Influence of Edmund Plowden's Succession Treatise." *Huntington Library Quarterly* 37 (1974): 209–226.

———. *The Queen's Two Bodies.* London: Royal Historical Society, 1977.

Bindoff, S. T. *The House of Commons, 1509–1558.* 3 vols. London: Secker and Warburg for the History of Parliament Trust, 1982.

Bruce, John. "Particulars Respecting Thomas Sackville, Lord Buckhurst, with a Fragment of the 'Itinerarium ad Windsor' Written by Mr. Serjeant Fleetwood, Recorder of London." *Archaeologia* 37 (1856): 351–362.

Chambers, E. K., and W. W. Greg, eds. "Dramatic Records from the Lansdowne Manuscripts." *Collections* [Malone Society] 1, no. 2 (1908): 143–215.

Digests. Justiniani Digesta. Edited by T. Mommsen and P. Krieger. Dublin and Zurich: Weidmann, 1968.

Dunham, William Huse, Jr. "Regal Power and the Rule of Law." *Journal of British Studies* 3, no. 2 (1964): 24–56.

Ellis, Henry. *Original Letters Illustrative of English History.* Series 1 and 2. London, 1825–1827.

Fleetwood, William. *The Effect of the Declaration Made in the Guildhall by Master Recorder of London, Concerning the Late Attemptes of the Quenes Majesties Evill, Seditious, and Disobedient Subjectes.* London, 1571.

Foster, Frank F. "Merchants and Bureaucrats in Elizabethan London." *Guildhall Miscellany* 4 (1971–1973): 149–160.

———. *The Politics of Stability.* London: Royal Historical Society, 1977.

Graves, Michael A. R. *The House of Lords in the Parliaments of Edward VI and Mary I.* Cambridge: Cambridge University Press, 1981.

Harris, P. R. "William Fleetwood, Recorder of the City, and Catholicism in Elizabethan London." *Recusant History* 7 (1963): 106–122.

Hasler, P. W. *The House of Commons, 1558–1603.* 3 vols. London: Her Majesty's Stationers Office for the History of Parliament Trust, 1981.

Henderson, Katherine Usher, and Barbara F. McManus. *Half Humankind.* Urbana: University of Illinois Press, 1985.

Hogrefe, Pearl. *Tudor Women.* Ames: Iowa State University Press, 1975.

Holinshed, Raphael. *The Laste Volume of the Chronicles.* London, 1577.

Jewel, John. *A Defence of the Apologie of the Churche of Englande.* London, 1567.

Kantorowicz, Ernst. *The King's Two Bodies.* Princeton, N.J.: Princeton University Press, 1957.

Knox, John. *The First Blast of the Trumpet Against the Monstruous Regiment of Women.* Geneva, 1558.

Leicester's Commonwealth. Edited by D. C. Peck. Athens: Ohio University Press, 1985.

Leslie, John. *A Defence of the Honour of Marie Queene of Scotlande.* "London," 1569.

Lever, Christopher. *Queene Elizabeths Teares.* London, 1607.

Levine, Mortimer. *The Early Elizabethan Succession Question, 1558–1568.* Stanford, Calif.: Stanford University Press, 1966.

———. "The Place of Women in Tudor Government." In *Tudor Rule and Revolution,* edited by DeLloyd J. Guth and John W. McKenna, 109–123. Cambridge: Cambridge University Press, 1982.

List of Deacons and Major Canons of Durham, 1541–1900. Durham: The Prior's Kitchen, The College, 1974.

Moore, Dennis. *The Politics of Spenser's "Complaints" and Sidney's Philisides Poems.* Salzburg: Universität Salzburg, 1982.

Murdin, William. *A Collection of State Papers . . . Left by William Cecill, Lord Burghley.* London, 1759.

Neale, J. E. *Elizabeth I and Her Parliaments.* 2 vols. New York: St. Martin's Press, 1958.

Phillips, James E., Jr. "The Background of Spenser's Attitude toward Women Rulers." *Huntington Library Quarterly* 5 (1941): 5–32.

Pollack, Sir Frederick, and Frederic William Maitland. *The History of English Law before the Time of Edward I.* 2d ed. 2 vols. 1898. Cambridge: Cambridge University Press, 1968.

Scalingi, Paula Louise. "The Scepter or the Distaff: The Question of Female Sovereignty, 1516–1607." *The Historian* 41 (1978): 59–75.

Slavin, A. J. "The Fall of Lord Chancellor Wriothesley." *Albion* 7 (1975): 265–286.

Stow, John. *A Survey of London.* 2 vols. Edited by C. L. Kingsford. Oxford: Oxford University Press, 1908.

Strype, John. *Annals of the Reformation.* Vols. 1–4 of *Works.* 26 vols. Oxford, 1821–1840.

Taylor, Frank. *Supplementary Handlist of Western Manuscripts in the John Rylands Library. 1937.* Manchester: Manchester University Press, 1937.

Wood, Anthony. *Athenae Oxoniensis.* 4 vols. Edited by Phillip Bliss. London, 1813.

Woolrych, H. W. *Lives of the Eminent Serjeants-at-Law of the English Bar.* 2 vols. London, 1869.

Wright, Thomas. *Queen Elizabeth and Her Times.* 2 vols. London, 1838.

Bibliographic Essay

In the last few years, there has been an enormous amount of material produced on women in the Middle Ages and Renaissance. This essay, therefore, does not attempt to mention all the work that has been published but rather to discuss chronologically some of the more significant studies and collections of primary materials—in addition to those already discussed in the Introduction—that help place the essays in our collection in a scholarly context.

The impact of religion and other ideologies on women in the Middle Ages has been discussed extensively. Some major studies include Marina Warner, *Alone of All Her Sex: The Myth and Cult of the Virgin Mary* (New York: Random House, 1976); Penny Schine Gold, *The Lady and the Virgin: Image, Attitude, and Experience in Twelfth-Century France* (Chicago: University of Chicago Press, 1985); Leonard Swidler, *Biblical Affirmations of Women* (Philadelphia: The Westminster Press, 1979); and Elizabeth Petroff, *The Consolation of the Blessed* (New York: Alta Gaia Society, 1979). Petroff's recent collection of medieval women's mystical writings, *Medieval Women's Visionary Literature* (Oxford: Oxford University Press, 1986), is a most valuable introduction to the writings of the women themselves. Sister Prudence Allen's *The Concept of Woman:*

The Aristotelian Revolution, 750 BC–1250 AD (Toronto: University of Toronto Press, 1985) contains both original source material and analysis. Another useful collection of women's writing is Katherine Wilson's *Medieval Women Writers* (Athens: University of Georgia Press, 1984). Wilson includes not only the women writers but modern commentary on their work as well.

A number of essay collections have explored the full range of women's lives in the Middle Ages. Some that are especially valuable include Derek Baker, ed., *Medieval Women* (Oxford: Basil Blackwell, 1978); Mary Beth Rose, ed., *Women in the Middle Ages and Renaissance: Literary and Historical Perspectives* (Syracuse, N.Y.: Syracuse University Press, 1985); Susan Mosher Stuard, ed., *Women in Medieval Society* (Philadelphia: University of Pennsylvania Press, 1976); and Julius Kirshner and Suzanne Wemple, eds., *Women of the Medieval World* (New York: Basil Blackwell, 1985). Angela M. Lucas, *Women in the Middle Ages: Religion, Marriage, and Letters* (Sussex: The Harvester Press, 1983), also provides a helpful survey.

For an overview of English women both in the Middle Ages and Renaissance, one should consult a fine early text, Doris Mary Stenton's *The English Woman in History* (1957; reprint, New York: Schocken Books, 1977). More recent and more focused in its subject matter is Alan MacFarlane, *Marriage and Love in England, 1300–1840* (New York: Blackwell, 1986). Mary Prior's edited collection, *Women in English Society, 1500–1800* (New York: Methuen, 1985), also contains a number of useful essays.

Helpful Renaissance criticism includes first a bibliography on the sixteenth century by Merry Wiesner, *Women in the Sixteenth Century* (St. Louis: Center for Reformation Research, 1983). A very important early study is by Ruth Kelso, *Doctrine for the Lady of the Renaissance* (Urbana: University of Illinois Press, 1956). Another valuable resource is Elizabeth Hageman, "Recent Studies in Women Writers of Tudor England, Part I: Women Writers, 1485–1603, Excluding Mary Sidney, Countess of Pembroke," *English Literary Renaissance* 14 (1984): 426–439. Also useful is Kathy Lynn Emerson's biographical dictionary, *Wives and Daughters: The Women of Sixteenth Century England* (Troy, N.Y.: Whitson Publishing Co., 1984).

Recently, a number of books have been published that contain primary documents about the Renaissance debate over women's capabilities. Especially useful among these collections are Katherine Henderson and Barbara McManus, eds., *Half Humankind: Contexts and Texts of the Controversy about Women in England, 1540–1640* (Urbana: University of Illinois Press, 1985); Betty Travitsky, ed., *The Paradise of Women: Writings by English Women of the Renaissance* (Westport, Conn.: Greenwood Press, 1981); and Simon Shepherd, ed., *The Women's Sharp Revenge: Five Women's Pamphlets from the Renaissance, 1580–1640* (New York: St. Martin's Press, 1985). Linda Woodbridge's *Women and the English Renaissance: Literature and the Nature of Womankind, 1540–1620* (Urbana: University of Illinois Press, 1984) has a useful discussion of a number of these pamphlets. Suzanne W. Hull, *Chaste, Silent, and Obedient: English Books for Women, 1475–1640* (San Marino, Calif.: The Huntington Library, 1982), discusses the books written for women in Renaissance England. Retha Warnicke's *Women of the English Renaissance and Reformation* (Westport, Conn.: Greenwood Press, 1983) is also a very valuable study of several generations of educated women during the sixteenth century. On the topic of women and religion in Tudor England, Margaret Hannay's collection, *Silent but for the Word: Tudor Women as Patrons, Translators, and Writers of Religious Works* (Kent, Ohio: Kent State University Press, 1985), contains a number of valuable essays. A fine theoretical discussion can be found in Janis Butler Holm's "Toward a History of Women in Early Modern England," *Annals of Scholarship* 2, no. 2 (1981): 107–118. Another fascinating study that considers the question of gender and power is Louis Montrose, "Shaping Fantasies: Figuration of Gender and Power in Elizabethan Culture," *Representations* 1, no. 2 (1981): 61–94.

One of the first and finest collections to examine feminist interpretations of Shakespeare is Carolyn Lentz, Gayle Greene, and Carol Neely, eds., *The Woman's Part: Feminist Criticism of Shakespeare* (Urbana: University of Illinois Press, 1980). Other significant studies include Lisa Jardine, *Still Harping on Daughters: Women and Drama in the Age of Shakespeare* (Sussex: Harvester Press, 1983); Juliet Dusinberre, *Shakespeare and the Nature of Women*

(London: Macmillan, 1975); Linda Bamber, *Comic Women, Tragic Men: A Study of Gender and Genre in Shakespeare* (Stanford, Calif.: Stanford University Press, 1982); Carol Neely, *Broken Nuptials in Shakespeare's Plays* (New Haven, Conn.: Yale University Press, 1985); Simon Shepherd, *Amazons and Warrior Women: Varieties of Feminism in Seventeenth-Century Drama* (New York: St. Martin's Press, 1981); and Marianne Novy, *Love's Argument: Gender Relations in Shakespeare* (Chapel Hill: University of North Carolina Press, 1984).

Index

Carole Levin received her M.A. and Ph.D. degrees from Tufts University. An associate professor of history at State University of New York at New Paltz, Professor Levin has also taught at Arizona State University, University of Wisconsin—La Crosse, and University of Iowa.

Jeanie Watson received her M.A. from Midwestern State University and her Ph.D. from Ohio University. Professor Watson has taught at University of Nebraska, Stonehill College, Gustavus Adolphus College, Marshall University, and Rhodes College. She is now associate dean of arts and sciences and associate professor of English at Southwestern University.

The manuscript was edited by Catherine Thatcher. The book was designed by Joanne E. Kinney. The typeface for the text and the display is Garamond. The book is printed on 55-lb. Glatfelter text paper. The cloth edition is bound in Joanna Mills' Arrestox; the stock for the paper cover is Hopper Skytone Pewter.

Manufactured in the United States of America.